About the Author

John Mullen was born in Dundalk, Ireland, and now
lives in Southern Spain

Patrick
A Memoir

John Mullen

Patrick
A Memoir

Olympia Publishers
London

www.olympiapublishers.com
OLYMPIA PAPERBACK EDITION

A CIP catalogue record for this title is
available from the British Library.

ISBN: 978-1-78830-788-8

This book is memoir. It reflects the author's present recollections of
experiences over time. Some names and characteristics have been
changed, some events have been compressed, and some dialogue
has been recreated.

First Published in 2020

Olympia Publishers
Tallis House
2 Tallis Street
London
EC4Y 0AB

Printed in Great Britain

Dedication

FOR SHAUN

Acknowledgements

I would like to thank my dear wife, MARISOL, for her infinite patience and constructive help in the creation of this memoir

Memory is the diary that we all carry about with us
Oscar Wilde

Chapter One

It was hot, even for Spain. It was mid-March and yet the sand beneath me was warm to the touch. It had been a surprising start to the year altogether, what with January being the coldest on record. A smattering of snow had actually fallen around our communal swimming pool, enough for a friend of mine to build a small snowman —an unheard of, event. It had created much hilarity among our neighbours and many cameras were clicking to record the event. This was followed by torrential rain in February and, although badly needed, had caused a great deal of damage to property. Now we were into March and basking in glorious sunshine.

I was particularly pleased for my guest who had arrived the day before and was staying with me for a week. I glanced at him affectionately. It was a spur of the moment holiday for him as he usually came out to stay with me in Spain during the month of June. I wondered what had prompted this sudden departure from his usual practice, but I knew that it would be hopeless to question him on the subject. Never a great talker, the matter would remain his secret. Perhaps he had just got fed-up with waiting for June to come around and wanted to see me. The thought pleased me. Whatever the reason, I know that I was delighted to see him as I always enjoyed his company.

Was it just a coincidence or some deliberate plan for him to be here at this time of year, for both our birthdays fell in this, the third week of March? My birthday was the twentieth and his was the sixteenth. But I knew that it had to be just chance that he should show up at this time. I knew for certain that he never planned anything — things just happened with him. Anyway, whatever the reason, it was very fortuitous, for now we could celebrate our respective birthdays together.

We each looked forward to this annual visit with great anticipation. It was a time when we both, in a sense, relived our lives, remembered many battles fought and sometimes won, and brought back to mind incidents from the past which were as acute in my thoughts as though they had occurred yesterday. I was not sure if he could recall them as clearly as me; he did not say much, but I liked to think so.

Then again, he did not need to speak about them — his body language told me much — the wide grin of pleasure on seeing me waiting at the barrier at the airport, the tight embrace when he almost lifted me off my feet. He had muscles that seemed as hard as steel. The excited way in which he almost danced out to the car in the warm sunshine told me much. I, too, shared his excitement as I had been preparing for his arrival for days, getting in his favourite foods. I knew all of his likes and dislikes as well as I did my own. All these things told me more clearly than any words that Patrick remembered everything. Oh, I know he was very reticent about voicing his thoughts, but I knew that the memories were there, clear and sharp. They had been embedded in his subconscious just as deeply as they were implanted in my own.

The weather back in England when he had left yesterday had been atrocious, so the contrast for him could not have been greater. I remembered only too well what the weather could be like in the UK during the month of March. Just when you were beginning to think that the winter was at an end and the daffodils were pushing their way above the ground, a sharp frost would cut in like a knife and lay waste to young life. Whilst here, the sun was shining, and the sea was calm, with the waves gliding in gracefully, making their mark and retreating as though pleased with their signature. Far too cold to swim in yet, but the sight and sound was very reassuring and restful to the soul.

We could consider ourselves very lucky as the evidence was all about that a few days earlier the sea had been anything but calm — in fact, had been extremely agitated with debris of all kinds now littering the beach. The local authority had not as yet got around to clearing it, but then this was spring, and no emphasis would be put on beach cleaning until June when the tourist season was in full swing. A line of seaweed fifty metres above the present tide mark showed the extent of the sea's incursion when angry. The sky would have been a sharp blue today had it not been for the very thin layer of white cloud which had drifted over at high altitude from the coast of Africa. It changed what might otherwise have been a harsh tone, hurtful to the eyes, to one of soft Wedgwood.

The Costa del Sol's weather is always influenced by

its close proximity to the dark continent and those of us that live here have every reason to be grateful. Africa is less than fifty kilometres away at this point and it inevitably means long months of glorious sunshine without the burning intensity suffered by Africa itself. There were hardly any tourists at this time of year — the multitudes that normally invaded this coast each year would start arriving much later. Apart from a lone fisherman doing some repairs to his nets and a few squawking seagulls fighting over some fish pieces the seaman had chucked away, we had the beach to ourselves.

I watched a vapour trail in the sky made by an aircraft climbing away from Malaga airport and thought we had seven whole days together before my companion took off from that same airport. Laying aside the book I had been reading, I squirmed about in the sand to make myself more comfortable and studied the figure lying beside me.

It was that of a young man whose milk-white body was clear proof that he did not come from these parts. It was a well-developed body with rippling muscles that told of hard manual labour as a means of earning a living. His hands were rough but surprisingly well cared for considering the type of work that he carried out. But I recalled that he had always been fastidious in his appearance. He was a manual worker in a warehouse — mostly cleaning duties with occasional forays in a delivery truck when a strong pair of hands were needed to help the driver to unload heavy boxes. He was thirty-three years of age now, a powerfully built young man in the prime of life.

He was very fair and therefore vulnerable to the sun's rays which explained the copious amounts of sun cream that sought to protect that white body. I noticed how his hairline had receded since our last meeting, and it seemed likely that in a few years' time he would be very thin on top. Perhaps that was why he now sported, maybe as a defiant flourish, a well-groomed moustache which was another feature that was new to me.

He had eyes that matched the blueness of the sky — eyes that were always wary, ready for the unexpected, on guard for the next challenge. They helped to conceal a shyness with strangers which I knew was almost painful to him. He never knew when he might be tested again, or when an uncaring world might throw down the gauntlet once more. Every day he had to try and avoid the pitfalls that would bring him embarrassment and worry; pitfalls that would not cause a thought to you or me — in fact, would be brushed aside as though nothing of any note. It must be strange, I thought, to go through life like that, on the constant lookout for another obstacle that might impede your path, bring you down, almost as if one were blind.

I smiled at his profile. His hands drummed on the sand as he beat time to some pop music on his Walkman which clung to his ears, and he looked completely relaxed as he lay there with his eyes closed. I marvelled at the change in him over the years since I first held him in my arms and looked at the scrap of life for which I had been partly responsible.

He was my eldest child and we named him Patrick.

As though sensing that I was watching him, he opened one eye and, seeing me staring, grinned self-consciously. I smiled back and asked needlessly, 'Fancy a San Miguel, Patrick?'

Unable to hear me, he removed the earphones on seeing my lips move. I repeated the question.

'Yes please, Dad,' came the swift reply and he laughed at my expression. I was always pulling his leg about getting drunk when he rarely touched the stuff — only enjoying the odd beer now and then. The nearest beach bar was only a few hundred metres away, and gathering our few things together, we ambled in that direction. Would it be open, I wondered, thinking that it was still only March and not many customers about? Hardly worth it, I mused, as it was not even the weekend when the local people might be tempted to spend a few hours on the beach. But the open door suggested that the place was open, despite the fact that we were the only customers in view.

Remembering the ramshackle building with the tin roof that had, until recently, stood on this site, I smiled to myself. It was one of many such buildings along the coast that catered for the needs of hungry and thirsty tourists, with peeling paintwork that appeared to have been put on during the civil war and a shaky veranda that seemed in imminent danger of collapsing. Then the local authorities stepped in with a new edict that threatened the owner with closure if he did not pull down his rickety edifice and build a brand-new structure that was in step with EEC rules and regulations, particularly with regard to matters of hygiene and safety.

This particular owner had taken the warning seriously, for I was confronted with an attractive modern building that sported much stainless steel behind the bar and comfortable seating on the new stable veranda. I was pleased to see that the ancient fishing boat, filled to the brim with sand, still stood to one side, the remains of a fire still in evidence on top of the sand. This was where the sardines were grilled, and a faint aroma of this tasty dish still hung in the air. A heap of driftwood lay alongside in readiness for the next grilling. The place appeared deserted, but our footsteps on the new tiles swiftly brought the owner from the back.

'*Buenos dias, Señores,*' exclaimed the man, smiling broadly, clearly anxious to retrieve some of his recent and heavy investment. He had an extravagant moustache with an even more extravagant paunch which told the world of his contented lifestyle. He wiped his hands vigorously on a none too clean towel which demonstrated that, despite the brand-new surroundings and edicts from on high, old habits die hard.

'*Un café con leche y una cerveza, por favor,*' I said, smiling back, thus exhausting almost my entire Spanish vocabulary.

'*Si, Señor, enseguida*', declared the man, throwing the dirty towel to one side and moving with alacrity, as promised, to get our order. He had the happy knack of most Spanish of making us feel very welcome and I was glad that we had brought him at least a little business. I had little doubt that he spoke near perfect English, catering as he did to countless tourists from the UK every year. But like most of his countrymen, he appreciated it when visitors made some attempt to speak his language. I noticed that I always got better service when I made my request known in Spanish.

Soon, the delicious aroma of freshly blended coffee wafted out to the terrace and I could hear the whirr of the milk being heated to go with it.

The man appeared a few minutes later with our order and poured our drinks with a flourish. When he poured the milk into my coffee, the jug was fully two feet above the cup, and he did not spill a drop. As his eyes caught my look of admiration, they shone with pride at his own dexterity. He bowed as though hearing a burst of applause and disappeared off stage, leaving us to enjoy our drinks.

With Patrick in possession of his beer, I sat tipped back in my chair against the wall of the building, sipping my coffee. Looking down the beach to where we had lain out sprawled in the sand, I pondered on how my life had changed during the last thirty years. Plenty of ups and downs with the accent on the downs — I grimaced at the thought. But was that true, I asked myself? To be fair, were there not plenty of ups as well. Indeed, looking at my son now, I might even claim to have had a charmed life, and we had experienced many more ups than downs together. Every family has their share of good luck and bad. Compared to many, with regard to bad fortune, we had probably got off very lightly. Indeed, there were countless moments of pure joy to look back on.

One thing, however, had remained constant during all that time and that was Patrick's presence in my life.

Most of the important decisions I had taken had concerned Patrick in one way or another, and I sighed as though feeling the pain once more, thinking of how hard some of them had been. Many had been gut-wrenching and had distressed me greatly at the time.

Did I make the right choices, I often wondered, and I would grow angry for having had to make them at all. Did I have any choice when it came down to it? Fate had made the real choice and all I could do was follow the path chosen for me. Oh, there were minor roads leading off but only one main path.

Looking at the result of all those decisions sitting beside me enjoying his beer, I consoled myself that I had done as good a job as anyone could, given the hand I was dealt. It did no good to dwell on what might have been, but I could not help but wonder how my firstborn would have coped with the world if fate had not been so cruel. Would he have been a lawyer, an architect, a great sportsman? But it was useless to punish myself in this way and it was a habit which I thought I had put behind me. Like those other times when I had felt this way, I tried to count my blessings.

Other parents had seen their healthy and highly intelligent children end up as drug addicts or worse, maybe horribly maimed in a road accident. In this way, I always tried to envisage my glass being half full and not half empty. But it was hard to be cheerful in the face of such a disaster as Patrick had suffered. I had tortured myself, endlessly thinking back to see if there was anything that we had done or not done to have had this appalling stroke of bad luck inflicted on us as a family.

But nothing ever sprang to mind. We had done everything right, more right, than most — it was just how the cards had fallen on the day. It is almost certain that if the modern medical techniques being used today had been available at that time, none of what subsequently happened would have occurred at all.

Chapter Two

I had always wanted kids. I came from a typical Irish family. Three boys and three girls. There was always plenty of life in our house; life was never dull. Something was always happening even if it was only a row. The usual thing: the girls fighting over a dress that was worn without permission, my brothers arguing over I don't know what. I was the baby, being five years younger than my youngest sister, Carmel. I was told the story by my eldest sister, Peggy, only a few years ago in fact, that Mammy cried herself out when she discovered that she was pregnant with me. So you can say that I was something of a surprise to my mother, who clearly felt that she had already done her duty as a good Catholic mother should.

My father died from throat cancer when I was only four years of age, so I can hardly remember him at all. I have only a couple of clear recollections of him, one of which is when he gathered some newspapers together and rolled them up into a ball before tying them securely with a piece of string. Thus, he created a football for me and took me to a place known as the old polo field, a mile from our home. This was a relic from the days of the English army garrisoned in the town and Daddy played with me there. He could not afford to buy me a real football. Money was not to be used for frivolity in

Ireland in 1936.

I can also remember my daddy dancing with me. He would put my left foot on his right and my right on his left, and balancing me thus, he would waltz gaily around the room while Mammy sat laughing in the corner. Other than those couple of instances, I have only vague memories of a kind gentle man playing with me. I have only ever seen one photograph of him, and I can say with some feeling, thank God that I took after my mother in looks and not dear old Daddy. I missed him though. An old man myself now, I still do. Crazy, I know.

I can remember the funeral. Daddy was laid out in a coffin in what was our living room, the casket balanced on two kitchen chairs which formed a trestle. The lid had not yet been placed on the coffin. Mammy had to keep dragging me away from the body as I tried to wake Daddy up. I can remember the silence. A crowd had gathered by our front gate, but nobody spoke. I thought they looked frightened and I wondered why. I thought it was exciting. I had no clear idea of what was happening but the memory of the big black horses with the tassels on their heads is very clear.

The silence was only broken by the sound of the harness jingling when the horses moved restlessly between the shafts of the hearse. They kept chewing the things in their mouths like chewing gum, but it wasn't — a highly polished hoof pawing at the ground as it waited for its cargo. They looked magnificent, so huge, towering above me as I waited beside them for my father's coffin to be loaded on board. One of them did a 'kee kee', and as it fell to the ground, I could see the great cloud of steam rising from it. Years later, someone told me that these splendid beasts were specially bred in Holland — I wouldn't know.

Suddenly, a lone voice was heard. It was that of an itinerant street singer, a common enough sight in Ireland at that time. It was a woman in the next street, just round the corner, and she was singing a sad song, something I came to know as a lament. It was only long afterwards that my sister Carmel told me of the strange coincidence that the woman, who was quite unknown to us, was singing a song called 'Poor Old Joe'. My Daddy's name was Joe, so it must have seemed a bit eerie at the time, to say the least.

I can remember the driver of the hearse in his big hat who smiled down at me. He had some kind of rug across his knees; he looked warm and cosy sitting up there. I wished I could have ridden with him. There was a cold wind blowing. But I was destined for the single carriage behind with Mammy and my sisters, my brothers walking. It was a bit of a squash, I sat on Carmel's knee, but we all managed to get inside.

Looking back, I think Carmel must have been designated my minder for she always looked after me and often allowed me to play with her and the older children. I am sure I must have been a pain at times. Aunt Mary, Daddy's sister, had come down from the North for the funeral and brought me sweets, but Mammy made me share them with Philomena and Carmel. I was cross. I thought they were all for me.

It was great; it felt like a party, except that Mammy

was crying and my sisters did not look very happy. But I thought it was great. Tom was very serious. I had never seen him like that before. Mammy said he was the man of the house now that Daddy was gone. I asked where he had gone, and Mammy said 'Heaven' and cried some more. I hoped he would come back so Mammy would not cry again, but he never did.

My best pal was Binno, and he was one year older than me. He lived just round the corner in McSwiney Street, and he had four older sisters but no brothers. His Mammy and Daddy were both alive. We lived in an area called the demesne which, before the Free State came into being, had formed part of the old Lord Roden estate when England ruled. It had, at its centre, a large dense wood which was called 'the Clump'.

Well, before the war, it was dense, but by the end of hostilities in nineteen forty-five, I think there were about five trees left. This was despite the best efforts of a huge man, appointed by the town council, by the name of Morrisey to prevent the wholesale destruction of this important social amenity. He was about eight feet tall and wore a flat cap and carried a big stick. The war years were desperate times, for coal was unobtainable, and despite the availability of the locally-dug turf, many people could not afford it.

I used to accompany Seamus and Benny Toal, together with their father, up to Anaverna Mountain on a Saturday to dig the turf. This was done in the spring and left in stacks throughout the summer for it to dry in the sharp mountain winds which could cut like a knife. There is no more God-forsaken place on earth, like a bog on the top of a mountain, when the rain is pouring down, and a gale force wind is slanting it into your face like needle points. With the absence of any kind of dwelling within miles, it was a scene that would not have been different one thousand years ago.

When the autumn came round, Mr Toal would hire a lorry and bring the turf down off the mountain and store it in his big shed at the back of his house. He would pay me a shilling for my day's work. No shilling was ever harder earned for it was bitterly cold on the mountain top and I would be scantily clad. The turf would be dripping wet at the time of cutting and my hands would be red-raw with the coldest water you have ever touched in all your life. We used to heat some water in a billy can over a bit of a fire in order to make a pot of tea. It was absolutely vile and tasted, not surprisingly, of turf, but it was drunk anyway.

There was a coal yard — I suppose we should call it a turf yard — beside a small council estate not too far from where I lived, known as 'The Laurels'. Well, let's face it, all estates were council-owned in those days. The yard was owned by a man called T. M. McDougal who was always well dressed. He was a dapper little man and always wore a Homburg hat and a bow tie. It was rumoured that he often used to hose the turf down to make it weigh more, thereby adding to his profit — something which was very much against the law. Try burning wet turf. When you put it in the grate, the smell was overpowering and the smoke would refuse to go up the chimney, billowing back out into the room causing everyone present to cough their guts out.

'Open the window, Carmel,' Mammy would gasp, between hacks.

If this action was not taken quickly, then the smoke would drift rapidly up the stairs which opened off the sitting room and then it was almost impossible to get rid of the stuff. It would hang around in the bedrooms and the landing for days on end.

When my sister, Peggy, who worked in Halliday's shoe factory, was paid on a Thursday night, she would hurry home with her wages. Mammy would then send me haring off with a sack under my arm to buy four stone of turf for one shilling and seven pence halfpenny. It was quite a dash as the yard used to shut at seven o'clock. I then had the task of carrying the half hundredweight of often wet turf on my back the half a mile home. Not an easy job for a ten-year-old, but I managed it by taking a breather halfway to my destination and resting the load on Mrs. Kelly's garden wall which was about four feet high. If I put the sack down on the ground, I could not get it up on my back again without help. There was a great feeling of excitement when the rest of the family saw that I had made it to the yard in time, as we would now have some heat in the house — cause for celebration indeed, as it was wintertime.

So, in the middle of the night you would be woken by the sound of a tree crashing to the ground and the shouts of Big Morrisey chasing the miscreants. He never caught anyone except us kids climbing what was left standing upright the next day, and then we would get a lather across the arse from his big stick as we climbed down, fearfully, on his command.

After school and at weekends, Carmel and I would be dispatched up the Clump, armed with the turf sack together with a big hammer and a couple of chisels Tom scrounged from somewhere. We would attack one of the many substantial stumps which the treefellers had left behind and were often able to bring home a goodly collection of stout pieces of wood to Mammy, for the fire. It helped to burn the wet turf your man had sold me. Often a chisel would get stuck in the stump and then we were in trouble, as it was desperately important that we retrieve this invaluable tool. But we managed somehow, often by banging in a piece of stone to loosen the chisel by widening the cleft in which it was trapped.

Over the years and long after I had left to work in England, the old Clump, or what was left of it, became an eyesore, with rubbish being dumped indiscriminately everywhere. A sad downfall after its years of glory. It was a disgrace to the area until a few years ago when a generous benefactor appeared on the scene, his name, Martin Naughton, now one of Ireland's most prominent businessmen. I heard a story about him once, and I am not sure if it is true or not — maybe it is just one of those legendary tales that follow highly successful men about.

It was at a time when Martin was running a large electrical engineering concern, and he decided that it might be a good idea to add an electric kettle to his range of products. But first, he must find out how the general public felt about this idea, so he sent out his army of market researchers.

When asked the question, 'If you were going to buy an electric kettle, what make would you choose?", seven out of ten people replied, 'A Morphy-Richards.'

Like many others in the grip of a recession, this particular company was going through a very bad patch at the time and appeared vulnerable to a take-over which was when Martin Naughton moved in and bought it up.

Then he produced his lovely new electric kettle. Because of all the highly successful products that emerged from its factories throughout the years of its existence, Morphy-Richards never once produced an electric kettle. Martin Naughton was fully aware of the power of a brand name.

I love that particular story, for I think it epitomises the difference between the true entrepreneur and the rest of the pack.

But Martin wasn't always the great tycoon. Not when he was a little boy and did my mother and sister a favour one Sunday morning. He was the son of Garda Naughton, a local policeman, who, with his own hands, built a lovely house for his family a few doors away from us, just around the corner. I remember him very well — a big tall powerful man, I would see him arriving on site, having come off duty, riding his bicycle, to put in another hard stint on his new home. How that man could work. I never saw anyone else helping him and I am convinced that he built the entire house on his own. Martin must have been about twelve at the time when he helped my mother. Being appreciably older, I had long since left the town to seek my fortune in England.

Together with my sister Philomena, Mammy had attended early morning Mass but, on returning home, discovered that she had not taken the front door key with her and they found themselves locked out. Martin came to the rescue by fetching a ladder from home and climbing through an upstairs window, which had been left open, thereby gaining entry and coming down to open the front door.

Now, many years later, as a tribute to his late father and his fellow officers in the Gardai, Martin Naughton had the old Clump, comprising many acres, completely transformed at his own expense into a beautiful park which is the pride of the neighbourhood and, indeed, the whole town. When I returned to Dundalk on a visit a few years ago, I was amazed at the change in my old playground. I strolled around the newly laid pathways and admired the great work that had been done. But the magic had disappeared for me. Where had all the wee fellas gone that used to play here. Scattered to the four corners of the globe. The thought made me feel old which indeed I was. If I stood perfectly still, I could almost hear the shouts of laughter or maybe alarm as Big Morrisey chased us and we ran for our lives, Binno and me neck and neck.

'If he kills us, he'll have to pay for us, Johnny,' my pal would pant. But he never caught us, and we lived to tell the tale.

My sister Philomena attended the inauguration ceremony and had the opportunity of reminding Martin of his knightly gesture and they both had a good laugh about it. So the most important men in the land were wee fellas once and all the better for it.

There was another interesting chap lived round the corner, nearly opposite the Naughtons, whose name I never found out. He was a tailor by profession and looked nothing like you might imagine a tailor would look. I mean, I can visualize a small humpbacked figure, forever bending over, short-sightedly sewing away at somebody's trousers.

This man looked nothing like that — in fact, he was just the opposite. A tall commanding figure with iron grey hair and a bristle moustache, he might well have been a retired major from the army. He rode a racing bicycle — I never saw him walking — and he rode it like the wind. He was always hell-bent over the low-slung handlebars and wore a beret to keep his locks out of his eyes as he tore round the streets like a bat out of hell. He was a man in his early fifties, and he was known to all in the demesne as 'The Flying Tailor'.

The most amusing thing about this character was the extraordinary method he employed to mount his cycle. Most men put one foot on a pedal and use the other foot to push off in preparation to throwing their leg over the saddle and taking their seat. Nothing so straightforward for The Flying Tailor!

The axle on the rear wheel was at least six inches longer than was strictly necessary, and he used this extra length as a foothold to launch himself into the saddle for all the world as though he was mounting a horse. Maybe he had been in the cavalry. To watch him dismounting was even more spectacular, as he would vault into the air just like Frankie Dettori getting off his horse after another big win.

Years later, when I was a racing cyclist in my teens, I tried this method of mounting my bicycle to impress the girls and it is not to be recommended. I had great difficulty in walking, for days, without the tears forming in my eyes.

Chapter Three

When Binno and I prowled its shadowy depths in the thirties and early forties, the Clump was a magical place. It was the Belgian Congo, with lions under every bush waiting to pounce, it was the Mato Grozzo, with pygmies using blow pipes with poisoned darts — in fact, just about anything we wanted it to be.

Mammy would say, 'Where are you going?' and I would reply, 'Up the Clump.'

'Who with?'

'Binno.'

'You behave, mind!'

'Yes, Mammy,' and away I would charge to meet Binno for the start of another adventure.

As it was right on our doorstep, it proved a paradise for us kids, and great for playing cowboys and Indians. Nobody ever wanted to be an Indian as you were sure to be shot. I was always John Wayne which upset Seamus Toal, who had to be content with Gene Autrey. I thought he was just a sissy — Gene Autrey, I mean — singing and kissing girls. You never heard of John Wayne singing!

We became adept at making catapults using a piece of forked stick cut into shape with one of Mr Toal's knives we borrowed from his tool box in the shed. Two slivers of rubber cut from an old inner tube of a car tyre served as elastic and we found that the tongue from a disposed boot was perfect for holding the missile — a deadly weapon when defending yourself against a Roman legion.

Binno and I had great times in the Clump. He always had great ideas. He swiped a torch from home, and when it got dark, we would play a game we called 'Jack, Jack, show the light'. He would hide behind a tree and flash the torch and a crowd of us would chase him, but when we reached the spot he had moved elsewhere and then he would flash the torch again. I don't think we ever caught him.

Often, we would not notice how late it had become and Carmel would come looking for me.

'Mammy has been looking everywhere for you — you are going to be killed.'

Being killed was the prescribed punishment for almost any misdemeanour, however trivial, and nothing less would suffice.

Reason enough to stay out, you might think. My bowels loosened at the threat, and as I squatted down to relieve myself, I did not see the bed of nettles until too late, and I ended up with a badly blistered arse.

On one occasion, Binno and I were persuaded to accompany a much older boy, called Ross, to catch some pinnikins (wee fish) in the Rampart river, which was about one mile from my home — not that we needed much persuasion. This sounded very exciting, especially as the older boy had a big net and a bucket, but we neglected to inform anyone of our intentions. It was only when the ice cream man came around and

Mammy, feeling a bit rich for once, gave tuppence to Carmel to buy two sliders, one for herself and one for me, that the alarm went up. Johnny could not be found anywhere, and it did not take long to discover that his pal, Binno was also missing. Search parties were sent out and Carmel discovered us by the bank of the stream, having a great time.

We were both dragged home by the scruff of the neck and I can remember Mammy taking my trousers down and tanning my bottom to the plaintive appeals of my sister Carmel not to hurt the wee fella. Her appeals for mercy to be shown fell on stony ground, but what really upset me more than the smacking was the thought of having missed out on that ice cream which was a rare treat in those days — a memory that is etched clear in my mind even yet.

People say that children were much safer on the streets in those days; you could let them out to play and no harm ever came to them, and I suppose, up to a point, this is true. But there were plenty of dangers to be avoided and kids had to be on their guard even then.

Not much more than a year after I left to go to England, a young boy was found murdered just two hundred yards from my home.

One of my favourite characters was Harry, our milkman. He was a very cheery man, young, no more than thirty, and came from Dowdleshill. He drove the most attractive milk float in town, horse drawn, of course. It was painted white, with fancy gold writing on the side advertising the dairy and a nice low floor level so Harry could hop off and on easily on either side and so could I for that matter.

Although open at the sides for convenience, it boasted a kind of sunroof, or perhaps I should say rain roof, that protruded over the driver, so Harry and his illegal passenger were always in the dry. For Harry was always very kind to me, not only giving me a ride around the block but dropping me off on the corner of McSwiney Street, so I only had a few yards to run home. Most important of all, however, was the fact that he allowed me to take the reins of Dolly and drive the yoke, always with his steadying hand not too far off in case I might lose control.

Near the end of the run, we passed Binno's house, and I was forever on the lookout to wave to him and show off. Harry was always on time and I would listen for the clip clop of Dolly's hooves and the occasional clang of the churns in the back of the float as there were no milk bottles in those days. The milk was measured out in steel jugs of different measure and the housewives would come out with their own jugs for the milk to be poured into them.

It was a sad day for me when Harry said goodbye on his departure for America to seek his fortune. He was the only adult I ever met as a child, and I was only seven or eight at the time, who treated me with respect and trusted me with the responsibility of driving that milk float. I never saw him again.

There was one other interesting milkman who visited our street, and he was really different. I always had the impression that he was self-employed, a farmer maybe, because of the quaint manner by which he delivered the milk. He would ride a bicycle, steering with one hand, whilst with the other he held the reins of a Great Dane that was between the shafts of a small cart. Sitting in the cart was a large churn of milk and the usual selection of measuring jugs. The huge dog was well trained, for he would trot along quite docilely beside his master and never seemed to give any trouble. I guess he was cheaper to feed than a horse but only marginally, I would think.

I had three accidents as a child, all involving damage to my head. My enemies and possibly even my friends will say that that explains everything. The first was when I fell off a high wall surrounding the Toal's garden. We were acting out a Foreign Legion film we had seen at the previous Saturday matinee. I was standing aloft waving a flag, having just stormed the citadel, when my foot slipped on the wet surface and down I went to the pavement, with which my head made sickening contact. They say that you see stars when struck violently on the head, and I can confirm that this is so.

Mrs. McKenna was just cycling past on her upright bicycle, the basket in front filled with white bread from across the border. These were the early days of the war when many foodstuffs were scarce. Ireland was fairly self-sufficient but could not grow enough wheat to bake decent bread. So we were stuck with this almost black stuff you could hardly grace with the name of bread and it was vile. Even now, years later, I shudder when I think of it. Down across the border though, in Northern Ireland, you could buy lovely big white loaves which would melt in your mouth. Plenty of people made their way there and smuggled it over, and Mrs. McKenna was one of the most successful, making the twelve mile journey to Newry by bicycle at least once a week and filling the basket strapped to the handlebars with the delicious stuff which was then put on sale in her husband's shop.

The lady was the wife of Barney McKenna, who owned the shop round the corner in McSwiney Street, opposite Binno's house. It was Barney who would never sell you a packet of five 'Will's Woodbines' cigarettes, lamenting the fact that he only had some loose ones which he could let you have for a penny each. A packet of five cost threepence. Times were hard, he said. He would be glad when all this rationing was at an end, he said. Nobody believed him. Barney was one of those men you might call 'swarthy'. Whenever I hear of someone described as swarthy, I think of Barney. He needed to shave about three times a day. Every other man had seven o'clock shadow — Barney had one o'clock shadow.

There I lay, my head pounding, bawling my head off, seeing myriads of stars and becoming very frightened at the copious amounts of blood running into my collar. Yet, in the midst of all that pain and fear, I could still smell the delicious aroma emanating from the basket on the front of Mrs. McKenna's bicycle as she leaned it against the wall to come to my aid.

My second accident was down to Binno. I mentioned that we lived on a former demesne, now crammed with council estates, which had formed part of the old Lord Roden estate. His Lordship had dug out and created a canal, in the centre of his many acres, over which he built a stone bridge — all this to provide him with a pleasant view. On each side of the bridge was carved an effigy of a man's head which looked vaguely like that of a Chinaman. Hence the bridge was known to all and sundry as the 'China Bridge'.

A lone swan had made its home on the canal and led a sorry life as youngsters behaved very cruelly towards it, throwing stones and other missiles which often found their mark. Such behaviour incensed the swan and it became a danger to small children, on one occasion the victim being a little girl called Nancy Williams who was grabbed by the swan and half dragged into the water by the big bird. She was lucky not to be drowned. At least this near disaster deterred children for a long time from molesting the swan. The bird had one good friend, however — an old man who came every afternoon to feed it breadcrumbs. He was known simply as the 'Swan Man' — a small gentleman with a white moustache wearing a long black coat, winter or summer, and a bowler hat on his head.

Over the years, the local council gradually filled in this canal with debris and a lovely amenity was lost to the town forever. It became an eyesore filled with garbage and the poor swan was slowly but surely denied its stretch of water and departed. It became an area known as the 'slobland' and attracted a group of poor women clad in black shawls — almost a national garment which had all but disappeared, by this time, in Ireland. I remember they were always smoking short clay pipes.

They were called 'The Cinderpickers' due to the simple fact that that was exactly what they were after — cinders. The dustbins of the town, containing the ashes from the grates of many homes, were emptied here. The women would pick over what was dumped and quite often fill a sack, by the end of the morning, with usable fuel, not to mention any other items that might prove useful to them, although the poverty existing in the town at that time was such that I think that their pickings were bound to be very slim indeed. I have no idea where these women lived or where they came from — they just appeared from nowhere every morning and disappeared again just as mysteriously. They formed the lowest strata of society in the town and a barefooted child on his way to school in the depths of winter might well have felt superior to them.

Beyond the China Bridge and just before you joined the Long Walk, grew a magnificent chestnut tree which provided us with giant conkers every autumn. It straddled the creosoted fence that surrounded P.J. Carroll's football field. Carroll's was the tobacco factory that employed many local girls including my sister Carmel. Business must have been good, for the management were able to fund a sports club for its workers, doubtless wanting to be seen helping people to improve their breathing whilst slowly choking themselves to death on their product.

It was a fence that was only to last until the outbreak of World War Two when fuel became a very scarce commodity. Nothing helped to kindle wet turf better than a well creosoted piece of timber. The gaps that kept appearing were initially plugged with new pieces of planking, but it soon became obvious that it was like trying to stem the tide and the owners finally gave up the impossible struggle in despair.

The conkers were best when they fell of their own accord; it meant that they were ripe and at their biggest but there were never enough to go around, being snatched up as soon as they hit the ground by gangs of kids. We loved playing conkers and the owner of a chestnut that survived many contests earned considerable esteem from his peers. Binno said that they hardened if you put them in the oven for an hour, but it never worked for me. Maybe I should have switched the oven on.

Anyway, this day Binno and I were throwing stones up at the branches in an effort to bring some chestnuts down. I don't quite know how it happened, but I think this is the scenario. I was in front of Binno when he let fly with a good-sized rock just as I took a step backwards to see what effect my own missile had had. The rock bounced off my skull and the stars came out again for me and the blood flowed. But I survived — just.

I think Binno was more frightened than me. Thinking that maybe I was going to launch a retaliatory strike, Binno, with the solemn face of a seven-year-old declared, 'If you kill me, you will have to pay for me,' but I was too preoccupied with my flashing stars to bother.

The third accident I think could have been very

serious, but again I was lucky, if you can call being nearly decapitated lucky.

It was only my second day at work, and it meant an early start — something like seven o'clock in the morning. I had been taken on at the Magnet cinema as a trainee projectionist and part of my duties involved going to the railway station in the early morning to collect the can of film off the Dublin train for that night's performance. Arriving at the cinema, I was expected to make my entry through these steel mesh gates, you know, the security type. You remove the padlock and slide them back to the wall. These particular gates were extremely wide, requiring them to be in two parts with a pole in the middle upon which the iron bars rested.

I was just fourteen at the time, never having seen one these yokes before and, having pushed the gates to the wall, started wrestling with the pole in the middle. I was bending over almost on my knees when the bar was dislodged by my action and came down like a guillotine. I don't remember much about anything after that, as I lay there in a pool of blood until the caretaker, Paddy Kerley, found me. A great start to my career. Fortunately, I did not have to attend hospital, a few adept stitches being found sufficient to hold my brains together. I spent the next two weeks walking around with what looked like a turban on my head, which attracted many a ribald comment from my pals. When asked what had happened to my head, I would reply in a useless effort to be witty, 'I fell and trampled on it.'

I used to think that when I am old and bald,

everyone will see these scars and wonder about them. I am now old and pleased to confirm that I still have a great white thatch, so it looks like I am safe from any prying questions.

Chapter Four

Another great pastime we enjoyed as kids was catching bumblebees. To do this, you had to be equipped with a large jam jar. A one-pound size was no good — it had to be a two-pound jar and it required a lid, well, a piece of stiff cardboard would do the trick and often did. You put some flower heads, preferably thistle flowers, in the jar to keep the bees happy, they loved them. There were three types of bee you could catch, and they were all to be found gorging themselves every day in a big patch of thistles right by Hardy's orchard, which formed part of the old Roden estate in years gone by, really quite close to the aforementioned China bridge. It was an area we always referred to as the 'Big Field' — why it was called that forever remains a mystery to me because there was no such place as the small field from which to differentiate it.

'Have you seen Binno?'

'Yeah, he's up in the Big Field.'

'What's he doing up there?'

'Sure, he's catching bees, wouldn't you know.'

I remember once running away from the Sloan gang across the Big Field (that's how I came to be such a good runner — I was always running away from a fight) when my foot went into a pothole and I went down, and my knee becoming impaled on a broken porter bottle. I carry the scar to this day. Thankfully, the gang's attention was diverted by a hail of stones from Binno, who was never known to run away from anybody.

Back to the bees. First there were the wee brown fellas, but they were no good, too small. Binno said they lived in hives and you could get honey from them, but I don't know. Then there were the big black and yellow larriers that we called bruisers. These were just great. All you had to do was put the open mouth of the jar to the thistle that was the object of the bee's attention and scoop it in. Dead easy. The third and most attractive type, but the most rare and difficult to catch, were the big black ones with the crimson behind. We called them 'red arses' and the one who had the most of these was reckoned to be the best catcher. My sister Carmel really loved these and would swap two big bruisers for one 'red arse' any day of the week.

Returning home alone one day from one such foray in search of bees, I saw a mortal sin being committed. I was passing a small grove of trees near Hardy's orchard when I heard the sound of muffled laughter. Pausing to detect its source, it took me some time to locate the point from which it was coming. I then crept forward, being careful to avoid detection.

Without the company of Binno, I was more than a wee bit scared but determined to find out who was making the noise. Peering through some bushes, I saw a soldier and a woman behaving strangely. The woman was lying on the ground, her body partly obscured by the man who was standing over her. I could just see the lower part of the woman's legs and her knickers were around her ankles, a sight that made me freeze. As I watched, bug-eyed, the soldier unbuckled his big brown leather belt and, lowering his trousers, lay on top of the woman. I was just ten years old at the time, being brought up in a rigid Catholic community. There was no sex education lessons in those days. How things have changed — can you imagine the Christian Brothers... don't even think about it! Neither was it a subject my mother was ever likely to bring up in front of me!

Every Sunday, the priests in the pulpit giving the sermon at Mass were continually ranting on about the terrible sins of the flesh and none of us, certainly none of the boys my age, had a clue what they were talking about. What on earth was fornication? For ages, I had it confused with fortification. They would get quite worked up on the topic and people around me would stir uneasily under the tirade. Father Campbell, quite new to the parish at that time, was a particularly holy terror on the subject. He would grow hoarse with his shouting, waving his fists about as though beating the living daylights out of the devil for his behaviour. Anyone would think it was all our fault that the devil was always hanging around tempting us.

Personally, I found it all very boring and my attention would soon stray to something else. For example, I was far more intrigued by the little girl whose father was the manager of the Bank of Ireland just opposite the cathedral. She always attended ten o'clock Mass on Sundays with her father, and I could not help but admire the cute hat she wore. It was similar to the hat worn by the soldiers in the town — I think you might call it a forage cap — and hers had the embellishment of a colourful ribbon. I always made sure to be in the row in front of her and a little to one side so I could steal glances at her from time to time. It was not long before I noticed she was glancing back at me and with a smile. I made certain never to miss ten o'clock Mass on Sundays for ages, looking forward to it with a wildly beating heart. That is until her father got transferred to another branch and a great romance was ended. I never even found out her name.

We were continually being told that the devil appeared in many guises in order to tempt us into sin and we must be on our guard at all times. I was always on the lookout for him, but I never saw him nor did anybody else so far as I knew.

I knew next to nothing about the ways of the world other than overhearing the sniggering conversations of older boys in the schoolyard. Things that beggared belief, things that just had to be made up, there could be no truth in them whatsoever, sure you would have to be mad to believe them. I remember a fellow called Slattery, from somewhere out Cooley way, appeared in the yard one day and asked a group of us, with a lewd grin on his face, 'Here, have yis heard this one? What is love?'

We stared at him as though he was crazy, and when he could not elicit a reply, he answered his own question. 'Two in a bed, trying to make three.'

He gave a guffaw and swaggered off while his audience looked self-consciously at one another, not quite sure whether to laugh with him or not. We avoided eye contact with one another, none of us wanting to show that we were uncertain what Slattery was talking about. Then, someone sniggered, and the spell was broken, a punch was thrown, and it ended with the usual fracas in the schoolyard.

Now I was faced with this extraordinary scene, and my emotions ran riot. My face was burning, my throat constricted, and I don't think my eyes could get any bigger. I knew that I should not be looking, that what I was seeing was dirty and a mortal sin. But the man and woman were laughing, they were having fun and I could not understand it. I tried to move but I seemed to be paralysed, my legs were stuck to the ground.

But wait, the man was not laughing any more, he was moaning aloud as though in great pain, but the woman was giggling at him. My heart was pounding as though it would burst. Was this what the priests were always talking about — that the devil took many forms to lure us into temptation. The man`s groans were now terrible to listen to; he was in agony, yet the woman continued to laugh aloud at his misery. Frightened out of my wits now, because I knew with certainty that the woman was the devil, I managed, with a great effort of will, to tear myself free from my paralysis, and then I was running. Running as fast as I could, through bunches of nettles which made my knees sting, but I was beyond feeling pain. I just wanted to get away from here. The brambles tore at my ankles, slowing my pace, and I sobbed in terror as at last I was crossing the China Bridge and my home was in sight.

I slowed as my fear diminished, my mind filled with

anguish at what that soldier must be suffering for his sin. I never told anyone what I saw, not even Binno, but I vowed that the devil would never tempt me like that because I knew now what I was in for if I gave in to temptation.

My mother had had a hard job raising her brood, but she was a tough character and instilled in all of us a sense of dignity and honour. Apart from what Tom earned, which was not a great deal, she only had her pension on which she had to bring up her other five children. How she was able to manage it I could never understand to this day. The rent took three quarters of her widow's pension, which only left her a pittance on which to feed and clothe us. She was a very proud woman and always insisted, however ragged our clothes, at least they must be clean and well pressed.

In our house, the question, 'Where did I put my darned coat?' took on a whole new meaning, not to mention every other article of clothing.

My brother Tom was the family cobbler. From somewhere, he had procured a last, and many a Saturday morning would find him in the kitchen putting new soles or heels on someone's shoes. Mine were the most frequently repaired, as I seemed to wear out my boots quicker than anyone else. This might be due to the fact that I kicked more tin cans than anyone else in the family. I often wondered where Tom got the leather for all these repairs; perhaps the fact that he worked in a shoe factory had something to do with it. I enjoyed watching him as he used the deadly sharp little knife to trim the leather and fashion it into shape. I was always intrigued by the way he would put a handful of wee silver nails in his mouth and deftly extract one at a time as he went round the edge of the sole, tapping each nail into place. He would finish the job off by staining the edges of the new sole either brown or black depending on the colour of the footwear.

In the summer, my boots would be replaced by guttees — a type of plimsoll with heavy rubber soles. The canvas tops were never capable of sustaining the weight of the soles, which would come away with monotonous regularity. Then, Tom would heat this thick glue (I think this came from the same source as the leather) on the gas and stick them back on again. They lasted at least until the next game of football.

On the subject of footwear, we were indebted in no small way to the St. Vincent de Paul Society for many a pair of boots for me. In fact, although I was often glad to get a new pair, the old ones about to fall apart, yet I knew I would be in agony for weeks until the new ones were properly broken in. They would pinch my toes causing me untold agony and my heels would be red-raw from the ill-fitting harsh leather until I had kicked a good many tin cans to school and back.

There was one occasion when Frank Cole, the man from the St. Vincent de Paul, failed to come through with my new boots on time and Mammy was in a dilemma. My old pair had finally fallen to bits and I had no others to wear to school. What to do, that was the question. Several boys in class seldom wore shoes, even in winter, but this indicated that they were on a lower social level than everybody else. No child of Mammy

Mullen would ever dare to be seen without shoes of some sort — that display of poverty was not to be tolerated. I remember the ghastly wellingtons, that belonged to Carmel, I had to wear once. But, at this time, there were not even a pair of those in the house. However, Mammy solved the problem.

Going to her wardrobe, she reverently extracted her pair of flat heeled (thank God for small mercies) suede shoes wrapped in tissue paper. These were a relic from the days when my family was well off and Daddy had his own successful business. That was until the store burned down. Fire insurance was not the class act then that it is today, and he lost everything. Mammy would often bitterly relate how neighbours, under the guise of helping during the blaze, made off with all the stock that they removed. We were left destitute.

So it was that Johnny swanked off to school in his posh suede shoes, having made sure that I trod in every pile of mud that I could find on the way. I was terrified that the fancy footwear would be laughed at and there is nothing more disastrous for a little boy than to have his peers laugh at him. Sadly, the stitching on the back of the shoes could not withstand the pressure of young growing feet and very soon burst, but by that time, Frank Cole had come through with a big pair of hob-nailed boots.

Big Frank Cole played another role in our lives. He was an insurance agent and called every Saturday morning for the sixpence for Mammy's insurance policy. This was one expense that had to be met at all costs. We might starve to death but there would be no paupers grave for anyone living at number forty-three. We could always be assured of having the big black horses with the jingling harness in attendance.

Every morning, before I went to school, I had to pass inspection. For some unknown reason, the backs of ears drew my mother's attention like a magnet and woe betide me if she found any trace of dirt there.

'Have you done your ecker?' (homework)

'Yes, Mammy.

'Have you been to the lavatory?'

'Yes, Mammy.'

Shoes must be polished to a high lustre; never mind the hole in the sole — people cannot possibly see the piece of stiff cardboard residing there (Tom did not always have the leather). Hair must be combed back, before you go to school, with copious amounts of water, the parting like a razor.

So, in the thirties, thanks to Mammy, we learned how to starve in a dignified fashion. If you are going to faint from hunger, do it at home. Do not make an exhibition of yourself by lying down in the street. We were a fairly close family with seven people sharing three small bedrooms — work it out for yourself. So I knew the feeling of security and sharing that ensued from having siblings, not that there was ever very much to share.

Looking back, most of my time seemed to be taken up with thoughts of food or at least how to get hold of some. Friday night was cause for celebration when Tom brought home his wages and we could replenish our empty bellies.

My brother Tom was the eldest child and it fell to him to become the main support of the family with our father dead — no easy task for a young man barely seventeen years old. We were lucky to have him for a brother, because it was mainly thanks to him that we all survived the desolate years of the thirties and forties. He worked long hours in Rawson's shoe factory and handed his wage packet, unopened, to Mammy every Friday night. In addition, despite mass unemployment at the time, he always seemed to be able to find some little job at weekends or evenings that brought in a little extra money.

My other brother George, two years the younger, was quite different in character and could never find a job in Dundalk. Oh, he found one or two little part-time occupations, but they never lasted. I think that he felt envious of Tom, who was such a go-getter. George, for his part, was diffident in manner and could never push himself forward. It was a pity, for I think, because of this difference in character, that they never got on well and George wasted no time, when the opportunity presented itself, to leave home forever and settle down in England. I am delighted to say that he did very well in that country, married an English girl and had a fine daughter.

Mammy called Tom the 'Boss' after Daddy died, and I never heard her refer to him by any other name afterwards. In fact, we all called him the 'Boss' but we were never in fear of him — it was just another nickname and an affectionate one at that. Without ever raising his voice, he had the ability to command respect from the rest of us, and he never once raised his hand to me in his life, although I am sure that I deserved it on more than one occasion. When he died recently, I lost my best friend.

Chapter Five

It has been written elsewhere, with greater passion, about the poverty that existed in Ireland at that time. I can only say that somehow my family managed to stay reasonably healthy and we all lived to see much better days. Apart from poverty, TB was the great curse to be reckoned with in the country, and hardly a week went by, but we heard of some family or other being stricken with the disease. I say 'family' because it was never just the individual who was affected by it. It was known to be highly contagious and I can remember being warned by my mother never to enter the house of a sufferer. Indeed, I was positively warned off playing with children whose family was known to be afflicted with the malady.

It was a dreaded disease and I knew many who succumbed to its ferocity. Sadly, too it was often the young who died of the illness — often brothers and sisters from the same house. The sanatoriums were full to overflowing, reflecting the high number of persons who endured poor living conditions and were denied proper food for all of their lives.

One abiding memory I have of my home was the amount of singing that went on. My sisters, especially Carmel, were constantly singing the latest song hits, and although they had no formal training, they all had beautiful voices. I grew up to the sound of melody. George, too, had a splendid baritone voice and was often heard giving a rendering of his favourite tune — Cole Porter's, 'When They Begin The Beguine'.

Years after he had grown up and left home, if someone was heard to be singing that song on the radio, Mammy was immediately reduced to tears as George was forever her favourite child. Indeed, when Mammy died she left her most precious possession, her wedding ring, to George. Strange, when Tom, who had remained at home and was the bulwark of the whole family, who had made untold sacrifices for his mother, was never to enjoy that privileged position of his brother in Mammy's heart. Who knows what pulls at a mother's heartstrings?

Three years after Daddy, died Tom was still working in Rawson's, Peggy had a steady job in Halliday's shoe factory and my brother George, although not in a regular job, occasionally managed to find something part-time which brought in a few pounds to help things along.

We certainly were not rich, but at least, as a family, we were making ends meet and Mammy was able to put food on the table at meal times. Just as things were beginning to get a little brighter, and to ease the burden for Mammy, Tom did what his mother considered to be a very foolish thing.

When the Second World War broke out, my brother Tom, together with many thousands of other young men, hurried to join up when volunteers were asked to join the army. It was a very natural thing for any nineteen-year-old to do, full of bravado and derring-do as one is at that age, but his action nearly drove poor Mammy to despair.

It took six months but her many letters of entreaty that Tom might be released from the service, as he had other pressing responsibilities, finally bore fruit and he returned to his job at the shoe factory. But honour had been served and Tom had been seen to be willing to stand up and be counted when his country called. In a way, I think he was glad to be back home and away from the crushing boredom of army life on a desolate and windswept army camp.

I found it exciting to see him in uniform and looked forward to his odd weekend at home from the army camp at the Curragh. I can vividly recall one particular weekend leave he had when he came home to see us, and on departure he gave me threepence to spend on some sweets. He was no sooner out of sight than I was speeding to Scrooge Gaughran's shop (deadly competition for Barney McKenna) up the road, but not to buy confectionery. No, it was to buy a loaf of bread and a penny candle. I never knew why the old lady was called Scrooge as she was always kind to me. However often I entered her shop, which was pretty frequent, the greeting was always the same, 'Ah, Johnny, I hardly knew you.'

Her son Willie was an active IRA man and was charged, found guilty of causing explosions, and sentenced to a long term of imprisonment in England. Bearing in mind that this was during the war, he was lucky not to be hanged. He contracted TB whilst in Lincoln prison and obtained early release on compassionate grounds, but did not live long to enjoy his freedom. He died shortly after his release. Behind the shop was a small farm (yeah, yeah, you've guessed it), part of the old Lord Roden estate, and it was honeycombed with secret passages where it was rumoured IRA men on the run frequently found refuge. My sister Carmel used to help out on Saturdays on the farm collecting eggs and the like — they kept a huge flock of hens — and she reckoned it was true.

I can remember the night of Tom's largesse vividly as we celebrated having bread and light by which to eat it. I have been fortunate to subsequently attend banquets in some of the finest hotels in London and elsewhere, but no meal ever tasted as rich and fulfilling as our loaf of bread that night. The chandeliers in the banqueting room of Grosvenor House Hotel in London shone no brighter than the candle in 43 Oliver Plunkett Park. The memory of it lingers still.

Over all of this poverty-stricken country, hovered the brooding presence of the Catholic Church. When I was a little boy, the priest, to whom we all learned to touch our forelocks as soon as we could walk, would tour from house to house demanding the dues — money to be donated to the Church. Woe betide any family seeking to renege on this commitment. Being only six or seven years of age at the time but already vaguely aware of other religions, I was greatly puzzled as we did not know of any Jews living in Dundalk.

I can remember a Father Murray, famous for his loud voice, roaring like a bull inside 'Mobite' Martin's home (I don't know why he was called that nickname) because he had only been offered five shillings. He could clearly be heard out in the street, much to the chagrin of poor Mobite who could barely afford to have his boots mended. The clergy knew how to exploit pride.

Mobite was very friendly with old Mr Levens, who lived on the corner. They would often stand outside on the sidewalk after their morning stroll and have ferocious arguments. To hammer home his point, Mobite would pound on Mr Levens' back but never with the flat of his hand. I noticed he always used the back of his hand which must have left poor old Levens with bruises for days on end.

It was the same Father Murray who visited our class in school, when we were about thirteen or fourteen, to solicit new members for the Pioneer Total Abstinence Association. In a country notorious for hard drinkers, it never ceased to surprise me that they could find anyone to join. I never knew if the priest's teeth were his own — if not he should have sued the dentist. They were so enormous they would make a Great White envious.

After a sermon on the demons of drink, he demanded that all those wishing to enrol in the Association and make a pledge to abstain from alcohol, put up their hands. Needless to say, forty-three grubby hands shot into the air. We were not daft, we knew about diplomacy. Then Father Murray explained that there would be a two-year probationary period after which, if we had not taken a single alcoholic drink during that time, we were then entitled to call ourselves a true pioneer.

For some reason which I cannot explain — maybe it

was because I saw so much drunkenness on the streets on a Saturday night — hey, what am I saying — any night of the week, that to this day I have never broken that pledge. I honestly don't feel that I have lost out on anything — quite the reverse. I could always remember, the next morning, the fun of the night before, with a fuller wallet and a clearer head than my hard-drinking and free-spending associates.

If you thought Father Murray had a loud voice, let me tell you Father Downey's was stentorian in the extreme.

You avoided going to confession with Father Downey at all costs. He terrified everyone. It would not be unusual to hear him bellowing at the top of his voice from the confessional at one poor penitent or another upon hearing his sins,

'What, are you a Catholic at all?'

Fellow penitents, waiting to have their confessions heard, cringed and melted away to return only when another priest was on duty. On entering St Patrick's church, the new arrival would hear the whispered information that it was the dreaded Downey who was hearing confessions and the response would be immediate — 'Aw, be Jasus, I'm off to the Marist,' and they would scurry off to the other church.

Then, of course, for schooling I had the Christian Brothers, that august body of child beaters. But before that I had the Sisters of Mercy whom I found not to be very merciful.

My first day at the convent of the Sisters of Mercy is as clear to me today as if it was yesterday. I was five years of age and my mother, being very religious, decided to stop off at the Redemptorist Church to say a few prayers before enrolling me that morning in school. There were not many in the church as it was a weekday and very early in the morning. I was conscious of my new boots with the steel studs on the heels as our footsteps echoed on the stone floor when Mammy marched me up to the front pew. There was a short-sighted woman creeping about on the altar who kept peering at things she had polished, and as we knelt down, I noticed an old man several pews away who was familiar to me.

At my age, I suppose everybody over the age of twenty was old, but this man really was old. The poor old chap suffered from a serious eye defect which caused it to keep constantly watering. Nicknames were almost as common as Christian names in our town and this old fellow was known to all the children of the demesne where I lived as Jemmy Juicy Eye. You may think it a cruel nickname, and I suppose that it was, but then there were plenty of others to make him feel in very good company. Names such as Mad Watters, Limp McKittrik or even Hook Ball Kirby — the list is endless. I will not attempt to enlighten you as to the reasons for these eloquent sobriquets — I will let your imagination do that for you.

Bum Bum Traynor was another. No, you would be quite wrong about that, he was a grand old gentleman. He lived on the corner of our street at number forty-six. He walked very upright, always wearing a trilby hat, and in his spare time, he played the big drum in the local brass band, otherwise known as the Emmet band — so named after a great Irish patriot called Robert Emmet who led an insurrection in Dublin in 1803. The English said it was no more than a fracas — well they would, wouldn't they — but they hanged him anyway. He achieved immortal fame, however, by his speech from the dock when he said, among other things, 'Not until my country has taken her place among the nations of the earth, then, and not until then, shall my epitaph be written.'

Something like that — I wasn't there but great stuff all the same. The Brothers drummed it into us as children.

Bum Bum was in the habit, while striding out on his afternoon marches, of pretending he was beating his big drum and humming aloud, 'bum, bum, bum, bum, bum, bum.' So there you have it. Easy, wasn't it?

I attended the convent for two years in a boys-only class until transferring to a boys' school proper. My teacher during all that time was a nun called, among other things, Sister Gabriel. She had the whitest face I have ever seen, completely bloodless, her thin lips and pinched cheeks making her face almost a death mask. I wondered afterwards what nickname they might have given her.

Her wimple was starched as stiff as a board so that she was unable to turn her head without turning her whole body with it. There was a girls' school nearby, but we never saw anything of its pupils. The nuns also ran a laundry next door and you could smell the steam when it was windy.

I had only been in Sister Gabriel's class a matter of weeks when I learned my first and most memorable lesson in life. We were asked to copy down something which she had written on the blackboard, in our jotters. We were to use a pencil and were warned that if we made an error, we were to use an eraser to rub it out and not our fingers or the cuff of our sleeve as the page must appear clean and tidy.

You've guessed it. Mullen made a mistake, and not possessing an eraser, borrowed one from the boy in front whose name was Matthews. Sadly, the rubber was dirty and made a mess of my nice clean page. When Sister Gabriel saw the mess, she accused me of using either my finger or the sleeve of my jersey.

I told her I used a rubber as instructed and with all the confidence of a five-year-old who was always told by his mammy to tell the truth, I pointed straight at Matthews and asked for his corroboration of my story. Seeing the bad-tempered look on the teacher's face, little Matthews could see a load of trouble ahead of him and decided that the best way to avoid it was to deny any knowledge of the matter.

The nun was furious at what she conceived to be my obvious lie and kept me in after school.

'You will remain here until you tell the truth,' she commanded.

Crestfallen and bewildered at the turn of events, I watched all the others depart home whilst Sister Gabriel sat behind her desk and glowered at me.

'Are you ready to admit that you lied?' she demanded several times.

'I am telling the truth, Sister, I used the rubber,' I insisted, my confidence ebbing fast.

After several of these exchanges, she lost patience with this recalcitrant child and commanded, 'Come with me, we will see what the Mother Superior has to say about this,' and she swept out with one now badly frightened five-year-old in tow. I had a job to keep up with her, her long black gown swishing angrily and the huge set of rosary beads, big enough to moor a medium-sized oil tanker, which were tied around her waist, clacking against her knees as she stamped along.

We marched across the school yard and through a large wooden gate, which she closed after us with an ominous bang, and entered the convent garden. I looked around fearfully; I felt completely cut off from the outside world and totally alone with this frightening creature. Who knew what dreadful punishments might be handed out in this strange place? But I had not done anything wrong, I tried to console myself. Mammy had always said that God was a kind person and only punished the guilty. But Mammy's assurances were beginning to wear a bit thin by now.

This garden was an area which I had only caught glimpses of before when the gate was left open, and which led to the nuns' domestic quarters. It was summertime, I was hot and sticky, and Mammy had promised me an ice cream when I got home from school. I could hear lots of bees buzzing and the garden seemed full of roses — the smell was so overpowering I nearly choked. To this day, the smell of any kind of rose brings back memories of fear, a wildly beating heart and wet pants.

I was brought before Mother Patrick, who was ensconced in some kind of sitting room. This was my first and, thank God, my last meeting with the great lady. If Sister Gabriel had the whitest face in the world then surely her superior had the reddest. She was sitting down — I don't think she could get up, she was so fat.

'What have we here, Sister?' she gasped, her breath coming in short pants.

'We have a boy here who tells lies, Mother Patrick. I have told him he can go home when he tells the truth and not before,' Sister Gabriel snapped, eyeing me balefully.

I was an intelligent child, if a badly frightened one, and I was trying hard not to cry — I felt so alone. I was also extremely bewildered. But the message was becoming all too clear. Mammy had been wrong all along — it does not pay to tell the truth. Quite the reverse in fact. If I told the nun that I had not used the rubber, I could go home straight away and tell Mammy the truth. Maybe she would believe me.

So it was that I told a whopping lie and was released from captivity at once with dire warnings of what might happen to me in future if I were caught lying again. I raced home, sobbing with relief, as fast as my little legs could carry me. Mammy believed my story of events and for years afterwards, even when I was grown up, she would recall, with great resentment, the day when her son was forced to lie to get some form of justice. I have long since forgiven the mean-hearted nun as it was my first serious lesson of what to expect in the outside world — indeed, it was a lesson that stood me in good stead for the rest of my life.

Chapter Six

I had the great misfortune of attending the Irish Christian Brothers (and what a misnomer that is) school after I left the convent. I had the option of attending the De La Salle school instead — it was, in fact, somewhat nearer to my home — but for some reason, Mammy decided that it was to be the Christian Brothers and thereby, as it were, sealed my fate. I can honestly say that the only thing I learned there in seven years was to how to keep my head down and thereby keep it on my shoulders. This was a very necessary attribute if you wanted to survive in this house of horrors. I was more skilled than most. I could make myself shrink almost to the point of being invisible in class, but ultimately, I received my fair share of vicious beatings at the hands of these enlightened educationalists.

The school was housed in a brand-new red brick building, purpose built with light airy classrooms and decent lavatories and cloakrooms. Before this, it was located in an old Victorian building close by, which had outlived its usefulness. For one thing, it was now far too small for a rapidly rising population, for, despite the huge number of people emigrating, there was still no shortage of children.

I had commenced my first term in this old edifice and had been there only three or four days when the ancient solid fuel boiler, used for heating the place, blew up. This caused massive flooding and so much disruption — it was a bitterly cold winter's day — that it was decided to move in at once to the new school which was almost complete but had not yet been officially opened, or indeed blessed. In view of the savagery I was to witness over the next seven years in that building, I guessed they missed out on the latter ceremony altogether.

We marched across Wrighton's lane, which divided the old and the new, in single file through the gate into the school yard and I was the second boy to make the historic entrance to the new edifice, the first boy being a lad named Matthews (no relation to the dastardly Matthews). I always remember that a small brick building no more than the size of a decent shed, had survived the onslaught, of the planners and this stood right by the entrance to the school playground. It looked incongruous, jutting in as it did to an otherwise square playing area. It was, in fact, a workshop that had been allowed to remain and was the property of a little man called Wee Sands. I describe him as little because he was the smallest man in town — not a dwarf, you understand — just very tiny. He could not have been more than five feet tall and not surprisingly walked with a very erect bearing. He always wore a cap and had a very grave, if not indeed a very sad, face but then who would not if you had to look up to all those cheeky children.

In later years, I got to know another chap who lived further up near the top of Wrighton's Lane which was not a very salubrious quarter of the town. It was one of the older parts providing a short cut between Clanbrassil Street and Chapel Street. It was composed of little whitewashed cottages and had been let run down very badly. Putting it bluntly, it was a slum. But I do remember it for one very good reason. In someone's yard grew a huge pear tree, the branches of which greatly overhung the wall of the yard into the lane. When ripe, the pears were not only the biggest but the juiciest I have ever tasted, and my prowess as a high jumper stems from those days. With great agility, I managed to pluck a pear for myself most mornings on my way to school.

The fellow I want to tell you about was a character called Peter Rawlings.

I did not know him very well but was on nodding acquaintance with him due to the fact that he was a regular attendant, like me, at the Sunday afternoon dances at the Pavilion Ballroom, Blackrock — a village near Dundalk. These were held during the summer months only and were a legend for bare legs and budding bosoms. If you wanted to get off the mark, this was the place to do it. It took me no more than ten minutes or so on my racing bicycle, riding like a bat out of hell, to cover the three miles from Dundalk in a wave of anticipation of exciting female company. Seventeen years of age, hair Brylcreemed like treacle to offset the wind as it tore at my ears, I could not wait to swing into action.

Here at the Pavilion, we would stand and size up the talent on show, many of whom would have made the journey from north of the border for an enjoyable day out at the seaside. Peter was a tall youth with a huge coif, well-oiled, that stood forth like the bows of a destroyer. His suit was a disaster, and although the trousers were threadbare, with the turn-ups all ragged, he had a crease in them that could cut your throat. His shirt was not much better, with a well frayed collar, and he wore brown sandals, the buckles of which were inexpertly repaired with thick rubber bands.

Not a very bright spark to pick up the girls, you might think, but all that shines is not gold. For Peter could dance like he could give Fred Astaire lessons, and it was a treat to see him in action if he could find a good enough partner, even if he did have a patch in the arse of his trousers. He would not dance with just anybody — she had to be a right little Ginger Rogers before Peter would ask her out on the floor.

I remember one Sunday when he must have found his princess, for he nudged me in the ribs and declared proudly, 'I have got a special request coming up from the band, Johnny. You will have to get out on the floor for this one,' and he winked at me, which could be an alarming experience to the beholder since Peter had a bad cast in one eye.

Requests were not unusual, the bandleader always happy to oblige a customer.

When I heard it read out, it was a very popular song of the day. I had great difficulty in not laughing aloud as the bandleader announced through the loudspeakers, 'Ladies and Gentlemen, and now a request from Peter Rawlings of Wrighton's Lane for his lady friend, entitled

'We Won't Live In a Castle'.

Bearing in mind Peter's family's long-time residency in Wrighton's Lane, and the fact that most newly married young couples at that time were forced, through poverty, to live with their in-laws, I think the girl could take that as a promise.

It was during my first week in the new school that I was introduced to PT. Our instructor was an ex-army sergeant named Sullivan. I thought he was short for a soldier, having always thought that fighting men were big. He wore a polo neck sweater that might have been white once, a pair of baggy trousers and canvas shoes — what we used to call guttees. He had a very red face which fronted a stumpy skull which sprouted hair like a porcupine's quills, and he continually tried to suck in his huge belly which was overflowing from the waistband of his trousers. He always looked angry, as though someone had just upset him. As this was ten o'clock in the morning, I suspect that he was suffering from the effects of too much Guinness the night before. He stood on an upturned crate to give himself altitude and bawled at us as though we were a new bunch of recruits on the barrack square. He had a shrill high-pitched voice which made him sound more like a fishwife than an ex-army instructor.

He made us carry out various exercises, stretching, touching our toes and so on. I noticed he made no attempt to do any of this himself and then ordered us to march, 'Cle, Cle, Cle Deas Cle. Left, left, left right left.'

I could not help but notice that the boy in front of me seemed to have difficulty with his co-ordination.

Instead of each arm swinging forward alternatively, they were both going forward and back together giving him a curious clockwork gait.

'Halt!'

Someone else had noticed the strange march as a furious shout from our instructor brought us to a shuddering stop, and he leaped off his plinth to confront the boy who he thought was taking the mickey out of him.

Sullivan looked as if he was going to have apoplexy as he tried in vain to get the seven-year-old boy, whose name was Lorenzo Daly, to march properly in a straightforward manner. Try as he would, nothing appeared to succeed, and in the end, the bad-tempered ex-sergeant had to admit defeat and Lorenzo blithely continued on his way, quite happily swinging both arms together which is not an easy thing to do. Try it sometime if you do not believe me.

It was a great pity that the same high quality that was to be found in the new school building was not matched by the standard of its teaching staff. Where did they manage to find them? You would be hard put to find such a collection of misfits in a psychiatric ward of a mental hospital, which is where most, if not all, of them should have been kept under lock and key.

On admission to the school, I had been placed in first class along with all the other seven-year-olds and settled in quite happily under the tutelage of a kind man named Mr Cooper, from Broughton Street, who was in charge of us for most of the time. Even after I had left his class, he remembered me when staging a school play and gave me the role of a headmaster. I can recall his kind sister going to a lot of trouble, specially kitting me out in a cassock and mortar board for the role. It was the most exciting moment of my young life, finding myself in front of an audience. It was to be nearly forty years later that I took up amateur dramatics, and when I first walked out on stage, I felt the same thrill that I experienced all those years before. Why did I wait so long? I don't know, just too busy, I guess.

One or two other teachers came in, at times, to take us for some lessons, but I do not remember anything about them. I was very happy there, coping quite well, but this was not to last for more than a week or two before some well-meaning soul decided that I was far too intelligent to remain in the first class and should be placed straight away in second class.

What the genius overlooked was the fact that the basics of the Gaelic language was taught in first class — a very necessary first step, since all lessons in this school were taught in the native language of which I knew not a single word. The exception to this routine, naturally enough, was English grammar.

This decision was a disaster for me as I struggled for the next seven years trying to understand what the blazes they were talking about. Not only did I not know the answers — I had not a clue what the questions were about. I never caught up with Irish grammar and apart from the English lesson at which, mercifully, I seemed to excel, and arithmetic, which was not too bad, I had a terrible time. I remember once one of my essays was read out at school assembly one Monday morning as an example of good composition, but it was cold comfort when I was regularly flogged for my lack of knowledge of history and geography. This was doubly sad since I adored history, it has always intrigued me, and I felt sure I could have been good at it.

For hours after a beating, I was unable to hold a pen as my hands were so swollen after the cruel cuts of the leather strap which was the favourite instrument of torture. Approximately fifteen inches long, it was two inches across by half an inch thick. It was probably meant to make contact with the victim's palm by the broad side but if the attacker saw that it was not having the desired affect (screams of pain), he turned it round and used the narrow edge to inflict more serious injury. If that, too, failed to elicit at least whimpers of distress from the victim, then the assailant had the fail-safe solution of turning the child's hand over and beating the backs of the hand.

I remember that that was a favourite tactic of Brother 'Spud' Murphy. Much more effective, the sadistic brute quickly discovered. Ten cuts on each hand was quite a normal chastisement for not being able to answer a question correctly. Being confused between the capitals of Yugoslavia and Romania was always good for a five-minute thrashing.

The record, however, is held by a boy called Luke Begley who was dragged out in front of the class and received thirty-six cuts in one frenzied attack by a demented Brother Rehill.

Nicknamed 'The Butcher', and aptly named, the man was a nightmare come to life.

The Brothers normally wore a long black coat, nearly to their ankles and buttoned all the way down the front, in addition to a broad sash wrapped around their waist. Short and red-faced, Rehill was forever hitching up his sash as though getting ready for action, which indeed he often was. Behind his horn-rimmed glasses, his eyes had a crazed glint and his whole body oozed aggression. His thin hair was plastered straight back on his head, and there was always the trace of a smirk on his lips as though he knew what was coming and we didn't. He was wrong about that. He was the only person I have ever met who truly frightened me.

This boy Begley was unusual in the fact that we had never seen him struck before this day for the simple reason that he was the brightest boy in the class. His desk was at the front (he had no reason to hide), mine was second from the rear, and his work was always of the highest standard. Unlike most of us, he was too well dressed and came from a good home. Surprising, too, for a boy who was so much of a swot, I never saw him bullied like the rest of us. I remember a toad called Clifford, with a club foot, who sat behind me for a whole year and who tormented me daily, without mercy, when I attended the convent. Maybe his disability made him anti-social — in any event, I seemed to bear the brunt of his anger. I cannot see it from here, but I think my back still bears the marks from his punches.

Begley never had to put up with anything like this treatment. In fact, he was extremely popular due perhaps to his quiet and self-effacing manner and his willingness to help others. I cannot recall the reason for the attack, but then with this hoodlum we had for a teacher, you did not have to do anything wrong. Like Dracula, I think he just wanted to taste some fresh blood. Spencer Tracy as Mr Hyde and having one of his bad days, is a good comparison for his normal behaviour.

We counted them as the blows fell mercilessly on the boy's hands. The victim appeared to be stoic and unmoving in the face of this assault, which only helped to drive his attacker to even greater heights of depravity. He could not hear the screams of pain that he craved. I did hear snuffling and looked around to see several boys openly crying in sympathy for their classmate. It was a demonstration of solidarity for another unfortunate boy; they were with him in his agony — something I had never seen in school before or indeed since.

It was only long afterwards that I realised that the eleven-year-old boy was in a state of total shock which was why he exhibited no signs of pain. It is a measure of the effort put into it that the pervert that inflicted this punishment fell back into his chair completely exhausted, or perhaps I should say sated, after his exertions. The sweat was pouring off him as he continually wiped his face with a large white handkerchief. Who was it said the happiest days of your life were spent in school (maybe if you were the teacher)? There were a number of lay teachers, in addition to the Brothers, teaching in this school, such as Mr Cooper. One I remember very well was Mr 'Boiler' McClune. It could be said that the lay teachers never exhibited the cruelty of the Brothers, but in his day, 'Boiler' did have quite a reputation for handing out some vicious beatings. My brother Tom, who passed through these portals thirteen years before me, remembered this man with revulsion. By the time I came along, I think he must have mellowed, however, for one could not compare him to any of the Brothers for sheer brutality. Apart from his career as a teacher, he also owned a pub on the corner of Church Street and Patrick Street known as Mickey Dawes. His wife seemed to run it most of the time, or at least, when her husband was at work.

Behind the pub was a large piece of waste ground where the gypsies encamped on fair days. Binno always referred to it as the Indian reservation, as with piebald horses roaming about and all the shawl-clad women smoking clay pipes, it definitely took on the appearance of an Apache village.

I remember Patrick Street for another reason. Once, when I was about sixteen, when riding my bicycle along it, I noticed Mr Moore, who lived just round the corner from us, walking along in front of me on his way to work as a baker at H. F. & J. McCann. I was about fifty yards behind him when he seemed to stumble and crumple to the ground. A crowd gathered around him at once, and it was determined that the poor man was dead. His son Gerry was a great pal of my brother George. They were in the boxing club together and it came as quite a shock to everybody who knew him.

Patrick Street possessed a far more lasting memory for me in the shapely form of a beautiful girl called Eva Byrne. Eva was about the same age as me and tall, with gorgeous jet-black hair which hung down her back.

Whenever I left the house to go anywhere, it did not matter what direction my journey took me — I always went via Patrick Street in the hope that I might catch a glimpse of my heart's desire. She did not know that I even existed, so there was never any chance of a nod, much less a chat. On those occasions when I did spot her, my mouth went dry, my heart speeded up to a dangerous degree and, from somewhere, the sound of a hundred-piece orchestra could be heard. But Eva never noticed me.

Seamus Toal, to whom I rashly confided my dreams, rarely missed an opportunity to taunt me.

'I saw your man McCourt chatting with Eva yesterday,' he would say, slyly watching, no doubt, the look of pain that crossed my face. 'Sure, he was there showing off his new racing bike — a Lenton Clubman no less — he looked great in his racing outfit.'

I sniffed, pretending it was no bother.

'I beat the lard out of him in the ten-mile time trial last Sunday morning on the Dublin Road, Lenton Clubman or not,' I retorted. 'He was a full minute behind me, even with the old yoke, an ASP (all spare parts), that I was riding.'

Seamus did not give up easily.

'They say your man McCourt has an outfit for every day of the week,' he would say, looking at my tattered clothes.

'So have I,' I would exclaim, 'this is it I am wearing.'

Over fifty years later, I am visiting my sister Carmel in

Canada when she says to me, when I have taken her out for a drive, 'Pull over here a minute.'

We are passing a rather nice detached house in a leafy avenue and she points it out to me and says, 'Guess who lives in there.'

But of course I have no idea and tell her so.

'Do you remember a girl called Eva Byrne from Patrick Street? She lives in that house and we have been friends a long time, since we discovered that we both came from Dundalk. We met at an Irish hop here in Hamilton. She is a widow — her husband died a couple of years ago.'

My throat went terribly dry, my heart started beating perilously fast and, somewhere, an orchestra had started playing.

I was a widower, Eva was a widow. Was there some great force at work here?

Could it be, after all these years, that fate was going to step in and take a hand in my destiny?

'Are we calling on her?' I managed to stutter.

'Oh, I don't think so,' says Carmel. I wouldn't dream of barging in without letting her know I was coming. Better drive on.'

So I was not privileged to meet the desirable Eva after all. I guess some things are just not meant to be. Anyway, I hope she is very happy.

Being an arrant coward, I tried to miss school as often as I could. I would play on Mammy's sympathy and say that I did not feel very well, which indeed held an element of truth. I often felt physically sick just looking at the fury building up on Rehill's face. A boy would be sent out to the house to find out why Johnny had not attended school for the past three days and Mammy would say that I was ill. If this occurred too often, we would then attract a visit from Garda Corry, the school attendance officer.

He would arrive on his bicycle, lean it against the railings, and come up the path to the door whilst I hid upstairs and tried to still my wildly beating heart. He was a stout red-faced man and I always used to wonder why everybody in authority had a red face and a big belly.

'The school informs me that Johnny is missing a lot from his class. Is there any reason for this?' he would say, in his Cavan accent.

Mammy would say that I had been ill.

'He seems to be ill a lot. Maybe he needs good exercise. Does he play any football at all?' — Cavan being a great county for its Gaelic football. 'You know, sure I used to be a bit of an athletic meself,' the Garda would say proudly. Mammy was a charmer and used to get him chatting and he would ride away on his bike with a friendly warning.

'You know what will happen, Mrs. Mullen, if you get summoned and have to appear in court,' he would say, looking at her significantly.

Mammy would get the message loud and clear and I knew that the game was up, and it would be back to school the very next morning. Mammy knew that she would almost certainly receive a fine and that was something that did not bear thinking about in her straitened circumstances.

Of course, it was even harder when I did return after missing several days as I would have missed a lot of lessons and got even further behind. Fuel indeed for Butcher Rehill to get his strap out and lay it on thick and plentiful.

'Bear that in mind, O'Maolain,' I can still hear him panting as he swung the leather from on high with all of his might.

Garda Corry had another official function to perform for the neighbourhood, and that was the collection of dog licence fees. If he found someone with a dog who was not prepared to pay the fee, he would take the dog away from them and remove it to the pound, presumably to have it put down.

I was six years old when I had a dog given to me by a neighbour who found himself with a litter of six to look after. They were mongrels, of course, and those for whom he could not find a home would be summarily drowned, just as kittens invariably went the same way. I called the puppy 'Tricks', not knowing when I did so that he would turn out to be quite easily the stupidest dog in the town.

But he could fight, and that more than made up for everything else. He could beat the living daylights out of every dog in the demesne and I was so proud of him. I thought he was invincible — that is, until one day he met up with a dog he had not seen or smelled before, from O'Hanlon Park. I was with Tricks when this confrontation took place, and I was mortified by the grovelling, cowering, tail wagging display of my champion. The other dog had not even threatened him, yet here he was, lying on his back and offering his balls to be chewed — I could not believe what I was seeing. The other dog, which was a pit bull terrier, a breed I was to learn about when I was much older, just stood over Tricks, growling deep in his throat.

Tricks was ahead of me. He already knew all there was to know about pit bulls and wanted no part of this killer. The other dog trotted off as though attacking my mongrel was beneath his dignity, and Tricks turned his attention to me. I was so ashamed of him and embarrassed for him at this display of abject cowardice, that the tears stung my eyes at his downfall. My great champion humbled without even a fight taking place.

Tricks slunk towards me almost on his belly, his tail wagging in such desperation for forgiveness that the whole rear end of him bent under the strain. He was well aware of his contemptuous behaviour, and when I aimed a half-hearted kick, he made no attempt to dodge, taking it bravely in the ribs. Then I was on my knees beside him, the tears really flowing now, cuddling him to me — for I knew only too well what it was like to be afraid, the memory of Clifford with the club foot sharp in my thoughts.

Not long after that episode, I came home from school one day to find that Garda Corry had called and taken Tricks away as Mammy could not afford the five shillings for the licence fee. I cried my eyes out, railing at Mammy for allowing it to happen. At six years of age, no excuse could be tolerated for such a blow, and I never saw Tricks again.

I had one other dog which I found wandering alone

one day in Kitsy's wood, and it followed me home. It was a poor wee thing, thin and emaciated, and dragging one leg behind it. Mammy said it must go as we could not look after it, but I cried, and she relented. There was no question of taking him to the vet. Indeed, if there was one in the town, he could probably be found among the cinder pickers on the slobland. Mammy said it needed good wholesome food — something we could not afford as we had barely enough for ourselves.

It was my task before going to school, when we could afford it, to run up to Frank Hamilton's butcher shop at the square to buy the meat for the dinner. I asked Frank, on those occasions, if I could have a bone for my dog, and he would give me a big juicy one. I gave it to Rex, which is what I christened my new pet, without Mammy seeing me. When she saw the dog gnawing away contentedly in the back yard, she exclaimed almost enviously, 'Where did that dog get the bone?'

'Oh, maybe he dug it up in the garden, Mammy, he is a great wee hunter you know,' I would say innocently.

After a week, however, it was painfully obvious even to me at my tender age, that Rex's days were numbered. Mammy was adamant.

'It is cruel to keep him — he is in great pain, and he must be drowned and put out of his misery.'

So it was with a heavy heart that I took an old sack, filled it with some stones and, taking Rex, headed for the slipway on the Castletown river just by the Fair Green. It flowed from here into Dundalk Bay, and at high tide, small boats could be launched from this spot. When told the news, Binno agreed to accompany me, feeling that I could do with some moral support. The drama of the occasion was not lost on him either — Binno loved a bit of drama.

So two small boys had the task of putting the wretched dog in the sack, tying the end and throwing it into the river, which fortunately Mammy had made sure was at high tide. It was quite dark, there was a strong wind blowing, spray was thrown up over the wall and into our eyes so we could hardly see what we were doing, and we got very wet. We watched the sack hit the water, float for a few seconds and then disappear below the surface. We quickly came away from the scene, and for two normally very talkative little boys, we were strangely silent on the way home.

It was the last dog I have ever owned. Years later, when my own children broached the subject of owning a dog, I always had a ready excuse for not having one in the house. That incident lasted long in my memory — not a task for which a nine-year-old should be made responsible.

Chapter Seven

There was another boy in our class called Lonnie Gaskin. Although not the oldest boy in the school, Lonnie was indisputably the best fighter. That is not to say that he was a troublemaker; on the contrary, more than one bully was quickly put to rout by the power of Lonnie's fists. Nobody messed with Lonnie.

Brother Rehill was well aware of Lonnie's reputation and was always challenging the boy in a supposedly playful fashion. Sitting at his desk, Lonnie was at a great disadvantage as he would try to parry Rehill's punches as the Brother stood over him with a sick smile on his lips. 'Sure, I hear you're a great wee fighter, Gaskin,' he would say, whilst throwing a vicious punch underneath Lonnie's armpit — a blow that would make his victim wince in pain.

How I longed for the day that Lonnie would leap to his feet and lay the brute out on the floor. Although only a boy, I was certain that he was quite capable of doing so as he had a punch like a sledgehammer. But it never happened. Time and again, the boy had to put up with this form of torture while the bully stood over him, taunting him, fully aware that he was safe from any form of retaliation.

Another boy who came in for some appalling beatings was Jimmy 'Daisy' Conroy. What can I say about Jimmy without mentioning how he smelled? I firmly believe that the little boy, and he was small, could not have been washed since the day he was born. The jersey which he wore, and I am certain never removed from his body, stank to high heaven. The cuffs of the sleeves were as stiff as cardboard with the snots and tears that had accrued there over who knows how long. Daisy could almost have used them as weapons. I never gave a whole lot of thought to his nickname at the time, but now, over half a century later, it seems to make a lot of sense.

Knowing the Irish sense of humour, the saying, 'As fresh as a daisy' would be wholly appropriate for the young boy. I was glad, for obvious reasons, that my desk was a couple of rows away from him.

If young Quigley held the record for the mother and father of all beatings, then Daisy, indisputably, was the record holder for the greatest number of floggings. Hardly a day would go by without him being dragged out in front of the class and thrashed unmercifully for the slightest excuse. I was always shaking with fear when this happened, for it was almost like a drug with Rehill. Once he got started on a beating, it was as though he had an appetite for it that could not be assuaged easily. When through with his current victim, he would glare round the classroom looking for another likely candidate for a thrashing, and everybody tried desperately not to catch his eye.

I have to say here, that it was most noticeable that the better off among the pupils hardly ever got the strap. For besides being the most cruel of men, the Brothers were the most appalling snobs. Shop owner's sons like Walsh, McKenna or the posh O'Hagan twins, all nice kids mind you, were seldom beaten.

A classic example of this form of snobbery could be found in the presence in the class of a boy called Soirse Plunkett. I have probably spelled his Christian name wrongly but who cares. His family lived in a mansion out at Ballymascanlon, and I believe he was related to the famous Count Plunkett who was a leader of the 1916 rebellion. No beatings for young Plunkett in his beautiful suit, let me tell you. Who was going to swing the leather at him? Are you codding? No Christian Brother that was for sure! Their grovelling attitude towards him was nauseating to say the least. Rehill, in particular, would have considered it a favour to be allowed to wipe his arse.

The poorer boys were not so lucky. Daisy, however, could not be broken easily. He never lost his cheeky grin, even after some terrible hidings. He would often wink at me through his pain on his way back to his seat, and of all the boys in the class, I think I liked Daisy the best. He was as tough as nails. Only a little chap, he could and did hold his own against much bigger boys who left him severely alone when they discovered that he never gave in when embroiled in a scrap.

Out of many such incidents, I can remember one other particularly vicious attack I can attribute to Butcher Rehill.

There was a boy in our class by the name of Kenny Heery, who lived far outside the town in the village of Dromiskin. He was a mild-mannered chap, well dressed, wore glasses and was very quiet and inoffensive. Someone said his father was a farmer, but he looked more like a college professor's son. Because he had to come to school by bus, a service which could not get him to school by the correct time of half past nine, he was permitted to arrive twenty minutes later than anyone else. On this particular morning, the weather was bad and the bus was nearly an hour late.

On this Monday morning, Butcher Rehill had gone totally berserk. He completely lost it. Again, I cannot remember the cause — does it matter? Suffice to say that the Butcher was having one of his bad days.

This generally happened about five days a week anyway, and the prelude to this explosion of anger would be a frantic pacing up and down the front of the class, gnashing his teeth. Rehill was a great teeth gnasher. He would throw up his hands in the air, exhorting the Almighty for patience to deal with his problems — namely us, his pupils — but we knew from long experience that God would not respond to his request and resigned ourselves for what was to come.

Everyone began to cower down in the face of the inevitable. I heard someone whimper in terror and glanced around to see who it was and found everyone staring at me. My knees knocked together under the desk, and I put my hands on them to stop them quivering, so great was my fear.

The smell of piss was everywhere as children could not control their trepidation, as something seemed to snap within him and, with a wild cry, the Butcher leaped for his desk and grabbed the weapon.

Screaming like a dervish on this particular morning, our teacher had snatched his strap and was running up and down the aisles between the desks, belabouring everyone in sight, slashing out left and right, determined not to miss anyone. The man's energy was amazing. We squirmed down in our desks, desperately trying to cover our most vulnerable parts, our ears, and taking the blows on our heads and backs.

If he thought he had missed someone in his delirium, the madman would turn around and flay the unlucky boy. Not one boy out of forty-four escaped his wrath. Looking back, I often wonder how he did not come to cause really serious injury to one of these very young boys, for he would lash out with every bit of strength in his body and he was a man in his prime, no more than forty years old. He missed his vocation; he really would have been in his element in the German S.S.

It was at this moment that Kenny Heery entered the room to behold a scene that must have made him quake in his shoes.

He just had time to blurt out, 'The bus was late, sir,' before Rehill was upon him.

Dispensing with the strap which he obviously considered inadequate for the task, he hurled it at the desk in his fury. This was cause for some really serious brutality. He grabbed the boy by the coat collar and the seat of his pants and threw his victim bodily down the aisle towards his desk, which was the third from the front row.

Stumbling and unable to keep his balance, his

satchel still entangled in one arm (he must have been the scion of a wealthy family to possess one), Kenny Heery fell and split his head open on the corner of the desk. By the grace of God his glasses went flying, otherwise he must surely have lost an eye.

We all sat transfixed as the blood spurted forth and ran down the boy's face. Then it was that this lunatic, who called himself a teacher, faced the class and shouted, 'Now look what you made me do.'

But he got away with it.

Somehow, he got Kenny cleaned up and spent the rest of the day toadying up to the boy in his grisly fashion.

All the Brothers were guilty of the worst kind of brutality, but Rehill had the edge on all of them. At least the others would wait until you failed to answer the question correctly before striking you. The Butcher's blow came as he asked the question, almost as though he was afraid you might be right and there would be no reason to hit you.

'O'Maolain, (that's me in Gaelic) what river runs through Paris?'

I know the answer to this one and I almost sigh with relief but before my lips could frame the answer, Smash!

A blow to the side of the head, delivered with full force of the open hand and encompassing my ear, sent my brain whirling. Dazed and confused, my ear already swelling to what seemed like cauliflower size, I could only stand and stammer, all my confidence gone, whereupon I was dragged out in front of the class and given six cuts on each hand from the strap.

'I'll teach you to pay attention in future,' my teacher would shout. 'Let that be a lesson for you.' And his favourite remark as he finished the punishment, 'Bear that in mind, O'Maolain.'

I had good reason to remember his words, as quite early in life I began to lose the power of hearing in my left ear. The most extraordinary thing was that you never dared to complain at home about this treatment as the Brothers were considered omnipotent. The teacher was always right. No, I am wrong, there was one exception.

The school normally broke up for lunch between one o'clock and one forty-five, when most of us hared home for some well-earned nourishment. We bolted what little food was put on the table and ran all the way back again as fast as we could to play in the schoolyard until the bell went.

Not so the boys who came in from the country, the distance for them to travel in just forty-five minutes being too great. They were provided with a snack consisting of a rock cake and a glass of milk. For some reason which I never understood, they were expected to partake of this feast shortly before the normal break-up time, usually at about twelve forty-five or thereabouts. A boy was delegated to go around the different classrooms and announce that lunch was being served, and those entitled to this free bonanza got up and left the classroom.

This particular day, the delegated boy for the mission was a lad called Tommy Traynor. I was in the class of a Brother Doyle, otherwise known as 'Lightning' Doyle — a young man in his early twenties, newly admitted to the august body of the Christian Brothers. It was clear to all of us at once that he was extremely well qualified to join this brotherhood. We reckoned that he had the fastest draw in the school — that is to say that you could not see his fist moving until it had actually made contact with the side of your head. Even then, it was only the ringing tone in your ear that warned you of the pain that was to follow immediately, that told you that he had struck home.

On this day, he was in the middle of some dissertation when the door of the classroom suddenly opened and our Tommy stuck his head around the door and called out the usual greeting in that gravelly voice for which he was well known, 'Bun and milk, everybody.'

In three strides, Doyle was across the floor and on the boy like a panther, grabbing him by the coat collar and hauling him into the room, slamming the door shut. He then set about Tommy with both fists, beating him about the head and body whilst the boy tried desperately to cover up. Doyle was a fit young man and made his punches tell.

'I'll teach you some better manners, interrupting me in the middle of a lesson,' the Christian Brother shouted, his voice hoarse with fury.

Somehow, Tommy managed to wriggle free when his attacker paused for breath, got the door open and legged it down the corridor, with Doyle in hot pursuit, but the prey got away.

It was widely reported the next day that old man Traynor had stormed into the school, determined to sort out Brother Doyle for the unprovoked attack on his young son. I was not present at this supposed confrontation, so can offer no evidence that such an encounter took place, but certainly the good Brother was very subdued for a long time afterwards.

Brother Doyle quite fancied himself as a footballer, but he was not fit to lace the boots of his quarry, for Tommy Traynor went on to become a great professional footballer, playing for Southampton and his country. Strangely enough, I was to bump into him many years later at Southampton Municipal Swimming pool where I had taken my kids for an afternoon swimming lesson. Tommy was on the same mission with his young offspring, and I had no need to turn around to find out who was there when I heard that familiar gravelly voice say, 'It's Johnny Mullen.'

We reminisced about the old days before shaking hands and going our separate ways. 'Lightning' Doyle was not mentioned.

The headmaster of this enlightened school was one Brother Ryan. Blind as a bat and with a long, hooked nose, you've guessed it, he was simply known as 'Rhino'. He was a tall spare figure of a man wearing rimless glasses who walked with a long bouncy stride. He did not have a class of his own, merely taking a class, I suppose, when someone was ill or away for some reason. He was usually to be found fussing around in the school shop where boys could go to buy exercise books, jotters or pencils and the like. I can still smell the quite unique aroma of new stationary when I think of the place.

We were beginning to think that 'Rhino' was past it or at least going soft, since he had not been known to have beaten anyone for a long time, when we were proved unequivocally wrong. I was in the shop buying a jotter, I think, when, hearing a commotion in the passageway — someone was laughing — for God's sake, how dare they — 'Rhino' hurried out of his shop to investigate. A crowd of boys were gathered round a figure on the ground who appeared to be making an eegit of himself, much to the amusement of his fellows. The gang quickly scattered as the angry head approached and proceeded to beat the shite out of the figure on the ground, thumping him with his fists as he was not armed with a weapon, demanding that he rise and take it like a man.

Failing to get the response he desired, 'Rhino' began dragging his victim by the hair out of the narrow corridor into the front hall a few yards from the entrance where there was more light. It was only then that the short-sighted teacher recognised the boy whom he had grabbed. It was only big O'Reilly who suffered from not-infrequent fits of epilepsy, one of which he was having right now and, with the cruelty of some children, was the butt of sick humour when this occurred.

'Rhino' then tried to make out that he was only trying to bring him out of the fit which was the cause of much hilarity when the story broke. Big O'Reilly was back in class the following morning, not a bother on him and remembering little of the debacle of the day before. His only memento of the occasion was a small bald patch by his right ear where a tuft of hair had been ripped out.

The standing joke for days afterwards was, 'How do you cure an epileptic?'

'By tearing his hair out by the roots.'

Another weird character to be leery of was Brother Sullivan.

'Sully' was a thin bald-headed man who had the unspeakable habit of spitting yellow mucous into his handkerchief all day long. We would watch him, fascinated, in the morning, shortly after he entered the classroom, when he would take from his pocket an immaculately pressed Irish lawn handkerchief into which he would deposit his first gobbet of phlegm of the day. By late afternoon, he was carrying around with him a gooey green mess and you could see him searching for a dry spot in his desperate need to offload another gobbet. Sometimes he had difficulty getting rid of it as it would adhere to his tongue, and he would turn his back to the class and surreptitiously lick the, by now, soggy handkerchief. Very genteel. I often wondered why he never carried a spare. Even more thought provoking, who had the unenviable task of washing them!

Apart from his vile personal habits, Sully had long before decided to forego the use of the dreaded strap. Not from any sense of kindness I may hasten to add, for he had discovered a more effective tool. It was a very pliant stick, about a metre long, which we in Ireland called a sally rod. Believe me, there was no more vicious weapon in the teachers' armoury than this, especially when wielded with all the strength of a grown man. 'Sully' — I never heard him called anything else

— christened it Bronco.

'Where is my Broncho,' he would say, licking his lips in anticipation of handing out a hiding.

Six welts across your arse, for that was Sully's chosen target — never anywhere else, and it was almost impossible to sit down afterwards. The painful red weals it left would last for days.

For singing lessons, we had the good fortune to have the services of a lay teacher who came to the school once or twice a week. He was a gifted organist and choirmaster named Van Dessel whose two sons attended the school. I remember Michael and Jan well. The family lived right next door to a grocer's shop owned by the Corr family, the younger members of which went on to find worldwide fame, as 'The Corrs', for their hugely popular music. I distinctly recall the gifted organist giving me a whack for not standing up straight at choir practice. Some punishments were well deserved as he caught me leaning on the shoulder of young Baxter. Walking or running was never a problem for me, but I have always loathed standing for any length of time.

Yet for some reason that I cannot remember, it was 'Sully' and not Van Dessel who managed to place me on the Town Hall stage with some others to sing something from 'The Tales of Hoffman'. I think that that was probably 'Sully's' greatest single act of cruelty — inflicting this braying chorus of schoolboys on a paying and unsuspecting audience.

Once a year, the school assembly hall was out of use for two weeks as the Brothers had it converted into a gambling casino. No school assembly for this period — this was usually in the month of February, I recall. All the usual games of chance were on hand, including roulette and slot machines, to part the already impoverished locals from their few pennies. I was never quite sure to what use the money, inveigled in this way from the suckers, was put — to help the poor or to make them poorer?

The other evening, I watched, fascinated, a television report of a lady head teacher who was charged with assault. A dedicated teacher for thirty years, this dignified and totally innocent lady had been merely trying to restrain an attack by a ten-year-old hoodlum who insisted on trying to kick her. She was found guilty by an unbelievably stupid magistrate and given a suspended prison sentence. Although shocked, I could not restrain a guffaw, to a look of reproof from my companion, as I tried to imagine Butcher Rehill's reaction to the boy's attack. He would probably have thrown him out of the window, even if it was the second floor. Why is it that the pendulum never stops in the middle?

Chapter Eight

It was almost inevitable that in the face of such grinding poverty and lack of opportunity, that some of my family emigrated: my sister Carmel to Ontario, Canada and my brother George to England. I followed suit as soon as I was old enough.

Immediately on leaving school, however, just as soon as I possibly could, at the age of fourteen, I obtained a job at a local cinema. My brother George had long since departed for England where he soon joined the merchant navy and fulfilled a dream of travelling the world. We would get the odd postcard from exotic places like Rio de Janeiro and I would spend long minutes examining it and trying to get the taste of adventure which I always associated with foreign sounding places. How I envied him.

Tom and my sisters were all working in local factories. But even so, every little extra coming in helped to swell the meagre coffers at forty-three and my small contribution made a difference. The war in Europe might have been over, but the war on poverty was still very much in progress in Ireland in 1946. It was my go-getter brother Tom who tipped me off where there was a job going, and I hurried along for an interview which turned out to be successful.

My employer was, wait for it, the local parish priest

— or, more accurately, the administrator or ADM. as he was known — the parish priest being, in fact, the Archbishop of Armagh in whose diocese we lived. I know, I know, but what could I do? It was almost impossible to escape from the clutches of the clergy. They were into everything. Wherever there was a buck to be made, there they were, smiling sweetly, hand out. In the front of the building that housed the cinema, the clergy operated the St. Patrick's Hall snooker club — one shilling a game, no credit. I should know. It was the scene of my misspent youth. Gambling was rife, with poker games continually in progress from ten o'clock in the morning until eleven at night when the hall closed.

Most snooker games involved betting, often with eight or nine players taking part in the same match, each player putting a shilling in the pot. The highest score won the kitty. Some of the players were so skilful that you were lucky to pay a visit to the table more than once before all the balls had been potted. Half the unemployed men of the town gathered there, and the dole money was frequently lost the same day it was picked up. It was a centre for no-hopers. Fights would often break out, but nobody paid much attention to a fist fight in those days, as arguments were quickly settled in this way. It was a matter of honour that no weapon be used in such an altercation, and a man might as well leave the town as use his boot to settle a score. He would be completely ostracized for taking this action.

There were four or five cinemas in the town, each trying to compete against the unfair competition of the Magnet Cinema run by our august Very Reverend J. F.

Stokes. John Francis himself. This cinema was awash with voluntary workers, I being one of the very few to be paid any money, and I can tell you ten shillings (fifty pence) was not a lot even in those days for a forty-eight-hour week. But you took whatever job you could get.

I can remember, on one occasion, I had to accompany the great John F. to Dublin in his Rover to pick up a film that should have arrived by train that morning. It was quite a rush to get it back to Dundalk in time for that evening's showing and, in his hurry coming down Park Street, the redoubtable priest had a chap off his bike by cutting in too sharp to take the corner at Lucy Soraghan's corner sweet shop.

The man was only shaken up, but finding himself the centre of attention, put on an Oscar winning performance for the bunch of unemployed characters who normally congregated at this corner to discuss world events. This was pure theatre, with the man moaning and groaning on the ground. There were scathing comments about John F.'s driving skills, or lack of them, coming thick and fast from who knew which quarter.

'Aw, very bad driving there, Father.'

'Is he drunk, do you think?

'Aw, you're coddin, I never knew he drank.'

', go on with you, and I thought it was all just rumour.'

'Be Jasus, and him a priest, are you coddin me?'

'I think we should send for the Guards, it's an open and shut case.'

The rapier-like wit came thick and fast, from a

group in a class by themselves, to take advantage of this situation. These men with, let's face it, nothing else to do, had honed the famous Irish 'craic' to a fine art.

The immensely dignified priest, who fully believed in his own supreme importance, was on a hiding to nothing as he found himself the butt of such pungent humour. Unable to identify where the different voices were coming from, so great was the crowd by now, he was shredded unmercifully as he tried to bluster his way out of the most embarrassing situation of his life. He finally managed to extricate himself and moved off with a grinding of gears to the guffaws of his tormentors. His plight was the subject of much humorous gossip in the town for days afterwards. The star of the show made a miraculous recovery on the priest's departure and was stood a good many free rounds in 'Jimmy's' bar, on the opposite corner to Lucy Soraghan's, as he regaled his audience with a blow by blow account of his fictional injuries.

Despite the fact of there being five cinemas in the town to serve a population of fourteen thousand, at times that hardly seemed enough, especially on a Sunday night when there was only one performance given in each cinema at nine o'clock. I think this was to give everyone time to go to devotions at seven o'clock before going to the pictures.

If the best film was being shown at the Magnet, for instance, huge queues would form early in the evening and, despite the presence of a steel barrier and two commissionaires, often the queue would break and there would be a tremendous surge forward towards the box office. A near riot would ensue as the sweating staff tried to restore order.

Then the cry would go up

'All full!'

Immediately, the few hundred disappointed customers remaining would turn around and a 'Charge of the Light Brigade' proportions would head towards Park Street Cinema, where perhaps the next best film was being shown. Seeing the wave of humanity approaching, the queue at this cinema would panic and surge around the pay desk and the same near riot ensued.

Eventually, the same call would go out, 'All seats full', and the mob would then head towards the Adelphi. This in turn would be followed by the Town Hall, by which time the army of disappointed fans would have greatly diminished. Those finally left had to reluctantly turn their faces towards the only cinema left, which was the Oriel, otherwise known as 'The Fleapit'. The saying went, 'If you go in at eight, you came out half ate'.

Aptly named, this was a god-forsaken establishment situated on Market Street, and the two bouncers outside would grin delightedly and shout, 'Plenty of room, lads,' as the few dozen exhausted stragglers appeared in sight.

Hard to believe when you blundered your way into the dimly lit interior, as the place appeared to be packed to the rafters. The first six or seven rows, however, were not individual seats but wooden forms, the front one about three feet from the screen. Here, the new arrivals were squashed into an already jam-packed row with exhortations from the bouncers to, 'Move along there, sure there's plenty of room, yis'l all get in, no trouble at all.'

The screen was about ten feet square and those near the front suffered neck strain for a week afterwards as they gazed ceilingward at the moving shadows. Those at the side were probably worse off as they had a sharp sideways view as well as looking upwards — a field day the following morning for an army of physiotherapists if they could only be afforded. With clouds of smoke hanging in the air — everybody smoked in those days — you were lucky to see the screen at all or indeed hear anything with the amount of coughing going on. Since the film was probably made the week after the invention of sound, you were probably not missing much anyway. But even this trial was preferable to being left in the street on a Sunday night, which did not bear thinking about.

Talking about Park street cinema reminds me of one night, or rather early one morning — about two o'clock in the morning to be precise. I was walking home along Park Street, not a soul about, after walking Lily Toal home from a dance, when I became vaguely aware of someone shouting. Lily later married, dammit, 'Gingser' Murray (pronounced with a hard 'g') — he was a counter hopper at either McClean's or Deerey's drapery store — I can't remember which at the time. OK, I'll explain. At that time, drapery stores had big long counters down each side of the shop, and young assistants could not be bothered to walk around. Need I say more?

I remember one time, Gingser actually accosted me

in the street and accused me of trying to wipe his eye with Lily. He was quite upset and threatened to give me a black eye if I did not leave him a clear field.

'You and what army,' I sneered.

This was my normal defensive strategy of acting with naked aggression since schoolyard days, when threatened with having the shite beaten out of me. It was my only defence, since I could not punch a hole in a paper bag and desperately hoped that the long yellow streak, that I knew was there, did not show. It did not always work out but this time it did, and Gingser backed off uncertainly, leaving me to swagger off, having given another Oscar winning performance.

Talking of acting, I actually saw him a couple of times on the stage, at talent competitions, giving what he thought was an impression of Al Jolson — black face, bow tie, the lot. It was enough to make a horse laugh, but I guess it was enough to dazzle Lily, for he won her in the end.

I wasn't taking much notice of anything — neither would you if you had just been kissed goodnight by Lily — when this shouting penetrated my consciousness. It was coming from the direction of the cinema which had the same sliding mesh gates, of which I spoke earlier, enclosing the foyer and which opened directly onto the sidewalk. The manager of the theatre at that time was a fellow called Stanton, from Cork, and he it was who was doing the shouting. It transpired later that he fell asleep in his office and, the show over, the caretaker, not aware of the sleeping prince, locked up and went home.

When Stanton woke up hours later, the street was

deserted and, without a set of keys for the rail gate, was a prisoner for the night. At the moment that I became aware of him shouting, he had just caught sight of big Garda Sergeant O'Sullivan, another Cork man as it happened, pacing along on his beat, and called out to him.

Approaching the gate, the sergeant peered through the mesh grill to be greeted by the prisoner.

'Can you get me out, Sergeant, I am locked in,' he pleaded.

Apparently, there was no love lost between these two men from the southern city. I heard the bad feeling went back quite a way.

Glaring back at the manager, O'Sullivan barked in his thick Cork accent, 'Hoo (you) are in the right fockin' place, Stanton — behind bars,' and he continued on his way at a leisurely pace.

Sergeant O'Sullivan was a legend in the town at that time. I remember one Saturday night, when I was much younger, I was running along Crowe street with Binno on our way to the Town Hall cinema where my sister Phil was an usherette — you have guessed it — she used to let me and Binno in for nothing — it was great!

We were just passing the pub next to the Queen's Hotel, I forget the name of it, when I saw Sergeant O'Sullivan getting off his bicycle outside, and he was not alone. He had Garda Joe Gaffney with him. Joe was an Irish boxing champion with a jaw that resembled an outcrop of rock one might find on one of the steeper slopes of K9. Many a fist had been broken making contact with it, to the derision of its owner, before a crashing right sent his opponent to the canvas.

They were answering a call to a disturbance at the pub. The use of bicycles suggested that it was urgent, and I clutched Binno by the arm as the formidable duo went through the door without even removing their bicycle clips.

'Let's watch, this could be better than the film,' I suggested, and we waited across the street for the action to begin. We did not have to wait long as the doors suddenly opened and a gyppo was hurled head first onto the street, followed in quick succession by one, two, three, and finally a fourth of his ilk. The gypsies were known not to be able to hold their drink and would often start fighting among themselves, so this was nothing more than routine for the two boyos.

The presence of either one of these two Gardai was enough to frighten the wits out of any troublemaker. Together, standing shoulder to shoulder, working as a team, they were an awesome sight now — emerging from the inn, ties still straight, hats still on, not even breaking sweat — the only outward sign of annoyance the casual threat uttered by Joe to the last of the departing miscreants, 'If I am called out to you again, I will shove your head up your arse and make a wheelbarrow out of you.'

Together, the two policemen got back on their bicycles and ambled off slowly back to barracks. Time taken — about six minutes. Just another Saturday night on the streets of Dundalk town circa 1946.

I held the grand title of assistant projectionist at the Magnet and was witness to all this cinematic fervour.

Films at this time were generally changed three times a week. There were two shows nightly, at seven and nine, with a change of programme on Mondays, Thursdays and Sundays. During the week the latest films were on view, but Sundays some of the most awful films ever made, and a copy of which could be rented for next to nothing, would be on offer, for it did not matter what you showed — you knew the hall was going to be full.

I mentioned that performances were at seven and nine o'clock, and this often produced great problems for the chief projectionist and my immediate boss, Barney Gaughren, better known as Barney Gahon. Don't ask, I don't know why. Barney was a beefy man who was never to be seen without a cigarette in his mouth. He usually lit one from the other and did not remove it from his mouth until it was time to light another one. He would blow the loose ash from the cigarette through the corner of his mouth. As a result of this habit, his upper lip and the end of his nose was stained with nicotine.

Barney was always formally dressed in a pinstripe suit, which he bought in Burton's in Dublin. In all the years I knew him, I never once saw him in flannels or sports jacket — always the suit. In the winter time he would wear a big black leather overcoat which weighed a ton.

Usually, the programme consisted of the main feature lasting, say, one hour and forty minutes, plus the newsreel, ten minutes, and the trailers, making it at least feasible for the second show, or 'house' as we called it, to begin round about nine o'clock. I never once saw a house start precisely at nine o'clock.

Often, however, we had to contend with the inclusion of a twenty-minute comedy or general interest film in the programme which made reasonable timekeeping an impossibility. On these occasions, Barney had to do a little judicious editing, and together we would have a private showing of the short film in the afternoon to see how much we could cut out of it without too much distortion to the story line, replacing it later before dispatching it back to the rental people. Thus we managed to at least keep our times of showing within the bounds of possibilities — most of the time, I must say that we ran way over time.

There were other times when the programme advertised made it quite impossible for us to keep on schedule, and this was when we were obliged to show a double feature and still contain things to our seven and nine o'clock schedule. A film might contain eight reels, each of ten minutes duration, numbered one to eight. These were then spliced together in pairs to make up twenty minutes which was the running time of the size of spools we used in those days. Thus, you would have four spools of twenty minutes duration. Total length of film one hour and twenty minutes. Two projectors were used and almost at the end of the first spool running out, a simple mechanical device made it easy to change to the other projector, allowing the film to be seen uninterrupted by any stoppage. You would then insert spool three in the first projector in readiness for the next changeover.

When faced with this double feature dilemma, each of which might last eighty minutes, it is obvious that our normal system of editing or cutting made it quite impossible to curtail the length of the programme sufficiently. On such occasions, Barney adopted a simple solution by pointing to the second and less important feature, declaring with a vicious leer, 'OK, Johnny, nothing else for it — it's got to be reels one, two, seven and eight.'

The first time he said this to me, my hair almost stood up on end. Judicious extraction of unimportant material was one thing, but wholesale removal of reels three, four, five and six was absolute gutting. You could say it left me reeling!

I came to enjoy this disembowelment and always left the projection box to slip into the back row of the auditorium to see the reaction from the audience when we made the quantum leap from reel two to reel seven. If it was a western, we might leave our hero in his snow-white hat in the middle of serenading the beautiful damsel at the end of reel two and find ourselves suddenly, in reel seven, viewing a confrontation between two unshaven villains.

Dialogue: 'OK, what did you do with the gold?'

Distinct stirring in the audience.

'You killed Lefty for it, didn't you?'

Puzzled expressions on the faces of those around me as they tried to fathom out the plot.

Whispered queries between friends all around the hall, 'Who is Lefty, what gold?'

'I only went out for a minute, what have I missed.'

'I think you have to use your imagination in this one.'

You can say that again, was my thought, when I would creep out convulsed with laughter and assure Barney that nobody missed a thing.

'Told ya,' smirked Barney.

It was in 1947, when I was just fifteen years of age, that a bit of excitement entered the job. It was the occasion of the marriage of Princess Elizabeth and the Duke of Edinburgh, and no, I was not invited to the wedding. A film recording the event went on general release and we were scheduled to play it at the Magnet cinema for six days — no television in those days.

The authorities were concerned that the showing of this very English event might attract the displeasure of the IRA and instructions went out regarding security for the occasion. This took the form of an armed guard being placed over the most vulnerable person concerned with looking after the film. As I was the person who collected it from the local railway station on arrival and delivered it back again on completion of its run, I was regarded as the weakest link in the chain. I was in possession, too, of the keys to the cinema, so I suppose I was looked upon as a sitting duck for any terrorist operation.

So it was that for one whole week I swaggered around town with my own armed guard for company, and I made the most of it with the girls, too stupid to realise the danger I was in. Detective Kavanagh would escort me home every night after sitting for hours squeezed up in a corner of the projection room, his big gun sticking out of its holster.

On more than one night, I felt really sorry for him

because Barney was in the throes of one of his fairly regular stomach upsets. When my boss surreptitiously broke wind, which he did with distressing frequency, the atmosphere in the tiny eight feet by ten room became quite fulsome. I would glance across at my protector and his eyes would be watering under the strain of breathing in the fetid air. I had the greatest difficulty not to burst out laughing as poor Detective Kavanagh almost gagged in distress. My week of minor glory soon passed but not soon enough for my long-suffering bodyguard.

Sadly, Barney died from cancer, at the early age of forty-three, the year after I left Ireland. Maybe the sixty Afton Majors he smoked every day had something to do with it.

Chapter Nine

Although my wages were increased slightly over the next few years, I just could not afford to live on the pittance I was paid. I could see no future in the job I was in, and certainly my employer held out no hope of any advancement. The work was boring in the extreme and I felt that I was capable of handling much greater responsibility. The future stretched before me and I felt trapped, unable to escape the deprivation I could see all around me. Many of my friends had already made the decision and departed and I knew that it was only a matter of time before I, too, must follow their example.

It is hard to describe the feeling of hopelessness that pervaded the town at that time, especially among the young people. There was a yearning, almost amounting to desperation, to escape from the poverty that existed everywhere. I would lie awake in bed at night dreaming of a different life in another country where your background was of no account. It was a fact of life that good jobs were only to be had in Ireland on the basis of who you knew, not what you knew. For such a poverty-ridden country, it was astonishing the amount of snobbery one had to contend with too. Many a time I felt frozen out because I came from the demesne and lived in a council house. Your home address condemned you.

But there was always money to be found for drink.

Although I did not drink myself, there were occasions when, for one reason or another, some celebration perhaps, I found myself in a bar, and I would be content with a lemonade, which drew a few laughs from the drunks present. The picture that stayed in my mind afterwards was that of the line of men, most wearing caps, sitting at the long bar with huge glasses of porter in front of them. The red-rimmed, almost unseeing eyes that stared out of the bloated red faces was, for me, the stuff of nightmares. I could not bear the thought of living out a life of such wretchedness

'Please, God,' I would mutter to myself, lying in bed at night, 'do not let that happen to me.'

The sweat would break out on my forehead at the thought of ending up like one of those poor no-hopers. There had to be a better life, there just had to be. The feeling that I had was almost claustrophobic as I viewed a future imprisoned in this impoverished society.

There was high unemployment in the town at that time, indeed in the whole country, which meant that there was a huge exodus of young people abroad to find work. Very few of them ever returned and it represented a huge loss to the country as it was the most ambitious and bright ones that left. England and North America were the beneficiaries of all this talent, and I am sure were duly grateful as these were the sort of people who produced wealth for the country of their adoption.

Every day I would hear that so and so, whom I had known all my life, had left for the United States or Canada, and I would positively groan with envy. Even worse was when a former friend or acquaintance would return from New York or some such exciting place we had seen only on film. He would arrive for a holiday wearing a gorgeous powder-blue suit and, obviously loaded with money, could be found buying drinks for all and sundry out at Blackrock at weekends.

The prettiest girls in town would throw themselves at him and the rest of us eegits who stayed at home could only grind our teeth with envy at his success. The more I thought about it, the more certain I became that going abroad remained my one hope of getting on in the world and making something of myself.

Long queues were the order of the day at the local unemployment bureau (The "Buru") and were to remain so for many years. Apart from the local shoe factories, the Great Northern Railway or Carroll's tobacco factory, there was nothing else the young people of the town could look to for a future. The building trade hardly existed as many commodities were still scarce, and one hardly ever saw a house being built due to the dearth of materials.

The local snooker halls were full at any hour of the day or night and the pubs did a roaring trade. Men could always find money, it seemed, for drink and gambling, even if not for food for their children's bellies. The cinemas, too, were full every night as people flocked to them for a bit of escapism and to try and forget, for a couple of hours, the squalor of their own lives.

I remember making an appointment to see the ADM, the Very Reverend Father McDonald, who was my employer, the dignified Fr. Stokes having been moved to Drogheda. The purpose of my visit was to seek a small increase in wages, and I pointed out meekly that I had to help support my mother on what I earned.

Fr. McDonald's response was typical of the arrogance of the clergy at that time, and I was not the least bit surprised to be told, 'If you are not satisfied with what I pay you, then you can get out,' he barked and stalked out of the room, leaving me trembling at the manner in which he spoke to me after giving seven years' service. But there was never any negotiation with the haughty priest and shortly afterwards I took his advice.

A footnote to this confrontation came four years later on the occasion of my wedding, when I wrote to him to obtain my permission to marry. At that time, when a Catholic moved away from the diocese in which he was born, it was necessary for him to obtain this certificate to prove that he was a single man and entitled to marry. I don't know if that rule still applies. The good priest wrote back saying he was not happy to do so and required proof of some sort that I was still single. Under the rules that existed for Catholics who wished to remain so, he knew that it would have been impossible for me to get married in a Catholic church without the knowledge of the diocese in which I was born. I wrote back at once telling him that as he was unable to furnish me with the necessary form, I had now made arrangements to get married at St. Mary's Protestant Church in Andover by Dr Ivor Machin, the local Vicar. My certificate arrived by return of post without any covering letter.

Restless and frustrated like a lot of young people in

Ireland at that time, I was forced to leave my homeland to find work which offered some kind of future. This is how I ended up in England in the early fifties and my first stop, like so many before me, was London.

I found the vast metropolis overpowering after life in a quiet country town, but I was lucky and managed to find a job in the Rex Cinema in Islington as a projectionist, which I only regarded as temporary. It was poorly paid, but it was a start, and I found myself a room not too far away in Therberton Street, which meant that I could walk to work without the necessity of using public transport. I arrived exactly one week after the coronation of Queen Elizabeth and the debris from the festivities was still being removed by council dustcarts.

My new employers were Jewish — the Bloom brothers, Alex, Janis and Bernard, and their head office was in Battersea. They owned a number of cinemas in London, the Rex in Islington being one of them. Bernard, the youngest, was my immediate boss and a very snappy dresser, always with a silk handkerchief peeping out of the cuff of his shirt. Although they were tough hard-headed businessmen who paid only as much as they had to, yet they had an old-world gentlemanly manner about them. Bernard, I was told, had an exemplary war record. Having been employed solely by priests during my short working life, I was not certain how I would be treated in the outside world by barefaced capitalists.

It was a revelation to me, because at all times I found myself treated with the greatest respect by my new employers — an experience that was entirely new to me. No touching of the forelock here, I found, as Bernard greeted me with a, 'Good morning, Mr Mullen, how are you today?' as he arrived, driving his little blue Triumph Mayflower.

I only stayed in that job six months, having decided to give in my notice for a more attractive position, and on the day I was due to leave, I was requested to go to Battersea to see the big boss, Alex. Wondering what on earth he would want with me at this stage of the game, just as I was leaving his employ, I was ushered into his office and invited to take a chair. I had only met him once, and I vividly remember how his eyes had rested on me for a long moment while he fully took stock of me. He was nearly bald and sported a big luxurious moustache and reminded me of the comedian Jimmy Edwards.

Now he asked me all about my new job, my reasons for leaving, and I was completely honest with him and told him that I could never settle in London. He chatted with me for a while and then rose to shake my hand and wish me the best of luck.

'I don't think you are going to be happy in the country, Mr Mullen,' he declared, smiling at me. 'When you have had enough, come back and see me. We will always have a job for you here.'

Leaving his office, I should have been thinking how poor the wages had been, but somehow, at that moment, money seemed irrelevant. I was thinking instead how differently I had been treated by the Very Rev. Fr. McDonald.

A strange thing happened during my first few days

in London. The husband of my landlady, one Albert Gunter, was a bus driver for London Transport. One day, when driving across Tower Bridge in his bus, it started to open up to shipping. Too late to brake, he put his foot down and the bus only just made it in time. It could have turned out to be an appalling disaster, but thanks to the quick reaction of the driver, a terrible tragedy was avoided. The incident turned Albert into a nine-day wonder as the media had a field day. The house was besieged by reporters and cameramen as Albert preened himself in his new-found glory.

Another more frightening incident occurred that involved me when I was on duty one night at the cinema. It was the manager's night off and I was in charge of things in his absence. It was a responsibility I was delighted to take on as it gave me a bit of experience at dealing with the public. It was a sign too that my employers thought enough of me to trust me with the job of looking after things.

The foyer opened out onto the sidewalk, and I was standing there in my new finery, a dinner suit being thought most essential, at the time, for any self-respecting manager. At least I looked the part, I told myself, admiring my reflection in the glass doors.

It was late, coming up to the end of the programme, when I saw a figure running for his life on the other side of the road heading towards Islington Green. He was being chased by two men who were clearly eager to get hold of their quarry. They disappeared from my view, and I thought no more about it until a few minutes later I heard an awful moaning coming from the steps leading to the pavement. I turned to see a man desperately crawling up into the foyer and he was covered in blood. I rushed to his assistance, to discover that one of his ears had been almost severed from his head — it seemed to be just hanging there by a piece of skin.

Of course, it was the man I had seen chased a short while before, and it was clear that he had not been able to run fast enough to escape from his pursuers. He obviously had not had my training at evading trouble! I called an ambulance and the police, and I made a statement. There was a great deal of excitement for half an hour whilst the police made their enquiries. Then all was quiet once more — just another evening in the big city. Having only been in London a couple of months, it gave me something exciting to write home about to my pals. Eat your hearts out, this is living. How are things going in Dullsville?

Having been brought up in a small town, I found life in the metropolis to be totally different and not the sort life I was looking for.

The noise, the dirt, the constant rushing for bus or tube, everything was all so much different to what I had been used to. The John Halliday Christie murder case filled the newspapers that summer and to me there seemed talk of little else. Fortunately, it was the month of June when I arrived, so at least the weather was fairly kind with a fair amount of sunshine every day. I spent as much time as I could in the city parks where I found the pace of things considerably slower. It was here, in a quiet arbour, that I could sit and think and work out what the future held for me. I was very homesick and badly in need of friendship. I wrote a letter to my mother almost every other day as I knew how much she would be worrying about me. Being the youngest, I was well aware that I had been a bit spoiled, and I was missing my home comforts very much.

I knew that I could never settle down in a large city, having been born and bred in a small country town. I missed the easy friendship, the camaraderie of being greeted in the street by people who knew me. In short, I wanted to put down roots somewhere that I felt I could live for the rest of my life.

Of course, I found some things exciting — what youngster wouldn't. On my days off, I would tramp to the West End to see the sights which, up until then, I had only seen in films. There was always an air of excitement about the place. Even without any money, I could trawl around the theatres watching the people arriving in their finery and wonder if I would ever afford to go one of these grand affairs. In fact, it was but four short years later that I was able to return and join the throng going into Covent Garden opera house to attend a performance of *Carmen*. But that was all in the distant future.

One evening, while on one of my strolls through Leicester Square, I met a chap whom I recognised from back home. He spotted me at the same time and, although I had forgotten his name, I knew that he had been a delivery boy in Joey Donnely's, the greengrocers. Joey had a great business in Church Street opposite the 'Green Church'. It helped that Joey had been captain of Dundalk Football Club and had captained the League of

Ireland more than once. The 'Green Church' was so called because it was covered in ivy. We were always warned, as children, not to ever go near this bastion of Protestantism under pain of mortal sin, but I used to duck through the adjacent graveyard when using it as a shortcut if late for Mass at the Marist Church.

My young acquaintance proceeded to try and impress me by boasting of the huge salary he was now earning in the great metropolis and asked me to join him for a drink. As graciously as possible I declined, owing to the fact that I only had my bus fare back to my digs and of course I was still strictly teetotal. I bade him farewell and hardly expected to ever see him again. However, two years later when I was back in Dundalk on holiday, I was walking down Park Street when I saw a herd of cows being driven towards me. This was still a common sight in those days, but my attention was drawn to the drover who walked behind his charges carrying a stick. It was none other than your man from London and I called out a greeting to him. His face reddened at my shout, but he pretended not to hear me and continued on his way to the Fair Green where the cattle market was held. I guess the big money that he had talked about had dried up.

I gained valuable experience in London and I learned a great deal about the world — in short, I had the corners knocked off me, which is an old Irish saying. I kept my eyes open for vacant positions in the cinema industry through a trade magazine called 'The Kinematograph Weekly,' and would scour through its 'situations vacant' columns every week with great determination. A few acquaintances to whom I mentioned my intentions thought that I was mad to leave London and its bright lights, but I had had enough of the big city. So it was that after six months, having seen a position of assistant manager advertised for a cinema in Andover, Hampshire, I successfully applied for the job.

Chapter Ten

It really was like a breath of fresh air moving to the country after living in London for six months. In the city, I felt like a lost soul cut off from everybody around me. Yes, I spoke to people, but I did not make contact with them — we were just people who passed each other on the way to some distant place where we might take up residence and start living again.

Everything seemed temporary, I felt as though I was in transit, on my way to somewhere else, which is exactly how it turned out. I had lived in the city for a total of six months and had not made a single friend. Of course, I had met people in the course of my work, but it was not only me I found that was in transit — everybody else was on the move as well. Within a matter of weeks, it seemed, of meeting someone with whom I found I had a certain rapport, they were gone, evidently seeking fresh pastures to conquer.

Andover was very much the same size town as Dundalk in Ireland where I had lived all my life, and in a sense, it felt like coming home. Of course, things were very different. It was a lovely little market town at that time before the town council decided on a policy of taking the London overspill under its wing. It ruined the town completely. Perhaps it could be said that I was one of the first to take advantage of this new policy of replacement. Naturally, I did not know a soul when I arrived, but I hoped that that would soon change and indeed it did.

I found digs with a very genteel widow called Mrs. Nutley, in Station Road, who had four children — a boy and three girls. They were a charming family and I settled in very quickly. I was very happy there for the six months that I remained with them.

Here again I found myself in the employ of a perfect English gentleman whose name was Maurice Overmass. He was kindness itself and very quickly promoted me to manage one of his other cinemas at Whitchurch. I remained with him for nearly four years before moving on. Long after I had left his employ, my wife and I were welcome guests at his dinner table on many occasions. Maurice was a very wealthy man and travelled the world, but sadly never found what he was looking for and ended his life by his own hand at the age of sixty-four. I always held him in the greatest esteem.

I met Anthea, the English girl I eventually married, not long after I arrived in the town. She worked in a local bank where I paid in the takings, from the cinema where I worked, every morning — plenty of opportunity, therefore, to chat. She had the most engaging manner, friendly and outgoing, and it was not long before I was under her spell. For a young man in a strange country, not long away from home for the first time and desperate for company, I was completely enthralled.

She was pretty rather than beautiful, but her wonderful smile and vivacious personality ensured that she was never short of admirers. She possessed a great sense of humour, seeming to find something funny in most situations. If I ever found myself a bit down, she soon dispelled my despondency — it was like a tonic being in her company.

Despite the fierce competition, I managed to persuade her to go out with me. We soon found that we both liked the same things, sport playing a large part in our lives. My future wife was a brilliant table tennis player, turning out for the town team many times and won countless medals at her sport.

Anthea wanted kids as well — maybe not six but a couple anyway. It was one of the things her parents threw at her when they first heard we wanted to get married.

'Do you want to end up with ten children, become like a cow,' her mother wailed at her, aware of my Catholicism.

You can tell from this remark that I was not their first choice of a husband for their daughter — no, nor their second, third or even one hundred and third.

Anthea's parents were very strict Baptists and compared to an Irish Catholic, would have viewed a coloured Jew with a serious drug problem as a welcome addition to the family. You think I am exaggerating? Well, I had a sneaking suspicion on our very first date that my intentions were viewed with a certain amount of suspicion when her mother and aunt insisted on coming along as well. I had just eleven pounds in my pocket that night which was all the money I had in the world and I hoped it would be enough. This being nineteen fifty-four, it proved to be sufficient but only just.

A first date with a girl with whom you want to make a good impression is tortuous enough, but when she is accompanied by her mother and aunt the whole thing becomes a living nightmare. I was just twenty-one and still wet behind the ears, as they say, and the sight of these two formidable ladies taking stock of me was extremely nerve-wracking. I went through the agony of introductions, trying to appear suave and a man of the world, and hoped nobody noticed the quiver in my voice. I had been on dates before, but these were with girls back home with whom I had grown up and who knew all about me and my family. No pretence needed there on either side.

But that had just been fun without any serious intent — certainly no thought of any long-standing commitment. We were just living for the day and having a good time. This was different, I knew that already. I felt drawn strongly towards this young woman and felt that she could be my life partner. First, however, I had to convince her that I was the right man for her, and indeed it looked as if I might have even more trouble convincing her family. Fortunately, her father was not present for this first confrontation otherwise I might have fled against such overwhelming odds.

I had met the great man only briefly when I had called to collect my triple date. He had glared at me fiercely and sized me up suspiciously through a cloud of cigar smoke. Through the blue haze, a pair of cold grey eyes took stock of me. I remember his first words very clearly which told me of his ambitions for his elder daughter.

'So you are the manager of a cinema. What are your chances of a directorship?' he asked, sucking at his cigar importantly.

Thinking that honesty would be the best policy against such an astute man, I answered meekly, 'Not very good, sir, I should think,' leaving him looking at me quizzically, unsure whether to admire my honesty or censure me for my apparent lack of ambition.

In the years that followed, we seemed to reach an uneasy truce but neither one of us truly cared for the other. He could be very charming when it suited him, but he never fooled me. It was in the interests of my wife's happiness and his relationship with our children that forced us to get along. There were many times when I felt tempted to challenge his sometimes rude intervention in my affairs, but for the sake of harmony I always let it pass. The happiness of my wife and children overrode any feelings of pride that I might have had.

I thought that, for a first date, I would take my future wife to something uplifting, something that would quite erroneously suggest that I was a man of culture. I gave the matter a great deal of thought and decided that this momentous occasion deserved no less than the one man show staged by that great actor Sir Donald Wolfitt in the local guildhall. He performed some of the great Shakespearean roles for which he was famous including, I remember, Falstaff.

I thought that by taking her to something Shakespearean that I might impress her with my knowledge of the legitimate theatre (which was about

127

zero). Even the acting of the great man failed to hold my attention as I sat almost mute between Anthea and her mother. I squirmed and sweated for the entire evening and wondered how I could survive it. Every time I tried to whisper some comment to Anthea, her mother would glare at me suspiciously, and I quickly gave up any attempt at conversation.

I will draw a veil over the rest of that evening. Suffice to say that I must have really been smitten with the girl to want to continue to press my suit, as they were wont to say in those days. Still not convinced that I was viewed with great suspicion by her parents? Still think I am exaggerating? OK, let me run this by you.

One might have already been forming the opinion of me that perhaps I was an uneducated bum, too gross for the pretty twenty-one-year-old girl, or maybe I was inflicted with a hideous skin complaint so that her parents had every good reason to be wary of me. In fact, I was the same age as Anthea, had a responsible job as the manager of a cinema and was, not to put too fine a point on it, considered to be fair of countenance. Anyway, I managed to see Anthea a couple more times, happily on her own and it was, I think, about our fourth date that I want to tell you about.

It was the occasion of the annual police ball in the small town of Whitchurch where I managed the local cinema and where I now lived. This was shortly before the onset of mass television viewing and the demise of the local cinema had not yet taken place. The last rites would be performed in the not too distant future. At this time, the cinema still played an important part in the life of the community, being a major source of entertainment. So I was an easily recognised and respected member of the local business sector.

Whitchurch is not much more than a large village and a very agreeable place in which to live. Its most famous resident being Lord Denning, the former Master of the Rolls, who had lived all his life in the area. Another very well-known character at the time who resided there was the very amiable late James Robertson Justice, the popular actor, famous for his role in the hit film, *Doctor in the House*. He would often stroll along the street, swipe a carrot from the display stand in front of the local greengrocers and, chewing contentedly, stop to have a word with me on the steps of the cinema.

It is doubtful if we took much notice of the sixteen-year-old boy erecting a poster in the foyer behind us. He was employed by me as a trainee projectionist and was later to find world fame for making that great award-winning nature film, 'The Private Life of the Kingfisher.' His name was Ronald Eastman.

This was before the advent of the zoom lens and Ron would tell me, enthusiastically, how he was digging a hole in the bank of the Test river, which flowed near his home, in order to get better close-up views of his subjects. What I remember most about Ron was his enthusiasm for his hobby. He spent every penny he had on buying film for his camera which, at the beginning, I think was just a little 8 mm job which produced only in black and white. He soon progressed to something larger which gave him colour shots and he was over the moon. Paid on a Friday, by Monday he was broke and asking for a 'sub' on his wages to buy more film. He truly earned his enormous success the hard way.

But who takes any notice of the ramblings of a sixteen-year-old! I took more notice of him on another occasion. Catching me at a moment when I was very busy, he asked if he might build a boat in his spare time on the flat roof of the cinema as he had not the space to work at home. I nodded absentmindedly and thought no more about it until six months later when his mother, a tall lady with a commanding presence, called to see me and gave me a telling off for making her son work so many hours. She stormed off, leaving me perplexed and not a little shaken.

Going upstairs to my office, I suddenly heard the noise of hammering. It seemed to be coming from the roof, access to which was via a ladder from the projection room. Climbing up, an astonishing sight met my eyes as I emerged into the sunlight. I had assumed that when Ron had asked me about building a boat that he had meant a scale model. But what was laid out before me was a full-sized river craft destined, I think he said later, for the Thames at Pangbourne! No wonder his mother was up in arms. He must have spent every spare minute of his time up here, well out of the way of everyone. How he ever managed to get the thing down off the roof I never did find out as, after warning him that he had better get rid of it before the owners found out, I went off on holiday.

Ignore genius at your peril! By a strange coincidence, some years later, Ron, by now rich and famous, bought the water mill in which James

Robertson Justice was living in at the time of which I write. Sadly, it was the death by drowning in the mill race of his four-year-old son that forced the famous actor to sell up and move away.

Having consumed his carrot, James, a giant of a man, would squeeze into his tiny sports car with the top down, and my abiding memory of him was to see him screeching off, to all intents and purposes steering from the back seat. One of my favourite actors, he had a personality to match his size.

But I digress and I apologise, let's cut to the chase. I decided that I should support the police ball by buying two tickets, and we looked forward to an enjoyable evening. Whitchurch is situated seven miles from the town of Andover where my girlfriend lived (I liked to think of her now as my girlfriend), so transport presented a problem as I did not drive, let alone own a car. The answer was to hire a local taxi to collect my date and take her home again, a big expense for one evening but hell, you are only young once and this was a bit special. It was a gala event, evening dress was obligatory, and a splendid evening was promised.

The proprietor of the taxi service, Ron Clacy himself, drove me to collect Anthea and I knocked on her door looking, as I thought, resplendent in my tuxedo and bow tie and carrying a nosegay of flowers. Anthea looked beautiful in a long white dress with a thrilling décolletage. How did she manage to get away with that, I wondered, with such strict parents, and tried hard not to stare. There were severe admonitions from her parents to return their daughter to the safety of the family fold once the dance was over and we left with dire warnings ringing in my ears of what would happen to me if I fell short of their expectations. We were both twenty-two years of age at this time.

We had a wonderful evening; the scene was very colourful with the lovely evening dresses worn by the ladies and many men in white tie and tails. White gloves for the men were almost 'de rigueur' at that time — how things have changed.

After the last dance was finished at one a.m., Ron collected us outside the hall and took us straight back to Andover. It was a beautiful moonlit night, and on the way, we sat in the back of the taxi and held hands. I had never felt happier. Anthea looked ravishing and her cleavage had me in a ferment. Dare I risk a caress, I asked myself, and wondered if wearing white gloves made the action less carnal. Having not even dared to try kissing her as yet, the thought remained just a dream as I was now madly in love and was terrified of losing her.

Entering Andover, we turned left at the traffic lights to go up Winchester road to her home — a route which took us past the police station. I sat bolt upright as I recognised her father's car outside the cop shop and pointed it out to Anthea in a panic. What could have happened, we wondered, and could hardly wait to get to her house to find out.

We discussed it animatedly as we continued up Winchester Road. Had there been a burglary? Perhaps someone had been injured. Anthea was clearly worried, and I tried to console her, but the truth was I could not think of anything that would have persuaded her father to visit the police station at that time of night. Then I had an idea. It was probably to do with his business and as the key holder, he had been called out if the burglar alarm had gone off. She brightened up at this thought and we eventually pulled into the driveway of her home.

Her mother was already at the door as we alighted and she screeched, 'Where have you been? Your father has gone to the police station to report you missing!'

To say that I was stunned was the under-statement of the year. I had done everything by the book. I had not arrived back drunk (I was a strict teetotal), and we had come straight from the dance in a taxi as soon as it had finished. I felt that I was in the presence of lunatics.

What I remember most about that evening, afterwards, was the look on Ron Clacey's face as we pulled out of the drive. What he must have been thinking afterwards I hardly dare imagine. It is hard to think of any parent behaving in such a bizarre fashion in the social climate in which we live today. However, even by the standards prevailing at the time, one must admit that the behaviour of Anthea's father was almost paranoiac. I was appalled at his lack of trust in me but, with Anthea's bubbly good humour to bolster me, we ended up afterwards laughing hysterically every time the incident came to mind.

Looking back, I must have been very brave to think that I might stand a chance of marrying Anthea, but they say that love is blind. I had not arrived in England long and was still trying to make my way in the world. To her parents, I must truly have appeared as one of those 'hicks from the sticks.' I had worked in London before finding a position in the town of Andover where I felt much more at home than in the big city. Having been brought up in a town of similar size, I felt that it was a place where I could put down roots. Bearing in mind the almost itinerant life I have lived since then, it is almost laughable to think how much I strayed from my original intention.

Chapter Eleven

Anthea's father, Philip Harcourt Ponting, was a popular and very successful business man. A short rotund man, he had a major weight problem and was always talking about his latest diet — unfortunately, these usually only lasted until the next meal. His constant habit of shaking his heavy jowls reminded me of an old bloodhound. I always thought he bore an uncanny resemblance to the old Aga Khan, grandfather of the present Aga Khan.

Despite his popularity, I always found him insincere, and behind his toothy grin, I felt that he was a very shallow man indeed. He was the mayor of Andover at this particular time, and a born showman, revelling in the attention this public office brought him.

His wife, the redoubtable Mabel, was a very different character and I suspect that it was from her that Anthea inherited her strong personality. Mabel was a leading light in the Inner Wheel movement, holding the position of world president of the association at one time.

No wonder this very successful couple looked askance at this penniless intruder into their daughter's life. Strangely, in later years, Mabel and I came to have a great respect for one another and she would sometimes ask me to escort her to official functions when her husband was indisposed. A large erudite woman, she was an excellent public speaker with great presence — a feature which I found very intimidating at the beginning of our relationship. I think she grew to like me when she discovered that she could hold an intelligent conversation with me.

She had a great love of music and was conductor, for many years, of the Andover Choral Society, having studied under Sir Adrian Boult. In her new son-in-law, Mabel might have hoped that she had a new recruit to the ranks of her choir, but when she first heard my throaty warble, she blanched visibly and the subject was never brought up again! Her excellent choir went on to win many awards in competition without the benefit of my corncrake voice.

Such was the beginning of my courtship of Anthea, which was to last nearly three years, but true love was not to be denied, and we finally ended up at the altar despite the most desperate opposition from her parents. In fairness, I have to say that once the knot was tied, I was accepted into the family and always treated with the greatest respect.

They accepted gracefully that the marriage would take place under the rites of the Roman Catholic Church, which must have been anathema to them as they were committed Baptists.

Oddly enough, Anthea herself, although brought up a Baptist by her parents, had already forsaken the Baptist Church in favour of the Church of England long before I met her — a move, you may be sure, that greatly displeased Philip and Mabel.

Now yet again she was defying her parents in

marrying a Roman Catholic, which, from all this, you will gather that Anthea was a young woman who made up her own mind. I could only guess at the pressure that must have been put on her, over those three years of our courtship, to give up her friendship with me. Yet she never complained to me at any time — such was her loyalty to her family. Anthea walked her own path and had no time for whiners.

Living in the same house as her parents, life must have been very stressful to say the least. Philip and Mabel were strong-willed individuals not used to being defied, and it says a lot for my wife's strength of character that she would not be denied her right to choose her friends and especially her life partner.

Her family gave us a wonderful wedding, however, taking over the Andover Guildhall for the reception and generally sparing no expense. There were one hundred and fifty guests and we could not have wished for a more splendid send-off.

Money was extremely tight so there was no question of going abroad, but we did spend our short honeymoon in London and enjoyed the luxury of staying in a West End hotel. Really, neither of us cared very much where we spent our first few days as man and wife just so long as we were together. It had been a long three years to wait for this moment.

One morning at breakfast, I thought I recognised a young couple sitting at a nearby table. I say couple, but really it was the man I thought looked familiar. The more I stared at him, the more certain I was that it was an old school chum who shared a desk with me when we were no more than ten or twelve years old. Finally, as they rose to leave their table, I could contain my curiosity no longer and approached them.

Even before I spoke, I could see the look of recognition on his face, and he grasped my outstretched hand in welcome. His name was Tom McCabe and, of course, he had a nickname, always being known as 'Bunty'. His name was well known in football circles, having played for Dundalk and more than once for his country. By an extraordinary coincidence, he was also on his honeymoon and was due to sail from Tilbury for New Zealand the following day. He was emigrating and taking his young bride to start a new life on the other side of the world. We marvelled that we should meet again after so many years and under these circumstances, reminisced over our schooldays, shook hands and parted, wishing each other every good fortune. I often wondered how he fared in his new surroundings.

One further coincidence occurred during our stay in London that made me wonder just what a small world it is. For a period, back in. Ireland, I had worked in a cinema belonging to the clergy that occasionally held concerts, usually on Sunday nights. Mario Lanza had scored an enormous hit with his first film, 'The Great Caruso', and as part of the publicity build-up for its forthcoming premiere it was decided to hold a national singing competition to find 'Ireland's Mario Lanza'. I believe the first prize included a year of study in Italy.

It was eventually won by a brilliant young tenor named Dermot Troy. He embarked on a countrywide tour and was booked to appear at the theatre where I worked one Sunday night. It was part of my duties to meet him, and his lovely young accompanist, on arrival and generally look after them until show time. They were a delightful couple and very easy to please. He was a great success, and I said goodbye at the end of his performance.

Anthea and I had decided to visit Covent Garden during our honeymoon and were delighted that *Carmen* was the opera being staged that week. Standing amidst all the well-heeled theatregoers in the sumptuous foyer of the famous building, my mind could not help flying back to a few short years before when I would stand outside, penniless and envious of the throng pouring into this very theatre. Well, I was no longer penniless, but I certainly could not afford two of the better class seats, having to be content with two far removed from the glittering stage.

Owing to a double booking, however, the assistant manager, apologising profusely, delivered us personally to a private box where he hoped we would be comfortable. Not surprisingly, I made light of the matter, squeezing my wife's hand in delight at this stroke of good fortune.

Studying my programme while waiting for the performance to begin, I was astounded to see the name of Dermot Troy in one of the leading roles. A wonderful singer, he had certainly come a long way since appearing at St. Nicholas's Hall in Dundalk. It lent an extra dimension to what was altogether an enchanting evening and one which we always cherished. A sad footnote to all of this was when, a few years later, I saw an article in an Irish newspaper where it referred to the late Dermot Troy. I never did find out what had happened to him.

It amused me that after several months of marriage I felt sure that I could detect Anthea's mother covertly staring at her daughter's tummy as though expecting quads to pop out. She had to wait fourteen months after our marriage for Patrick to arrive, about whose birth I will now tell you.

Happily, at that breath-taking moment of Patrick's birth, I could not have been aware of the heartbreak that was to follow when our son made his entrance into the world. This was what we had dreamed about, and in that joyous moment, my wife and I could have had no idea of the years of struggle that lay ahead as Patrick sought to find a place in life for himself. I had fantasized many times what it might be like to be a father. I was just twenty-six years old and still young enough to remember vividly how much I had missed having a father myself. I still did, as far as it went.

I was four years old when he died, and I could scarcely remember what he looked like, let alone recall having him around. It was a strange feeling hearing other children talking about their dads and there was no doubt that I was jealous, and at times angry, at being the only one without a dad. Whilst I could not quantify it, yet I felt there was something very important missing in the whole structure of my existence.

I was fortunate in having a strong woman for a mother, however, and being the youngest of six children,

I was well looked after and indeed spoiled by my siblings, so I cannot claim that I was lonely or neglected. Somehow, in spite of all the company and camaraderie that I enjoyed, there was a gap in my life.

It was a gap I was determined should not exist in my own child's life if I could help it. I was determined to be the best dad there ever was. I know — so says every expectant dad — but I did feel very strongly about it. For no particular reason, I always felt that my first born would be a boy and so it proved.

There were several other babies born that day in the same hospital, and I often wondered afterwards that if Patrick had been born to some other parents, how they would have coped. Would they have made the same decisions we were to make in bringing up our son? Would they even have survived as a family or would they have broken up under the strain and disappointment? I was to learn of cases such as that — equally, I was to come to know parents who sacrificed their entire lives looking after their child and spurning the assistance of any kind of institution, however benign and comforting.

There had to be a way that allowed the child to develop its full potential, and this often meant sending the child away, at least temporarily, to get the best that was on offer. The other extreme, which was too often the case, was keeping the child at home and performing every single function for him in the mistaken belief that parental love was enough.

The child then grew up totally incapable of looking after itself and dependent, for its entire life, on others. The parents made themselves martyrs, the quality of their own lives greatly diminished, and leaving their offspring an orphan when they themselves died, completely unable to cope with their loss. Then it invariably meant institutional life for the remainder of their days. It seems highly unlikely that every person would have chosen our way. Everyone has their own way of dealing with tragedy and this was a tragedy, there was no other way to describe it.

Like all young married couples, we had looked forward to the birth of our first child with a mixture of excitement and longing. We had decided not to wait until we had all the practical comforts of life most of us desire and opted to start a family without having the almost obligatory television, dishwasher etc. We felt that we would prefer to have our children while we ourselves were still young enough to remember what it was like to be a child. To us, that was more important than having all the creature comforts the advertising men insisted we should have in order to enjoy a fulfilling life.

Afterwards, I often wondered — were we right? Would it have made any difference if we had waited a couple of years before starting a family? Such thoughts come to torture you when the hand of fate strikes a blow. I don't suppose it would have made the slightest difference, but I was always left wondering at what might have been if we had waited.

A seagull screamed raucously overhead and, despite the warmth of the sun, as Patrick and I sipped our drinks I felt a distinct chill, and I shivered as my mind went back in time to that fateful day when Patrick was born.

Chapter Twelve

I was only sleeping lightly, my body seemingly poised to take wing at the slightest disturbance. I was living in a world divided between sleep and wakefulness, my body seemingly floating between the two halves. At times I thought that I was dreaming, only to be made aware, when I heard the clock strike its inordinately loud tone, that I was in fact awake, and my wife's breathing was not the sighing of the wind through the trees. It had been like this for several nights now.

It was hardly surprising, therefore, that the half gasp, half cry from the figure curled up alongside me had me sitting erect and wide awake in an instant.

I switched on the bedside lamp and turned to my wife lying beside me — the grimace of pain on her face told me quite clearly that this time it was the real thing. I looked at the clock — nearly four a.m. Why do babies always arrive in the middle of the night, I wondered? We had had one false alarm already — one which had forced me to telephone the district nurse who calmed me down and persuaded us to wait a little longer before rushing off to the hospital. She saved us from some embarrassment as it soon became clear that it was indeed a false alarm and that our first child was still not quite ready to enter the world.

Another groan from my wife galvanized me into

action, and I leapt from the bed as though spring loaded. Months earlier, we had kidded about this moment, imagining, in a jocular way, our panic when the time for the new baby to make his entrance into the world finally arrived. Suddenly, it was not the least bit funny as I struggled into my pants in the pre-dawn, where the hell was the other leg, hardly noticing that my shirt was inside out. Then helping Anthea to get dressed, which really only meant wrapping her in a warm dressing gown after literally dragging her out of the bed. My god, she was heavy. Getting her down the stairs was a feat of strength in itself, but we managed it eventually, with her leaning heavily on my shoulders as I staggered in front. Although a cold night in March, my wife was sweating which was as nothing compared to me — I was dripping. Finally, we were in the car and on our way to the hospital, and I had to restrain my desire to break every speed limit as we covered the mile and a half to our destination. Four hours later and I was wondering what all the panic had been about, as our first born had still not put in an appearance. One other man was sharing the waiting room with me, and I idly wondered if I looked as bad as him — he looked a wreck. I certainly felt like one with the anxiety of waiting beginning to take its toll on my nerves. Did it always take as long as this? Anthea had enjoyed excellent health during her pregnancy — continuing to take lots of exercise, never having smoked in her life, and could almost call herself teetotal as she rarely touched even a glass of wine. At weekends, I accompanied her on long walks as we tried to imagine whether it would be a boy or a girl. It was not customary to be told the sex of the baby, taking shape in the womb, in those days. Although not making a final decision about names, we had drawn up a shortlist about which we had endless and inconclusive discussions. We wrangled good-naturedly about it, but in the end my wife's favourite, if it was a girl, was to call her Fiona. If it turned out to be a boy, I had opted for Patrick. That was how we left it until the birth took place, but neither of us had really strong feelings on the matter as long as we were blessed with a healthy normal baby. Although we were naturally anxious that everything went well, we had never really imagined anything other than a smooth and trouble-free delivery. Now, at eight o'clock on a cold Monday morning, things did not look quite so rosy as I could not help noticing the anxious looks on the faces of the two nurses who emerged from time to time from the delivery room. I wanted to ask if everything was all right, but everybody appeared so busy that I did not have the courage to speak up. I kept telling myself that these were professionals who would not want to be bothered with hopeless fathers-to-be. I felt like a character out of a film, the butt of many jokes about the hapless male under these circumstances. Things were very different in those days — the current fashion for the dad being present at the birth of his heir was something that lay very much in the future. Being an abject coward, I doubt if I would have wanted to be present anyway, certainly not the way I was feeling at that moment. All the time, I was trying to put off the onset of a good old-fashioned panic attack. The smell of hospitals had always unnerved me and now, after five hours, I was on the verge of throwing up and shaming myself.

Suddenly, it was daylight, and with it came Doctor Hodges, Anthea's doctor, who accompanied one of the nurses to the delivery room. I was immediately aware that he had been sent for, and I knew also that it was my wife's condition that was causing concern. My fellow father-in-waiting was no longer waiting as he had been informed hours ago that he was now the proud father of a baby girl. It was amazing how that piece of news had changed him from a desperate-looking man into one without a care in the world, and I was pleased to congratulate him. He grasped my hand, his face a picture of joy, and almost ran from the room.

I had hoped that my transformation from a jittery hulk would be equally dramatic. Now I was not at all certain that it would be. It was claustrophobic sitting in the tiny waiting room, the smell of ether mixed with floor polish proving a bit too much, and suddenly I had an overwhelming desire for some fresh air. I stumbled out of the building and found a wrought iron seat by a bus stop on the pavement.

There was a light drizzle which I hardly noticed, the wet seat numbing my backside. There I sat for half an hour while buses came and went, bringing people to work, nurses getting off to take up their duties together with those with ancillary jobs at the hospital. It was too early for normal visiting, so I felt alone and cut off from this bustling world I saw all around me. Waves of panic assailed me, and my stomach churned as the awful thought struck me that I might lose Anthea. Sucking in deep breaths to quell my rising anxiety, I rose to my feet, suddenly filled with terror that they might be looking for me in the waiting room. Suppose there was a crisis and I was needed for something? What do you mean 'suppose', what the hell is this if not a crisis? My mind in a whirl, I hurried back inside.

The doctor emerged from the delivery room just as I took my seat, and the nurse with him pointed me out to him. I had never met the good doctor, being a newcomer to Andover, but he had been my wife's family's doctor for many years and had been in attendance when Anthea herself was born. He approached me with a grave look on his face, and my heart missed more than one beat in dread of what he was about to tell me.

'I am afraid there are complications,' he began. 'The baby has turned around in the womb and I think it advisable that your wife be transferred to Winchester without delay.'

He looked at me steadily, and from his expression, I garnered the news that there could be no doubt about the seriousness of the situation.

I groaned inwardly. Like any other expectant father, I had been more or less prepared for a certain amount of nail biting while awaiting the arrival of our offspring, but this was going far beyond my worst fears. Dramatic dashes from one hospital to another, a life, or maybe two lives, in peril was more than I felt I could cope with at the moment. Castigating myself for my utter selfishness and self-pity, I tried to think how dreadful it must be for Anthea who at this moment was in the delivery room suffering heaven knows how much pain and discomfort.

She must be worried stiff about the delay in the arrival of her baby and really concerned that she might lose it. Now this new departure from the normal, this sudden decision to transfer her to Winchester, must drive her to even greater fear.

Andover boasted only a cottage hospital and did not have the same range of facilities available as at the county hospital, and Doctor Hodges said he had already arranged for an ambulance to take my wife to Winchester straight away. He confirmed that I could accompany her, and in minutes, we had commenced the fifteen-mile journey to the ancient capital. I watched as she was wheeled out and transferred aboard the ambulance. I clambered in after her, the doors slammed shut and we were on our way.

My wife looked frightened, and I tried to reassure her on what seemed like an endless journey when, in fact, she was being wheeled into the labour ward in Winchester in less than half an hour. Then more waiting, and I tried to calm my nerves as my imagination went to work thinking of all the worst possible scenarios — the baby being still-born or, perhaps worst of all, losing my wife of fourteen months.

Women, especially women as fit as my wife, did not die in childbirth any more, did they — not when they were in the care of a leading hospital with all the modern equipment? Thus, I tried to reassure myself. I telephoned her parents to let them know what was happening and tried not to sound worried. Her father answered and I tried to explain as best I could what had happened. He started to ask inane questions for which I did not have the answers, the phone was quickly taken off him and Mabel came on the line, cool and efficient. She grasped the situation immediately and tried to comfort me, as she realised how helpless and frightened I must feel, at this time.

'There is nothing you can do, John, but wait it out. I know it is awful, but you have just got to be patient. Anthea is in the right place and will get the best of attention.'

Thus, my mother-in-law tried to reassure me. I knew she would be on to Doctor Hodges within minutes to find out more about what the chances were of Anthea losing the baby. I sweated it out for several more hours until told by a smiling nurse that I was now the father of a baby boy, that my wife was well and that I could go in to see her straight away.

The news left me feeling weak and trembling as a sense of euphoria swept over me. With stumbling steps, I followed the nurse to my wife's bedside and could hardly speak as I looked at Anthea's exhausted face on the pillow — she really had had a tough time of it. Her eyes, which were all puffed up as though she had been crying, were closed.

She appeared to be sleeping and the nurse nodded reassuringly as I looked questioningly at her. I glanced at the cot beside the bed, which was empty, and the nurse explained that our new-born was in an incubator which was quite normal for a baby born after such a struggle. He would be joining his mother very soon and, in the meantime, perhaps I would care to come with her, and she would show him to me.

Kissing Anthea, I accompanied the nurse down a corridor and caught my first glimpse of our son, soon to be christened Patrick. He looked beautiful, with blonde silky hair, and his face did not appear as wrinkled as those few new-born babies (nephews and nieces) I had seen in the past. He was sleeping peacefully, regaining his strength, the nurse informed me, after his extended battle to make his debut.

Later, I was to hear the full story from my wife about how dangerous the whole situation had become when the baby had turned round in the womb. The gynaecologist had gone to great lengths to rectify the situation but finally had no option but to use forceps to assist the delivery in the final stages. Everything had turned out well in the end, however, and we appeared to be blessed with a normal healthy little boy. He weighed seven pounds twelve ounces and had all the required bits to lead a normal healthy life. We were assured that his heart and lungs were fine, and he was breathing without difficulty. All this was wonderful news to us, and we hugged each other in delight. It was to be months later before the awful truth began to dawn on us that all was not well with our lovely little boy.

To someone more experienced than his blissfully unaware parents, the clear indentations made by the forceps on each temple of our son might have seemed an omen, but no warning was given to us by any of the medical staff of any future difficulties.

But that was to be much later, and this was now, and the joy of a successful outcome left me tearful and shaken with relief. We were a family! It is often said that a woman does not feel truly fulfilled until she has produced a baby, but I can honestly say that that moment was like no other in my life. I really felt complete and whole. I was the father of a child and life would never be the same again, whatever happened. I can quite unequivocally state that throughout the crisis I was like a rock (a dense inert mass).

Anthea remained in hospital for several days whilst she recovered from the delivery of her baby. When I visited her the day after the birth, she looked shaken but greatly relieved that it was all over. It was only then that she confided in me how worried she had been when they had rushed her to Winchester in the ambulance. She had been only vaguely aware of my presence at the time and it all seemed like a bad dream now.

She grasped my hand and said shakily, 'Thank you, husband.'

Remembering how small and unimportant a role I had played in the whole crisis, I averted my eyes with guilt. I had brought her flowers and busied myself finding a nurse who would put them in water for me to hide my embarrassment. Our new baby was now sleeping peacefully in a cot beside his mother. I glanced from one to the other. It was a scene that I had always conjured up in my mind — that of a happy mother smiling down at her new-born child, everything joyful, after a normal birth — but in truth, it had been a close-run thing.

Chapter Thirteen

In a few days I took my family home, thrilled and excited to show off our new addition to all our friends and neighbours. We suffered the usual frights and qualms that most young parents have with a new baby. But my wife was very sensible and well organised, very soon getting into a routine. She was of the opinion that babies thrive on a strict routine — being fed at the same time, having a bath at the usual hour, and being put down to sleep at regular intervals. On the evidence, this proved to be more than a theory. Not for her lifting the baby from his cot every time he made a little noise — she was much too sensible for that. Our child was very contented and within a very short while was sleeping right through the night without waking.

For myself on the other hand, old panic-britches himself, when I was alone with him when perhaps his mother had gone to have her hair done, I would rush to the cot if I heard the slightest noise from the baby. He would probably only be clearing his throat, but my heart would be in my mouth thinking he was choking. I was always greatly relieved when his mother returned. I was not a very cool minder.

Patrick, however, was a quiet little tot on the whole and caused little anxiety except that he did not appear to thrive on his mother's milk. Within a short while, on the advice of the district nurse who paid us several visits after our homecoming, my wife decided to try powdered milk, and this was much more successful. Very quickly, Patrick began to steadily put on weight.

I never missed a chance to hold him in my arms and could appreciate how big he was becoming as his weight rapidly increased. In our great joy of becoming parents, we were oblivious to the fact that Patrick showed little animation as one might expect from a baby. We were now living in a lovely old cottage which was built circa 1550, and I had decorated the only spare room in a bizarre colour scheme with life-sized transfers of various animals pasted on the walls. Pictures of rabbits and ducks, not to mention Mickey Mouse and Superman, were totally out of keeping with the old place, but I figured dark oak beams and a generally medieval setting was not conducive to generating a bright happy atmosphere for baby Patrick.

My wife, who loved the old house and everything it represented, was not altogether happy with the result of my handiwork but had to admit that it was a great deal more cheerful for a baby who could hardly appreciate the history of the place.

As time went by, however, I had cause to wonder whether my work was all in vain, as Patrick showed not the slightest curiosity in his surroundings. The weeks grew into months, by which time we were beginning to be troubled by the fact that our baby showed little interest in any of the countless toys and rattles both our friends and family bought for him. He displayed a marked indifference to anything we tried to amuse him with, and I began to feel frustrated as he continued to just lie there placidly. This was not the reaction I was looking for, the memory of my siblings' babies clear in my mind. He should have been inquisitive, eyes darting to any movement near him, but not at all.

Everybody said he was just lazy, a late starter, he would soon be a right little tearaway, but a feeling within me told me something different. My frustration grew, and I became short-tempered as I was not able to enjoy my son in the way I had expected. Looking back, my wife was strangely silent on the matter — maybe she knew something I didn't, or sensed it at least. The euphoria of becoming parents was soon gone and a deepening sense of foreboding descended upon us.

We took him to the doctor on several occasions but, upon examining Patrick, he was non-committal, repeating the same story that Patrick was just slow and was taking his own time. He would rabbit on how we must be patient and how every child developed at a different rate. I noticed, not for the first time, that he examined our baby's hands very closely, particularly the palms, but this did not have any significance for me at the time. By ten months, Patrick had not sat up, despite being a very well-developed child, and showed very little inclination to do so despite all our cajoling. I had seen other babies pulling themselves up by their harness which kept them safely contained in their pram, but Patrick was not interested in this aid. In fact, he did not need a harness at all for the amount of movement he made at any time.

The district nurse was now a frequent visitor and

very gradually it was being accepted that Patrick had a problem, but nothing definitive was diagnosed. Eventually, our baby did sit up, and it was such a relief that for a little while my worries abated. Maybe what people had been saying was true — Patrick was just a late starter and would soon catch up with the others. But our rejoicing was short-lived. Still our child showed little interest in things about him, and my anxiety returned to plague me.

It was about this time, to my great astonishment and delight, that my mother decided to pay us a visit. I had been cajoling her for years to come over to England for a holiday without any real hope of success. Now, out of the blue, she wrote and said she was coming. Not only would this be her first time on an aircraft — it would be the first time she would ever have been out of the country. This was a first of monumental proportions and deserved to be celebrated in style.

It was with a great feeling of excitement that I drove up to Heathrow to meet her off her flight. In those days, it was possible to wander around what they called the 'waving base', which in effect was a large roof area where you could watch the arrival and departure of nearly all flights. Later, I believe it was closed to the public as a precaution against terrorism, just like the Post Office Tower. What a sick world we live in.

I was in place in plenty of time to see the Aer Lingus flight land, and it taxied right up immediately opposite to the point where I was standing. The doors opened and who should be the very first person to appear in the doorway, but Mammy. She looked straight at me and returned my frantic waves with a cheery wave of her own. It turned out that she had made friends with the air hostesses and they had looked after her as if she was their own mother. They helped her down the steps and saw her through into the arrival hall as if she was royalty.

Although it had only been less than two years since I had seen her, yet I was shocked at how old and frail she had become. Could this tiny little lady be the tall buxom woman who used to tan my backside — it seemed unbelievable. She was enchanted with her latest grandchild and made the most unholy fuss of him during her short stay with us. Having had six children of her own, I was extremely keen to get her opinion of Patrick's ability to function as a normal child. But I was disappointed. Ever religious, all Mammy would say was that the good Lord would look after Patrick, he was a lovely baby and I was not to worry. Easier said than done.

I frequently had to drive out into the surrounding villages to visit customers, and I would take my mother with me. She enjoyed these jaunts enormously and questioned me about every facet of life in England. She was quite happy to sit in the car whilst I went off to see my customer, and I would leave the radio playing for company. When I returned, after maybe twenty minutes, the radio would be switched off and she would have her rosary beads in her hands and be praying away contentedly. That was Mammy, she never changed until the day she died, and I did not have to wait very long for that sad event to occur.

She stayed with us for three weeks and it was a very happy time for me. Remembering all the poverty-stricken years of the thirties and forties when there was hardly ever any food in the house, it was such a pleasure to take her out in the car and stop somewhere for afternoon tea or visit a posh restaurant in the evening, although she would not eat enough to fill a mouse.

When we said goodbye, I had no idea that it would be for the last time, although I should have been able to see how thin and drawn, she had become. I should not have been surprised when the news came.

It was only a month after her holiday with us that there was a knocking at our front door one night after we had gone to bed. Awakened from a sound slumber, I peered out of the bedroom window to see a police constable standing on the front porch and staring up at me.

'Are you Mr Mullen?' he enquired.

I said that I was, puzzled by this visit by the police in the middle of the night.

'Could you come down a moment, I have a message for you,' he said.

Quickly putting on a dressing gown and leaving my wife sitting up in bed, equally puzzled, I hurried down to find out what the problem was about. I could not remember committing any driving offence of late, but in any case, it was unlikely that this would be the official manner of informing me if I had.

He was there, in fact, to tell me that they had received an urgent telephone call from my brother Tom in Ireland, asking them to let me know that our mother had passed away. It had been found impossible to get through to me direct which I could well understand as my telephone had been out of order all day. It was a tremendous blow, coming as it did so soon after she had spent such an idyllic three weeks with us, and I could only feel grateful that I had had that great pleasure and the memories of it would stay with me forever.

With the exception of my sister Carmel, who could not be contacted in Canada, in time, the whole family were gathered for the funeral. There was a service arranged in the hospital chapel for the repose of the soul of Mammy and another sad figure who was also laid out in her coffin.

It was that of a nineteen-year-old girl who had been knocked off the pillion of her boyfriend's motorcycle on the Newry road, the day previously, and killed outright. She was a truly beautiful girl with lustrous black hair, and there did not appear to be a mark on her face. Her boyfriend, who was a few pews away from me, was absolutely distraught with grief and was being comforted by the girl's brother. Where the rest of her family were, I had no idea. I kept comparing the two bodies side by side — one who had led a long but hard life and the other merely on the threshold of hers. However hard my mother's life had been, at least she had lived long enough to bring up a family, whilst the other had had her life snuffed out almost at the outset.

A nun from the local convent was in attendance, and it was she who began to say the rosary, to which the small congregation responded. Well, the woman must have had a most urgent appointment elsewhere or perhaps she was on piecework, for the words of the Hail Mary's erupted out of her mouth at such a speed as to represent so much drivel. Maybe she believed that the more prayers she could get through in a day earned her so many more indulgences. Whatever the reason, I felt sickened by the total lack of feeling displayed by this farce, but someone else felt even more strongly about it and that was my brother George. He it was who led the responses in a very loud voice but in the most exaggeratedly slow pace so that each word hung in the air, almost like a challenge. This earned continual glares from the impatient nun who could not take off on her sprint dirge before George had finished. I really admired my brother for his dignified action.

Mammy lay in her coffin, and I will swear that there was a trace of a smile on her face as her favourite baby — and George was her favourite — saw to it that some dignity was restored to the service. It has to be the saddest day for any family when the mother is laid to rest. It is the end of an era for them, nothing will ever be the same again. For the expatriate, there will not be quite the incentive to return home so often, or indeed ever again, now that the one who gave him life has gone from the scene.

Standing by the graveside, I looked at my brothers and sisters and I could bet their thoughts were identical to mine. That so familiar voice echoing round the kitchen, 'Have you washed your face?

'Yes, Mammy.'

'Have you done your ecker?'

'Yes, Mammy.'

'Let me see those ears.'

That voice was now stilled forever but would remain fresh in our memories until the day came for us to say farewell to this world, when our own children would occupy our present positions.

Back home again after the funeral of my mother, Anthea seemed much more relaxed about matters, but I am sure it was all an act. It was only much later that I came to realise that she was probably better at concealing her fears and her worries which even exceeded mine. Never one to show her true feelings very much, I am certain that in the long run that she was far more affected by our baby's condition and therefore suffered greater disappointment and hurt because she felt unable to talk about it, even with her husband. Seeing my acute disappointment, she probably wanted to hide her own anguish from me.

The next hurdle was persuading Patrick to crawl, and my wife and I spent countless hours playing, or trying to play with him, on the floor. But he continued to largely ignore his toys, refusing to play with them, just touching them in a desultory fashion when encouraged to do so.

It was nearly two years before Patrick took his first stumbling steps, and Anthea and I cried when he did so. At last it seemed that we were getting somewhere, and our hopes rose that our little boy would be able to lead a full and normal life. We would sit on the floor, for what seemed like hours at a time, helping to steady him as he tried desperately to hold his balance. Time and again he would crash down on his bottom, and it was only after a long struggle that he could walk across the floor unaided. By now, the indentations on Patrick's temples had faded somewhat but were still visible, and we were at last realising that it was the forceps delivery which had caused all the problems. But no doctor had ever suggested such a thing, and it was only our own common sense that made what should have been the simple connection. It was strange looking back but, in fact, no doctor ever diagnosed Patrick's condition or gave as much as an opinion as to what might have caused the problem. I can only surmise that it was just the medical profession closing ranks, not daring to suggest that it might have been caused by neglect, lack of skill on the part of the gynaecologist or even bad luck. We were on our own and had to make the best of things. It is hard, on reflection, to remember what my true feelings towards Patrick were. He was my son and I loved him, but being brutally honest, I must confess that I had to face up to the fact that I was ashamed of him and, at the same time, ashamed of myself for feeling as I did. I was one confused father.

He was my first child and it was not the fact that I wanted to father a genius or a child with great talent that disappointed me, although who would not have been pleased if that had been the case. All I wanted was a normal healthy baby who could play and learn and yes, even get into scrapes like all other children appeared to do.

But I was being denied that, and I had to watch, in envy, the enormous pleasure other children seemed able to give their parents which I could plainly see when we took Patrick to the local park or to a playground. In short, I felt gutted. I wallowed in self-pity and allowed my feelings to show, being short-tempered and quick to take offence, and no doubt made things even more difficult for Anthea who was suffering the same kind of disappointment. Now, I feel even more ashamed when I look back on how selfish I had been.

Chapter Fourteen

It seemed like we had to wait forever before our son uttered his first word. For a long time, I honestly believed that he would never speak. It seemed like that wherever I went I could hear babies, hardly out of their mother's womb, prattling away nineteen to the dozen. I found it infuriating.

We went through all the usual prompting one does with a little baby. 'Da da, say, dad da. Where is dad da?' I sometimes grew hoarse after a marathon session standing over the cot. Anthea would sit Patrick on her knee for what seemed like hours, patiently repeating the simplest of words to try and encourage him to speak. The tears were never very far away after one of these lengthy coaching lessons, as they always ended in failure.

Certainly, it was much later than other children, probably when he was about three years old, when the first words came. I wish I could say that it was a momentous moment, but in truth, by this time we were so disillusioned by Patrick's backwardness that it almost went by unnoticed. Looking back now, I can state that there was no precise moment in time when we could say that that was the exact minute when we realised that our son was backward. Rather, it was a long, very gradual erosion of our hopes and dreams.

It was the constant drip of disappointments and setbacks that eventually bored their way into our consciousness and made us come to terms with Patrick's learning difficulties. Despite the reassurances of family and friends to the effect that Patrick was just a bit slow and would soon catch up with things, we knew in our hearts that something was sadly amiss with our son. We changed from a happy outgoing couple, full of optimism about life, to two very different human beings. Yet Patrick was a beautiful baby, almost as if fate was determined to make amends in some way for the calamity it had brought about. His blonde hair was almost like silk and his eyes of the clearest blue. His rosy cheeks spelt out that he was of robust health, and when he smiled, which was often, it was of the most endearing quality and he was a very contented child. Never one to whine or whinge, he went to bed happily every night without giving any bother. We had so much for which to be grateful. But somehow or other it was not enough.

We were frustrated and, yes, angry that we had produced something less than perfect in our first born. How could this happen to us, I wondered? It was a long time before we dared to discuss the matter fully with each other, not able to face the awful fact of Patrick's disability. For myself, I was too cowardly, too frightened of the outcome of such a confrontation. I was too afraid for my marriage — that the baring of our innermost fears might upset Anthea still further and it would all get too much for her. So it was that we had an aching needing to comfort each other but were too scared to reach out in case the other would see how worried we were. We went to great efforts to keep up an optimistic front.

Nobody was in any doubt, by now, that our son had severe learning difficulties, and although the terrifying word 'retarded' had not been mentioned, it was certainly in my thoughts. Countless hours sitting on the floor with him and endlessly repeating the simplest of words to Patrick was to no avail. Time and again, I could see my own frustration mirrored in my wife's eyes, whereupon she would avert her gaze and turn her attention to something else. I can remember feeling bitter and in a weird fashion, betrayed, but why? Nobody was to blame, these things happened all the time. It was only with hindsight that I could see that my poor wife probably felt worse, and I should have been more supportive — instead I was thinking only of myself. Never one to voice her feelings much, did Anthea herself feel a sense of guilt in some way as the mother of the child, I wondered? Women do sometimes, and feel the weight of responsibility even greater.

Trying to hold some kind of conversation with our child would leave us exhausted and angry. Neither my wife nor I were the most patient of people. Anthea, especially, was so quick and intelligent herself it must have been a nightmare for her particularly as she was in his company all of the time, whilst I had a break when off at work.

Eventually, when he could manage to say a few words, it was no less frustrating. When asking our child a question, for instance, 'Patrick, would you like some cake?', he would always answer using the last word of the sentence, 'cake'.

It would be the same if you asked him if he wanted to go to the moon — he would always answer 'moon'. He would never answer yes or no. This went on for a couple of years, but eventually his vocabulary increased slightly. The district nurse who came to assess him was encouraged by his ability to answer some questions but failed to understand that it depended very much on how one posed the question as to what answer one would get. When asked if he would like some cake, he would nod happily and say 'cake,' whereas if you said, 'You don't want any cake, do you, Patrick,' he would smile and shake his head in refusal, equally happily.

It is very hard to understand the medical authorities' attitude at this time and even later. Despite my many trips to the surgery and my assertion that something was very wrong with my son, no doctor would ever admit that Patrick was handicapped. At my behest, when he was finally examined by a child psychologist, I kept insisting that the child was mentally handicapped. He looked at me strangely and admitted that he found my attitude refreshing because the huge problem he usually faced was in convincing the parents that their child was retarded. This made me feel something of a freak.

Three years after Patrick was born, Anthea gave birth to another boy whom we named Ian. We had discussed at considerable length, and during many a sleepless night, whether we should risk having another baby. We had been assured that Anthea had not suffered any damage during her first pregnancy and that it was just a million to one chance that there had been complications with her firstborn. There was no medical reason why she could not give birth to another child safely, if she wanted one. But what if something went wrong? How could anyone be sure that the same thing, or God forbid, something even worse, might not happen again? What would we do, how could we cope with such a situation — that of having two backward children to look after and, above all, love? Did we have enough love in us to go around? I doubted very much if I had that much resilience. The thought was enough to send cold shivers down my spine It was only after much heart-searching, therefore, that we decided to have another baby, having been so mauled emotionally by Patrick's disability.

Doctor Blythe, our family doctor, had encouraged us from the start, and I shall always be grateful to him for his support. I think he felt, quite rightly, that with another child of normal birth, we would be better equipped to look after Patrick and better balanced in our emotions generally. He was of the opinion that Anthea would give birth to a perfectly normal baby and he was to be proved right.

In fact, Ian, our second born, was everything we had dreamed about. A jolly happy little chap, as sharp as a razor, and a delight for any parents. But the vast difference between the two boys only served to highlight the tragic consequences of the bungled forceps delivery.

Here again, fate played a hand, as my wife had no time for drugs and refused any medication to relieve her discomfort during her pregnancy. She could not be persuaded to have even an aspirin to relieve a troublesome headache. She endured the usual early morning sickness and had no desire for artificial aids. Anthea preferred to soldier on unaided. This was the year when many babies were born severely handicapped due to mothers being prescribed the drug Thalidomide. I shudder when I think of what those parents had to go through when shown the appalling consequences of using what had been considered a 'safe' drug. How does one cope with that kind of situation? My wife and I consoled each other that that calamity at least had been avoided, but it did not help our dilemma over Patrick.

All this time, we were very much on our own with regard to the best way forward for Patrick. By the time he was four, we had had him examined by so many doctors, psychologists and assessors that we had no idea where to turn next since we were never given a definitive diagnosis by anyone. The one great dread that I carried around with me was the thought that someone might say in years to come, 'What a pity you did not try such and such or see so and so — it's too late now.'

That was the stuff of nightmares and something that I knew I could not live with, and so we tried just about every remedy and sought out every possible source of help in our predicament.

It was round about now that I had the opportunity of going to work in Canada for a year, on secondment to a company in Ontario. It was a wonderful chance to see a bit more of the world, and I discussed it excitedly with Anthea. Canada was a country I had long admired and had seriously considered emigrating to if things had not worked out so well for me in England. My youngest sister Carmel, with whom I always had a close relationship, resided there, and it would be great to see something of her again and meet her growing family for the first time.

It was now or never, as far as I was concerned — another opportunity like this one was unlikely to crop up again in the near future, if indeed it ever would. Patrick was our great concern; he was now four years of age and should be starting school shortly. Anthea was not certain about this move abroad, but there was just time, I argued, for us to have this sabbatical before our son's fifth birthday and his proper schooling commenced.

I thought that it was a great chance for all of us, not least Patrick, to broaden our horizons and to enjoy a complete change. My wife took some persuasion but, in the end, came around to my way of thinking, and so we made our plans for the spring of that year. It was an exciting time as we made preparations for our great adventure. There was so much to do — we had to make arrangements for our home to be taken care of in our absence, inoculations and temporary visas to obtain. Fortunately, we had no animals to worry about, which was one relief. We had often toyed with the idea of getting a dog for the children to spoil, but somehow, we had never gotten around to it, the reasons for which I have already explained, and a decision I was now grateful for having taken.

Air travel not having yet assumed its dominance of the market, we sailed from Southampton, towards the end of April, on Cunard's *SS Saxonia,* and Anthea's sister Gilda saw us off. We waved from the deck as the ship swung out into the Solent and the band played some stirring music from the pier. It was all very uplifting, as though we were setting out to conquer the new world.

We called in at Le Havre, to pick up those continental passengers who were making the journey, before setting off across the Atlantic. It was a very comfortable ship with plenty of entertainment. Children were made very welcome and a nursery, staffed by capable women, was much used by those with very young children who wanted to enjoy the amenities on board. We were no exception, and we would deposit our two offspring whenever we wanted to take part in any of the sporting events organised by the crew. Needless to say, my wife won the table tennis competition without much effort.

It was during that voyage that the full impact of Patrick's disability became all too clear to us. On those occasions when we left our two children in the nursery, we took the opportunity of studying their behaviour through the glass panel in the door. They could not see us, and with regard to Patrick, our worst fears were realised. Whilst Ian, although only eighteen months, became animated and joined in readily with the other children in the games organised by the staff, Patrick sat desultorily among a pile of soft toys and took no part in anything that was going on. The ladies in charge tried very hard to coax him into joining in the fun, but to no avail. He could not be cajoled into taking part, showing a complete lack of understanding of what was required, and the nurses soon gave up on him and left him to sit idly by on his own.

It certainly put a damper on our enjoyment of the trip, and even as we were steaming towards North America, my mind was already thinking of the journey back as I knew it was only in the UK that we were going to get the much-needed help for our son. I had harboured vague thoughts of perhaps settling down in Canada if we all liked it, but I knew now that that was never going to happen. I was in no doubt that the same facilities would be available in Canada, but at what cost? There was no National Health in that country, as we knew it, and I was certainly in no position to be able to afford private care for Patrick.

On the fourth day, after leaving Le Havre, we entered the Gulf of St. Lawrence and, towards evening, the temperature dropped dramatically. The word went around that there were icebergs in the vicinity and we hurried up on deck, my pulse quickening as thoughts of the *Titanic* came to the fore. Sure enough, by the light of the setting sun, the first of several great icebergs drifted into view a few miles from the ship. They appeared to glow with a bluish light and were a thrilling sight. We were assured by the officers who joined us that we were in no danger, the beautiful but perilous objects having been tracked by radar on board for some hours. Having taken the precaution of bringing our coats with us, as the air was freezing, we were able to watch them until they disappeared in the darkness — a memorable sight that still lives in my memory.

The next morning, we found ourselves ploughing

through loose pack-ice as we entered the mouth of the St. Lawrence river. We were told that ours was the first ship through that spring, the river not being navigable during the winter months due to it being frozen over. It was the first week of May as we docked at Quebec. It looked a fascinating city, but our destination was Montreal and so there was no time to go ashore to explore. Most of our French passengers were getting off here, obviously having strong connections with the French-speaking city.

Within a short time, we were on our way again, and the next day we ourselves departed the vessel, the ship having reached its final destination. We had planned to spend our first night in Canada in Montreal and having loaded our cases into the back of a taxi, we instructed the driver to take us to our hotel. He seemed a breezy sort of chap, and we drove around for a bit before pulling up in front of a charming building where we were booked for the night. Being in an expansive mood, jollied by being in a new environment and delighted by the good behaviour of our two sons, I gave the driver a generous tip. He thanked me with a smile and departed with a cheery wave.

As we reached the top of the steps at the entrance to the hotel, helped with our heavy luggage by a porter, I turned to look around to find our ship in full sight a mere four hundred yards away. I had paid for a costly half-hour trip for nothing. It was my first encounter with Canadian commerce. Happily, I came across many acts of kindness during our short stay in that country that more than made up for that taxi driver's deceit. But he did spoil my moment of arrival.

Our final destination being Toronto, we entrained the next day for the eight-hour journey to that city. The boys continued to be marvellous, little Ian enchanting the other passengers with his gurgle chuckle. Patrick, of course, was his usual quiet docile self, seemingly oblivious to everything that was going on around him but very obedient and certainly no trouble to anyone.

I remember one particular moment during that long train journey, and that was when I paid a visit to the toilet at the end of our carriage. There was a typed notice above the pan and, in true forthright Canadian fashion, it stated, 'Gentlemen, it is our aim to keep this toilet clean and tidy, your aim will help'. A touch of Canadian humour which I have never forgotten.

Although it was early May, it was our luck to arrive in the first heatwave of the year, and we discovered the humidity crushing. We found living near the lake akin to living in a sauna, but fortunately, the house we were destined to live in during our stay was equipped with air-conditioning. It was a detached property in a quiet tree-lined avenue close to the shops and all amenities and we loved it. It was here that Ian took his first steps before sitting down hard on his bottom on the lounge floor. Far from discouraging him, he laughed aloud at his own collapse, and within days was scampering around all over the place getting under his mother's feet at every turn.

The house was owned by my new employer whose mother had lived in it until her death the year before, and it had lain empty ever since. He was pleased to have someone in residence who would look after it until such time as he could make up his mind whether to sell it. Otherwise I do not think that we could have survived that summer as the heat was stifling.

We enjoyed our time in Canada. My boss was the main Ford dealer in the area, for American and Canadian models, and had just been awarded the franchise for the British counterparts, which was where I came in. Having had years of experience in England with Ford, it was felt that I could contribute some know-how to the company with regard to the marketing of these strange 'compact' models. Looking at the size of the enormous 'gas guzzlers' of North America, I could understand the aversion of the men who had to produce the sales of this new line of products.

I remember leaving our main place of business in Stoney Creek to visit our Hamilton showroom for the first time, and although I was entitled to the use of a superior type of car, I believed in practising what I was preaching and elected to drive the new Ford Anglia. On getting out of the car, I was greeted by two very laid-back car salesmen who shook hands cordially whilst eyeing this strange 'mini car' for the first time.

One of them walked around the vehicle, looking bemused, and asked, Gee, John, have they given you one for the other foot?', from which you will deduce that before converting the customers to a change of thinking and driving a smaller vehicle, I had a monumental task in educating my salesmen first of all.

We found people, in general, to be very friendly, especially when they discovered that we were new arrivals from England, and many went out of their way to be helpful.

My sister Carmel lived in the city of Hamilton and we saw much of her and her fast-growing family. It was a great help having her close by and a considerable comfort to my wife who had never been away from home for long before this trip. We did a lot of sightseeing, taking in Niagara Falls, the Shakespeare theatre at Stratford-upon-Avon and even venturing into the United States on one occasion. It was an exciting time for all of us, but the pressing need to have specialist help for Patrick overshadowed everything else and the decision was taken to return home earlier than planned in order to get things organised. We were very sorry to leave that lovely country; we had made lots of friends and they were genuinely sorry to see us go, but go we did.

We sailed on the sister ship of *SS Saxonia,* the *SS Franconia,* and it was a sad trip back, despite the comfort of the ship, as we could have very happily settled down in Canada.

We felt that, in leaving the country, there was one small advantage and that was in missing the savage Canadian winter of which we had been warned on numerous occasions. This turned out to be a joke as we experienced one of the worst winters on record in England that year. It started snowing on Boxing day and the ground was still covered with the stuff at the end of February.

When it did finally clear, I went for my first cross-country run in months, which took me out of town. The hedgerows were exposed for the first time and I could see that the bark of the shrubs and young trees was completely eaten away to a height of one metre. The small animals, in their desperation for food, had been driven to eating almost anything to avoid starvation. The sight of more than one half-eaten carcass was proof that not all had made it through to springtime.

With regard to Patrick, we were right back where we started, with a mountain to climb.

Chapter Fifteen

It was time now to think of school, but was Patrick educable? He had had an I.Q. test, one of many, and it had been shown that he was borderline at sixty-eight while seventy-two was considered normal. It was like coming fourth in an Olympic final — so frustratingly short of what was required to achieve success. We were desperate to find somewhere that could provide at least some kind of a start to his education, but where to go, that was the question.

We discussed the problem with friends who had children of a similar age and most of them recommended a toddlers' school located in 'The Avenue', a leafy road quite close to the railway station in Andover. On our return from Canada, we had bought an attractive bungalow in the town, so this location would prove very convenient, but this was the least important of our criteria. Far more important was how well this particular school could cope with Patrick's dire shortcomings. We were well aware that our son ideally required specialist teaching, but that definitely came under the 'We wish' category.

Even if we had had the money, which we didn't, there did not seem to be any such establishment in existence — certainly not in our neck of the woods. What did other people do under these circumstances, and we were left to wonder in vain.

There was really nowhere else even remotely suitable, so we enrolled him at this local kindergarten, with a splendid reputation, run by a very able Mrs. Smith. The school was housed in a lovely old building that had formerly been a very substantial family home but now catered for a much-extended family in its new role as a kindergarten. It had a lovely warm feel to it as the sound of children's laughter, echoed loudly every single time we paid a visit.

Here, among his peers, other three- and four-year-olds, Patrick performed very poorly, seemingly unable to grasp the simplest concept of drawing or brick-building or indeed, any creative activity. Despite the individual attention given by a dedicated teacher, he failed to make any noticeable headway. Mrs. Smith was a kind and patient tutor, and in my many conversations with her, I could see that she was frustrated. The lady could only give our son so much of her time, having other pupils to consider, and she hated to report failure. The unvarnished truth, however, was that our son needed more specialist attention, and we had to face up to the facts. He stayed at this school for nearly a year, but in the end, achieved very little except that it gave his mother a break and allowed her more time alone with Ian, who also demanded her attention.

It was with great regret that we had to take him away from Mrs. Smith, but in any event, he was now five and should be attending a normal school. Despite all our enquiries, we could not find a specialist school, so we decided to give the local primary school a trial to see if Patrick could make any progress there. So it was really with some trepidation that we took Patrick along to expose him to the much less sheltered surroundings of a local council school, Wolversdene, aptly named as it turned out.

I could remember very well my own experiences when I first started school and how traumatic it had been. Away from the loving arms of my mother for the first time and being bullied and pushed around by a bunch of young toughs, it took me some time to adjust. Later, I probably became one of the young toughs myself. Such is the way of the world.

We did not have to wait long before finding out just how traumatic our son was finding life in his new school. He had shown a reluctance to go to this new place of education, especially after the first day, but we put it down to a sense of loneliness and not being acquainted with any of the other children. When I dropped him off on my way to work, I could see him in my driving mirror, standing forlornly in the doorway looking after me, his teacher holding him by the hand. I had explained to the headmaster the difficulty we were having with our son, and he was kind enough to promise that his staff would do their best to see that Patrick was settled in as quickly as possible. But he did point out that they catered for a huge number of pupils and individual attention for any one child was impossible to achieve.

It was on the third or fourth day of Patrick's attendance that the headmaster of Wolversdene Primary School, who by coincidence happened to live in the same street as us, knocked on our door. I was at work and my wife opened it to find him standing on the doorstep, holding Patrick by the hand. He apologised, explaining that our son had had an accident and had soiled himself, and he had brought him home. Anthea was mortified as Patrick, if nothing else, was a very well-ordered child and could look after himself very well. Indeed, he was meticulous in his habits and appearance. When I came home from the office, I was very worried to hear of this lapse of behaviour on Patrick's part as I felt we had enough problems on our hands.

I felt sure there had to be a reason for it so the following day, when I knew that the children would be in the schoolyard on their lunch-time break, I made my way there. The play area was quite close to the street, and so I could observe all that was happening in the yard without getting out of the car. It did not take long to pick out Patrick, and the bile rose in my throat as I saw what was happening to my son.

They had him backed into a corner, at least six of his schoolmates, although one could hardly call them mates as they danced around him catcalling and taunting him. My son, although only five years old, had his fists up and I was in time to see one little toe rag, circle round behind him, only for Patrick to whirl round and catch his tormentor a good one on the ear. He let out a howl and the rest scattered for the moment, as my son charged them, and I was out of the car in an instant and hurried round to the entrance to the playground. The gang was returning to the sport when I reached Patrick's side, and I saw the relief on his face when he recognised me. The little cowards melted away when they realised the game was up, and I was furious that there was no teacher in sight to prevent this kind of bullying.

I had never seen my boy in this mood before, his blood was up, and he was trembling with what I think was a mixture of anger and fear. I took Patrick away from there that afternoon, never to return, as I knew only too well that it was the strain of being bullied that had caused his distress.

It was the first time that I had the unusual feeling of being very proud of my son, as he never cried, and had stood up to his cowardly attackers in a manner few could better. Remembering my own craven behaviour when I was being pushed around at school when much older than five, I could not help but marvel at his courage. I marvelled, too, how suddenly lucid he could become when he was faced with a crisis, when he was shocked or taken by surprise. Now the words tumbled out, and although disjointed, they made perfect sense. 'Those boys, Dad, they did call me names, calling me names, they did, rude those boys,' and then the tears came, and I was so upset because I realised that Patrick was crying because he thought he was in trouble with me for hitting one of the little horrors. Then we were in the car, and I hugged my son fiercely to me, the lump in my throat nearly choking me as I dried his tears.

'They are nasty boys, son,' I consoled him. 'You certainly gave that big guy a wallop on the ear.'

He gave me a toothy grin through the tears as he realised that he was not in any trouble. He clenched a little fist, suddenly feeling proud. 'I punched him on the face, I did, I gave him wallop,' and he gave a whoop, his blood still up, and he got excited.

'All right, Patrick, calm down now, you will not be going back to that nasty school any more,' I assured him.

'Nasty school, Daddy, nasty boys, they did punch me, they did. I punched them, wallop,' and he suddenly put his arms around me, and I could hardly see to drive as my eyes watered. This was more than he had ever said at once, and I was astounded.

Were we any better, I wondered, than the lowest form of animal life? Those children had behaved like hyenas or wolves, turning on one of their own kind because he was weaker or a little different from them. Beneath the thin veneer of so-called civilisation, there was always this basic primeval bloodlust — for that is what it was, pure and simple, no more no less. We were just animals and nothing else — thus I raged as I drove home.

I had a stormy meeting with the headmaster the next day when I told him that Patrick would not be returning to his school. He apologised for the lack of supervision on the part of his staff that allowed such blatant bullying to take place, but could not guarantee that it would not happen again. He suggested that perhaps a special school would be more appropriate for Patrick's education, as if such a place existed in every town in the country. If only pigs could fly.

I was in a dilemma and not for the first time. What to do about Patrick's education, that became the burning question. Anthea was adamant that he could not return to the local council school to be tortured daily by the other schoolchildren, a decision with which I wholeheartedly concurred. Despite the limited means at our disposal, we cast around for a private school which might specialize in taking on children with learning difficulties. There was none in our immediate locality, the nearest we could find being miles away in Hertfordshire. Nevertheless, we decided that distance should not be regarded as an obstacle if it proved to be the only solution.

We made an appointment to see the principal and drove up with Patrick to inspect the place. It did not take us long to realise that it was us who was under inspection, for after half an hour in the headmaster's study, being grilled about every facet of our existence, particularly about our financial status, we were told that we might be suitable. They were especially keen to learn about how well-trained Patrick was in taking care of himself. Was he good socially, no undesirable traits, not given to tantrums, no bed-wetting, heaven forbid, was he amenable to discipline, and on it went. It seemed, when we talked it over later, that they were prepared to take Patrick in if we were willing to pay a king's ransom for the privilege and Patrick needed no looking after whatsoever. In other words, they wanted no hassle, just money. We did not take long to make up our minds and that school was a no-go area.

We did arouse the interest of a social worker by the name of Miss Collins, who was very sympathetic to our cause. On several occasions, she came to our house and put Patrick through many tests and was very supportive, though there again, like all the others, she never did give an opinion as to what might be wrong with Patrick.

She did, however, tell us about a new establishment which had opened recently near Winchester called 'The Compton Diagnostic Unit', which apparently was the first of its kind, certainly in our neck of the woods. This was a residential school where children were taken in for periods of up to six months and where they could be studied and appraised by suitably qualified staff. It could then be established what a child's capabilities were and decisions taken about his future.

The village of Compton was only about twenty miles from where we lived, so it was an easy task not only to take him there, but a convenient place for us when it came to visiting times. This seemed the ideal place for Patrick as I was very dubious about minds being made up on the basis of a two-hour examination, opinions formed which would affect our child for the remainder of his life. This would be a long-term diagnosis and a comprehensive in-depth study of our son's abilities, or lack of them.

Miss Collins made an appointment for us and it was with a great deal of excitement that we went along to the interview, taking Patrick with us. It was a large modern red brick building in the centre of Compton, a few miles outside of Winchester. We had passed it many times on the way to Southampton but had taken little notice of it, there being little reason to do so. We saw at once that it was a very well-run place, very much a school with caring teachers. The whole place had the right feel about it.

The pupils were all very young, the oldest not much older than our five-year-old. Ensconced in the principal's office, it was explained to us that the school was a completely new idea for children with learning difficulties to get first class and a long-term diagnosis of what each individual child was capable of. It was visited on a regular basis by doctors, psychiatrists and child psychologists, and we were told that Patrick's stay could be at least a month and anything up to six months. There would then be a full and frank consultation with us as to what was best for our child. We were delighted at this news as it was precisely the professional assessment, we had been looking for in our search for what was best for our son.

There seemed a good chance that Patrick would be admitted without much delay, and we came away happy that at last something really constructive was being done about Patrick's future. The unit's director was as good as his word and informed us within days that a place had been found for Patrick.

We were not prepared for Patrick's reaction to being left in this strange place, when a couple of weeks later, we took him along with his little suitcase. Right away, he sensed that we were leaving him, and we were dismayed when he started crying. Again, when faced with something which really upset him, he seemed to find the words in his panic to get away.

'No, no, don't like, don't like, want to go home, Mummy,' he cried and clung to his mother's skirts quite fiercely.

I could see that my wife was already having second thoughts, and although I too was finding it distressing, I knew we had to be firm and leave him. His whole future was in the balance — this could be the most important decision we could ever make on his behalf, and we had to face up to it. We had already been told that we were very lucky to have got Patrick in so quickly as the unit was only just starting up, and there was certain to be a huge demand for places as soon as it became better known.

We had already discovered, to our amazement, the enormous number of families who had a member suffering from some form of learning difficulty. It represented one of the biggest drains on the resources of the National Health and there was never enough money to provide the necessary care for all these sad cases. It was particularly hard to see young children so afflicted, and yet it seemed so little could be done for them by way of providing facilities.

Our other son, Ian, who had accompanied us, was showing signs of alarm as he began to wonder if he was being deserted too, and I indicated to Anthea to take him out to the car and I would hand Patrick over to the matron, who was looking on sympathetically.

Tearfully, Anthea made her farewell to our son, and I hugged Patrick to me and assured him that it was only for a little while and that we would come and see him at the weekend. He cried as he clung to me, and I swear it was the hardest thing I had ever had to do in my life as the matron very kindly came to my rescue and took him from me.

I steeled myself to walk away through the door and cursed the fates that had forced this upon me. Ian was only two but knew that something was amiss, and sat on his mum's knee and sucked his thumb, a scared look on his cherubic little face. He, as much as ourselves, was going to miss his big brother who would often look after him for hours on end.

Chapter Sixteen

Throughout Patrick's six months at the diagnostic unit, we visited him every Sunday and took him out for a picnic or just a drive in the car, but the farewells never grew any easier.

On those days when it was wet, and there were many, it was a problem to know what to do or where to go. Very often we would go to Marwell Zoo, which was not too far away, and we were more than grateful for this amenity as both children enjoyed seeing the animals. We had many happy times there and the time would just fly past on those afternoons.

Other times we would drive into Southampton to see a Walt Disney film. I can remember how enchanted Patrick was with *One Hundred and One Dalmatians*. He would become animated when reminded about it afterwards, and seemingly could not get it out of his mind. If you asked him today what his favourite dog was, he would without doubt opt for the Dalmatian with all its spots. Another great favourite of his was *Jungle Book,* a film I took him to see several times.

It was always the same struggle to leave Patrick afterwards, however, and we all found it very exhausting emotionally. The more we enjoyed ourselves, the harder it seemed to say goodbye.

He would cry and cling to his mother when the time

came. Ian, too, would get very upset as he did not understand what was happening. He just could not see why his brother couldn't come home with us and he really missed him.

'Patrick, Patrick,' he would cry out, as his brother was led away. It was a nerve-crunching moment every week, and I came to dread it. But there was nothing we could do about it except soldier on. It was a sad little party that made the journey home, nobody speaking. Even Ian, always a little chatterer, would subside in his seat and sit sucking his thumb, bewildered by it all.

We continually made enquiries as to Patrick's progress or otherwise, desperate to find out if there was any cause for hope that our son might be educable. But the people in charge were non-committal, keeping their cards very close to their chest and saying very little. I could understand their reluctance — they were professional people and would not be drawn to make any hasty judgement. 'All in good time,' was as much as we could elicit from them. Whilst I admired their professionalism, it did not help to alleviate our worry and concern. The weeks became months, and I wondered how long all this was going to take. I began to dread the weekends as I am sure my wife did as well.

However, the great day came at last, when we were summoned by Mister Clarke, the principal, to see him in his office. He ushered us in and we sat down shakily, not daring to look at one another. We had agonized on the way over to Compton as to what we were likely to be told. Would it be good news or bad, what were the recommendations likely to contain — but we had come to no conclusion. But here we were at last in the office. We were going to receive Patrick's final report and the agony of waiting had come to an end.

The gist of it was that they found our son was below the normal I.Q. rating, but he was educable. The principal had many good things to say about our son — the fact that he was very obedient and no trouble whatsoever to the people who had to look after him — news that was balm to our ears.

He went to great lengths to impress on us how fortunate we were that we had such a fine boy. He was very good-looking, fit as a fiddle and showed an aptitude for learning which, while it was not great, held out much promise for the future. With patience and good teaching skills, much could be accomplished with Patrick. He was slow, certainly, but he gave an indication of wanting to please those in charge of him and this was a priceless asset for anyone. Routine was the answer. For someone who could not grasp things quickly, repetition was the way forward.

In his opinion, it was the constant repeating of instructions that would succeed, until they were imbedded in his memory, and then he would never forget them. The boy would pick things up gradually until they were second nature to him.

The difficulty now was to find him a suitable school for children who had learning difficulties and required special attention. Mister Clarke made a face and here told us the bad news that places of education such as we required were in very short supply indeed, and we might have to wait a considerable time before we struck lucky.

It seemed appalling that we had to rely on luck to find a place for our son when we had the National Health and all that seemed to imply. We were to find out that it meant very little, and that each county was a separate entity so far as facilities were concerned. Hampshire, where we lived, was not noted for its abundance of care centres. We were very fortunate indeed that they set up this particular facility as it pointed the way forward for our son.

We thanked Mister Clarke for his kindness and took our leave. Despondent, we returned home, taking Patrick with us, and he could hardly believe that his exile was at an end. As we drove out of the centre, I could see his eyes starting to light up, as he realised we were heading towards home, and of course he could see the all-important suitcase being put in the boot of the car. As we got nearer and he could recognise landmarks, he hopefully asked, 'Are we going home, Daddy, are we? Going home, Patrick going home, Dad?'

He looked at me desperately.

'Yes, Patrick, we are going home,' I replied, and his mother hugged him. Ian, not one to be left out of the act, hugged them both. He too seemed to realise that Patrick's exile was at an end, and that he would be available for him to play with. His eyes darted excitedly from one to another of us as he sucked his thumb triumphantly.

Weeks dragged by and we wondered if we would ever hear from Mister Clarke again. It had been left that should he hear of an opening anywhere he would let us know, but I was not holding my breath. Anthea was delighted to have Patrick back once more and we were a real family again, but soon the novelty wore off and I could see that my wife was becoming agitated at Patrick's reluctance to get involved in any playtime activities, always content to just sit and watch. To Anthea, who was a highly motivated person, this was anathema, and I could see the tears of frustration all too often in her eyes when I came home from work. She would have welcomed a few tantrums from our elder son instead of him just sitting there like a block of wood. The contrast with Ian was now stark, as he got into all kinds of mischief, and it would be true to say that he got away with murder as his behaviour was such a joyous relief compared to Patrick's.

Fortunately, this did not have to continue too long, as one day I received a telephone call from Mr Clarke, who asked if I could call and see him as soon as possible. We shot over to Compton the very next day and were shown into the principal's study.

He said, 'I do not want to get your hopes up too high, Mr Mullen, but I am right in saying that Patrick is a Roman Catholic?'

Puzzled, I nodded.

'Well,' he went on, 'the position is this. There is an order of nuns who run a special school for children such as Patrick in the Midlands. It is called Croome Court and it is for boys only, but the relevant point is that it is a Catholic school and therefore Patrick would qualify without difficulty. They have a vacancy at the moment, but I realise it is a long way from here and you may well feel that it is just too distant, especially for frequent visits.'

He leaned back in his chair and waited for our reaction.

I knew that he had gone to considerable difficulty on our behalf — there must be dozens of children who were desperately in need of this placing, but he had offered it to us.

I looked at my wife and saw the look of anxiety on her face. The principal clearly thought that we were extremely lucky to be given this opportunity. The solution was not perfect, but it was the only thing on offer. We might have to wait months, who knew how long before we might be offered something else.

I looked at Mister Clarke and asked, 'Does this school have a good reputation? Has it been in existence long?'

He assured me that it had and that it occupied a mansion which had formerly been the seat of the Duke of Leeds. The nuns had acquired it many years before and had put it to the best possible use. At present, several hundred boys were resident at the school. I was only going through the motions — I had already made up my mind.

I knew that my wife was really getting down from the strain of looking after Patrick and made a quick decision to accept the place at Croome Court. After all, we could always take him away if it proved unsatisfactory. It was a very long way to go, but whatever the distance, once he was away from home, ten miles or one hundred miles made very little difference to Patrick. Any inconvenience would be ours alone — such as the long journey to visit him. In any event, however close the school might have been, it was unlikely that we would be encouraged to see our son any more often than once a month. Our weekly trips to Compton proved conclusively that our visits were very unsettling for Patrick. They had always ended up in crying scenes and were very hard on all concerned, especially my wife. Far better to allow him to really settle in and feel at home.

We made the journey to Croome Court the following weekend, taking Patrick with us. He sat in the back of the car with Ian in his car seat and, as always, was the attentive big brother. We had always marvelled how wonderfully gentle he was with little Ian, very protective, always fearful that the baby might fall or put something in his mouth. Knowing Ian's propensity for food, that was always an ongoing hazard. Our younger son believed that everything had to be at least tried for taste, and as a consequence, he had had a few near escapes from choking.

It was drizzling when we arrived, but in spite of the poor weather, we could appreciate the magnificent house and the splendid surroundings in which it was set. Plenty of room here for young boys to run about and exercise, a far cry from its original use. It was not a day for outdoor pursuits, which explained the dearth of human beings in the area.

On our arrival at the school, we thought that we had blundered in on a riot. The enormous front door was wide open, and as we ventured inside, we saw a seething pile of young humanity on the floor of the large entry hall, akin to a rugby scrum, which turned out to be exactly what it was. Whilst we looked on in astonishment, the melee cleared sufficiently to allow a black-clad figure to emerge. A laughing red face looked up at us and we were able to identify a young nun who it transpired was called Sister Teresa. Seeing us standing there with bemused faces, she called out, 'All right, boys, enough, enough,' and she handed over the ball for which they were all wrestling for possession. She greeted us warmly and grasped our son by the hand, smiling at him, an action which had Patrick smiling back.

'This must be our new pupil. I hope you are good at rugby — we need some new blood. Patrick, isn't it?

I could see that Patrick, in spite of his shyness, liked her immediately. I felt that this initial sight of the staff in action, however unorthodox, was a very good omen. This young nun clearly loved her charges, and I could see that my wife was much impressed too. My mind could not help but think back to the infamous Sister Gabriel of my own childhood and I shuddered. What a difference — things certainly had changed in the nunnery. We were made to feel very welcome by the Mother Superior and looking at all the happy inquisitive faces around us, felt sure that Patrick would be very well looked after. Thus, began what was, on the whole, nine happy years for Patrick.

They were probably the most important of his life, as it would be here that he would learn how to cope with his learning difficulties and make his way in the world. The lessons he would absorb would be crucial to his future wellbeing.

When he was twelve, he would be moved on to the senior school at Besford Court, a few miles away, run by the same order of nuns.

Chapter Seventeen

A week later, we deposited our boy in the care of the nuns, and although we were saddened that this course of action was necessary, we were equally convinced that it was in Patrick's best interests. Although we were a young couple, yet the matter of what might happen to him should tragedy befall us — his parents — perhaps a fatal accident — what would his future be then without anyone to look out for him.

It was something Anthea and I discussed many times. We took the conscious decision that, come what may, Patrick must be given every opportunity to prepare himself to go out into the world. Maybe he would never be capable of standing on his own feet, but we felt very strongly that it was our duty to give him every assistance to do so. If that meant being hard on him or ourselves, in the short term, then so be it. We had to take the long-term view and think of his future.

At least the weather was mild, with fitful sunshine, as we drove the hundred odd miles to the new school. Patrick was in no doubt what was going to happen when he saw his suitcase being loaded in the boot of the car. He had come to recognise the signs all too well and it was a journey interrupted intermittently by the tearful entreaty, 'Patrick going away. Patrick not want to go. Want to stay at home.'

His small hands clutched at my coat collar as I drove, and I tried not to let it distract me from my driving, but it was difficult. Again, I could not help but marvel how lucid he became when he was emotionally upset. It almost seemed as though his brain was galvanized into action. His tears tore at my guts and the begging look in his eyes almost made me turn the car around and head for home. Our nerves were jumpy to say the least, and the trip seemed endless, with my wife and I snapping at each other for no reason whatever or, on second thoughts, for a very obvious reason.

The truth was the two of us were just feeling guilty at deserting our son and leaving him with strangers and such a long way from home. Remembering how he had been bullied at Wolversdene school, I had nightmares about the same thing happening to him here. However kind and vigilant the nuns were, could they be expected to watch out for him all the time in a school of several hundred children. I tried to console myself by remembering that all these children were in some way retarded, and would not possess the intelligence and cruelty of normal children.

I had not thought that the distance would be relevant, but now that the moment had come it was very important. It was a good three-hour car journey and it seemed endless. It seemed like we were depositing our son at the ends of the earth and leaving him there like an outcast.

At Compton, Patrick was only thirty minutes away by car and we had felt close to him, especially seeing him every weekend.

We had left Ian in the care of his grandparents, as the journey was such a long one, and although he was a good traveller, he was bound to get fractious and our nerves could only take so much. Little Ian knew something was up and clutched at his brother when it was time to say goodbye. He was confused, but he also instinctively realised that we were all feeling sad. He was not a cry-baby by nature, but his little chin wobbled uncontrollably when Patrick hugged him.

The Mother Superior was very gracious and could see that our farewell to Patrick was going to try us. She sent for Sister Teresa, who took Patrick by the hand and led him off to a play area.

I had worried, initially, that the black-robed figures of the nuns would prove frightening to our son, but he seemed not to mind. I remembered my own first days at school quite vividly, when I was taught by the Sisters of Mercy, and I don't remember them as being particularly merciful. In fact, I was terrified of them, but then I was only five years old. Sister Gabriel, a ruthless disciplinarian, she had chosen the wrong vocation and should have been a sergeant in the army instead of being in charge of small children. But these nuns could not have been more different, and above all, they had a great sense of humour which I valued above all else.

I think at this point, Patrick was somewhat bemused — in any event, he seemed content to be led away and we took our leave. Not a word was spoken between Anthea and me for what seemed like an eternity. I felt a raw acid feeling in my chest; I really felt that I had earned thirty pieces of silver as I drove away. Somehow,

I had to retain my composure for Anthea's sake, as she sat unmoving in her seat, her face ashen. Finally, I spoke, giving all the reasons why this was a good move for Patrick. His stay at the school might only be for a short while. With special tutelage, who knew what great progress he might make. The nuns were dedicated and loving teachers. Patrick would be in good company with kids no better equipped for life than he was. He would make lots of friends. The school had excellent facilities — I had taken note of the football pitches and cricket field. Patrick would take to sport with the proper encouragement.

In reciting all of this, I knew I was trying to ease my own conscience as much as trying to cheer up my wife. All to no avail on either count, as I continued to wrestle with the thought of turning the car right around and going back to retrieve our son. Anthea, for her part, sat white-faced and silent for most of the journey home. Nearly forty years later, I know for certain that it was the best decision I had ever made, but on that day, on that rain-filled journey home, it seemed like the worst decision of my life.

We had a letter from the Mother Superior a week later to inform us that Patrick had settled down well and was proving a very amenable boy, no tantrums or any signs of stress. This bit of news perked us up no end and did much for our peace of mind. Ian was most anxious to know what had happened to his brother and obviously missed him very much, as Patrick used to spend ages picking up his brother's toys — his young sibling took the greatest delight in chucking them all over the place.

His mother was not nearly so obliging, so he kept asking when Patrick was coming home. We could have visited Patrick a month later, but I discouraged such a visit to my wife, as I argued that he was settling down well and a visit from us could undo all the good already accomplished. I felt that he really needed to bond with the school and his schoolmates and to feel entirely comfortable there. Time was a great ally, and I pointed out that the day he left that school, he would be equally unhappy as he was to leave home. I was not sure that I believed that, but it was an argument I put forward to bolster my case.

Anthea was unconvinced but agreed to put off a visit until the school sports-day, when all the other parents would be showing up and Patrick would feel no different to the other boys. In the meantime, we had one stroke of good fortune in the form of an old friend by the name of Peter Lewis.

Peter had arrived to work in Andover from his home in Weston-Super-Mare as a sixteen-year-old and being a keen runner, had sought my assistance as a coach. Living in digs and far from home, my wife and I had taken him under our wing, and he was a frequent visitor to our home, where he was a great hit with our children.

For a young teenager, he showed endless patience with our kids, and he would play games with them for ages without a sign of boredom.

Peter was now based in Worcester, only a short distance from Patrick, and when he heard of his close proximity to Croome Court he made it his business to call and see our son. Together with his girlfriend at the time, they occasionally took him out to tea for a Sunday treat and were able to report to us that Patrick was thriving and in very good spirits. This cheered us up enormously and we were greatly in his debt. Now a world-renowned scientist in his field, Peter has remained one of my closest friends to this day.

Sports day arrived, and it was a great occasion when we loaded up the car with Ian and lots of presents for Patrick, some of which had been given by his grandparents, who had taken a sanguine view of our decision to send Patrick to boarding school. It was July and a really lovely warm day when we arrived at the school. Ideal for a sports day, and I thanked our blessings, for without decent weather these events could be a nightmare.

We had loads of food for a picnic in the spacious grounds, which covered many acres, and as I parked the car, we looked around eagerly for the first sign of our son. We were keen to see him before he saw us as we wanted to observe his demeanour, to see if his body language told us anything about his state of mind — whether he was happy, basically.

Suddenly, we spotted him with a group of similarly clad boys, all wearing the yellow shirt of his house. He looked anxious, looking all around him, clearly on the lookout for his parents. We felt guilty at holding out on him and rushed over to hug him. He did not know whether to laugh or cry, and we were all in the same boat with the exception of Ian, who gurgled happily to see his brother again. He still called him 'Hatrick,' finding the 'P' beyond him, and we kidded him that he was going to be a footballer.

Hundreds of parents had turned up for what was obviously a very popular annual event. Although we were early, the carpark was already well filled when we arrived. We could hear the sounds of a band playing somewhere and there was a great air of excitement. We opened the boot, and Patrick helped us to carry the food to a spot chosen by his mother. She had made sure to include all his favourites, and we picnicked in the shade of a massive oak tree which must have been planted centuries before. I marvelled again at the extent of the grounds which covered an enormous area. It had been the seat of the Dukes of Leeds for centuries, before being made over to the religious teaching order. No doubt, crippling death duties had been responsible for that, but thousands of handicapped youngsters had benefited as a result.

It was a joyous day, as it was obvious that Patrick had settled in very well. Many youngsters called out to him by name and it was clear that he was very much one of the lads. In spite of all that was going on, we did manage to have a short chat with Sister Teresa, who assured us that Patrick was making good progress, particularly in looking after himself. His locker and bunk were always neat and tidy and he himself was always smartly turned out. We were assured that these were real pluses which would stand him in good stead in later life when he would have to fend for himself. Later, our son showed us his dormitory where he slept and was obviously proud of his kit. He took us into his classroom and was pleased to show us his drawings and writing exercises. It was clear, however, that arithmetic was going to be a major problem for him, and so it proved all his life.

We watched him take part in several races, and although he did not win anything, he seemed to enjoy himself, especially in the piggyback race when he was mounted on the back of a young giant from Besford Court, who had combined their sports day with the younger children. It was a hectic day, and we could only admire the amount of hard work the nuns must have put into it to make the whole affair run so smoothly. Having been involved, myself, in the running of athletic meetings on many occasions, I could appreciate how much organising it must have taken, especially with children, most of whom had severe handicaps, either mental or physical.

By six o'clock, everyone was jaded, and many were making their way towards the exit to the park. It was time to say goodbye once more, and although there were tears, they were not of the same intensity as the last time, and we felt greatly relieved as we drove home. We congratulated ourselves on having made the right decision, as it was obvious that Patrick was getting the very best of attention and would continue to make good progress. What was even more heart-warming was the very clear evidence of affection that our son was receiving. Patrick and his friends were loved by the nuns — it was not just a duty that motivated these young women to undertake the arduous life of a nun. They actually enjoyed the life and it showed in their happy faces and the faces of their young charges.

Chapter Eighteen

It was only a matter of weeks later that we collected Patrick and took him home for the summer break. Six weeks which showed us that our young son had matured even in the short time since we had visited him. He had had his hair cut short and seemed to have grown an inch or two since we had last seen him. He was tanned and fit-looking, which suggested he spent a good deal of his time out of doors. He was pleased to see us and proudly showed us his drawings, which he took home with him. They seemed to consist mostly of farmyard animals and dinosaurs and were colourful, if nothing else.

Patrick was overjoyed to be reunited with his brother and made a fuss of Ian all the way home in the car. Ian, for his part, was delighted to receive all this attention and chuckled away happily on the back seat. The nuns had done a good job with our son and his room, when he was at home, was a model of tidiness. We laughed as we saw all his shoes lined up like soldiers on parade.

That particular summer was notable for its long days of seemingly endless sunshine. Day after day, there was not a cloud to be seen in the sky — a rarity indeed for England. Now living in the country for the first time in our lives, we spent every hour we could out of doors, even eating most evenings with an improvised barbecue

I had constructed in the orchard.

That summer was notable too for one fright that Ian gave his parents. We were living in an old thatch cottage in the village of Goodworth Clatford, on the outskirts of Andover at this time — an attractive old property I was doing up as time and money allowed. We had decided that we wanted something in the country with a bit of space for the kids to run around without having to go into the street.

My wife had seen this old thatch village property, standing back well off the road in an acre of ground, and fell in love with it. It even had an ancient orchard at the back which gave it the feel of family living. It was substantially built of a warm red brick and not the wattle of many country cottages, with its usual nightmare of rising damp. I was told by an old man in the village that it had formerly been a small farm at one time, and housed a large family.

It was completely coincidental that it was named 'Ford Acre', giving me an odd feeling as I was dealing with Ford cars at that time. For myself, I was wondering which two trees in the apple orchard would support my hammock. That was a great delusion that was soon established when we moved in and I discovered the amount of work involved in the refurbishment of the old place.

There were two small sitting rooms, either side of the front door, which were divided by an enclosed and rickety staircase. We demolished this creaky affair, opting for an open stairway giving us a large lounge with a fireplace at one end. It was my wife's idea to knock down the semi-modern green and ghastly tiled fireplace, and what a good decision that turned out to be. It exposed a bread oven and inglenook and was so huge that one could walk in and look up the chimney. The hooks where they used to hang the bacon to cure, were still in the wall. The whole thing was fronted by an enormous oak beam. It really made our day.

All the work had to be put in at weekends, or rather more precisely, on Sundays, as I had to be in the showroom all day Saturday which often was my busiest day of the week. In the summer months, we were often working out of doors every evening until darkness fell. Progress was slow, but we loved what we were doing and did not feel that we denied ourselves anything in the way of living a more carefree existence. It was a very pretty village with a good number of thatch properties in it — one which had not been spoiled like so many others in Hampshire.

At one time, the old Andover-Southampton railway ran at the back of our house, but this had long since been closed down and the lines torn up during the Beeching era. It used to be called the Sprat and Winkle line as it was used to bring fresh fish up from the coast. We now had, in its place, a very pleasant walk which presented occasional views of the Anton river which joined the famous trout stream, the Test, near Stockbridge.

It was Patrick's first viewing of his new home into which we had moved a couple of months before, and he raced around inspecting everything. Being very old, it was full of nooks and crannies and seemed designed for hide and seek. He seemed thrilled to be living in the country after the early years of our marriage in town. He was obviously proud to have his own bedroom without having to share it with his younger brother.

We decided we could at last afford to have the cottage re-thatched and a local craftsman was commissioned to do the job. We had seen examples of his work and were greatly looking forward to what was, without doubt, the most important piece of work connected with our project. It was our single most expensive outlay, but we did not stint and requested Norfolk reed, which was the best for the purpose. Although the most expensive, it also gave a life of something like thirty years, and we felt that we would save in the long run. At this time, we were assuming that we would spend the rest of our life in the house. Little did we know!

The thatcher lived at the other end of the village and his home was sufficiently near to allow him to go home to lunch. One day, when he was halfway through the job, he disappeared around mid-day for some well-earned refreshment. We had collected Patrick the day before, and thoughtlessly, the thatcher had not taken any precautions with his ladders which had been left in place leaning against the cottage. It was only when I went outside that I heard a voice, seemingly coming from mid-air, calling, 'Daddy, Daddy, I can see, I can see.'

Looking around and upwards, my legs turned to jelly when I saw Ian sitting on the ridge of the roof right next to the chimney, oblivious to any danger. I tried to stay calm — whatever I did, I must not panic the boy or to let him know that I was scared stiff.

'What a clever boy you are, Ian,' I croaked, as I gingerly set off up the ladder to the roof. The thatcher had tied a smaller ladder to the top of the long one and it was stretched out over the thatch to allow him to work on the pitch of the roof, and by this route, the boy had clambered all the way up to the ridge at the very top of the house.

Never one to like heights at any time, I was forced to forget my own fear as I crawled over the thatch to reach Ian. He was chortling away, thoroughly enjoying my discomfort as I reached out to get hold of him. I had just grasped him to me when I heard a scream and turned with a start, almost toppling over, to see my wife looking up at me.

'What on earth do you think you are doing taking the child up there — you must be mad. Come down at once,' she shouted at me.

I will refrain from recording my reply. I will just say that I managed to get down safely with my son's help — he seemed much more at home with heights than his father ever will be.

One further incident remains in my memory from that summer — fortunately something less frightening and, at the time, amusing. It had been deemed necessary to replace the ancient cesspit, which had served the property for many years, with a new septic tank. Although the old cottage was situated in the village, it was not connected to the main drainage. I had been fortunate to obtain the services of a small and very competent builder who would come, when I could afford him, to do those jobs I was not capable of doing myself (of which there were many).

Trevor, for that was his name, agreed to carry out the work for a price I could just about scrape together. It meant considerable excavation and he promised he would start on Saturday morning and would be along first thing with the big digger. I told the boys, who were very excited at the prospect of all this activity, and at eight o'clock that morning, holding Ian by the hand, I went out to open the five-barred gate to the main entrance that I had fitted myself, in readiness for the arrival of the big digger.

Patrick sat on top of the gate and we all stared up the road to see who would be the first to see the big digger. True to his word, within five minutes, Trevor's little Ford Escort appeared up the road and I knew the big digger could not be far behind. I made a mental note to tell my builder that his car needed some attention to the suspension as it seemed to be dangerously low on one side. Pulling into the drive, the car came to a stop and a figure of a man extricated himself from the passenger side. I gaped at this apparition, for it was no ordinary man. He was young, certainly, had to be in his early twenties, but the size of him left me speechless. He was a Goliath, easily two metres tall with shoulders that beggared belief.

As we stared at him in astonishment, Trevor, noting our expressions, introduced us with a twinkle in his eye.

'This is Fred, the big digger,' and he laughed.

I gathered that this was a standing joke with Trevor, for Fred nodded amiably and removed his spade, which must have been specially crafted to fit comfortably into his vast hands, from the roof rack. Shown the site for the septic tank, which had to be sunk deep in the ground, Fred set to work. When I brought out some refreshment for him, two hours later, he was out sight, only huge dollops of soil being tossed into the sky betraying his presence deep in the bowels of the earth.

By a strange coincidence, the cottage next door, which had come up for sale, had been bought by the daughter of Lord Denning, who still continued to live at Whitchurch where I had been employed ten or twelve years earlier. I never met the great man, but I did have a few conversations with his son-in-law, one of which involved giving him permission to install a bathroom window, in a wall of his cottage, which overlooked my front lawn. I was only too pleased to agree, anxious to cement good relations with my neighbours, provided he glazed it with opaque glass.

He too was up to his eyes in refurbishing what was a very pretty cottage, and I was in no doubt that I would be, in part, the beneficiary of his efforts so far as the resale value of my own house was concerned. It did no harm for the next-door property to be of a very desirable nature to would be purchasers of my own house, should I ever decide to sell it.

On another occasion, when I commenced building my new garage, which I have to confess was a whopper, he came hotfooting round to see what I was erecting. Straight-faced, I told him that it was a small canning factory, but I was certain that it would not cause him any bother. He blanched visibly until he realised that I was only kidding. He did go on to say that he was sorry that it would partly obscure his view of my garden from his bedroom window. Tough!

Chapter Nineteen

It would be nice to report that apart from these episodes, it was a tranquil period, but sadly, after a few weeks, the strain on my wife's face had returned. She loved Patrick dearly, but after the initial pleasure of seeing him and having him around, the novelty quickly wore off. He could not seem to please her. He would come downstairs wearing a heavy jumper on the hottest of days and she would angrily send him back up to take it off. Left to himself, he would probably have spent the day puffing and blowing and lathered in sweat.

His day had to be carefully organised for him or otherwise he would just sit around and invariably get under his mother's feet and on her nerves. Being very organised herself, she would invariably endeavour to set him some tasks which he was capable of doing without supervision, but that was not always possible for various reasons. It always led to frustrations on both sides and there would be a falling out.

For all his backwardness, Patrick knew when he was in the doghouse, and although he would never dream of creating a scene or answering back, he had a knack of doing whatever was required of him at a snail's pace. He was a past master at this little piece of rebellious behaviour.

This would infuriate my wife, who would

remonstrate with me. 'You tell him to get a move on — he will not do it for me, he is terrified of you.' Words which horrified me, as I regarded myself as a pushover to all my family. I would try to placate Anthea, reminding her that we were supposed to be the intelligent ones and Patrick was backward. We should deflect his attention onto something else rather than meet him head on when he behaved in this unseemly fashion.

She would look at me accusingly. 'You always take his side — he is not that backward that he does not know how to annoy me.'

I always found it a difficult path to tread when matters came to a head between them as I loved them both dearly, and I could see both points of view. It made the atmosphere in the home unpleasant for everyone, as little Ian was very aware when things were not going well, and he suffered too.

Anthea could become quite bitter on the subject, but I knew that it all boiled down to acute disappointment at her eldest son's disability. She was a woman who never cried, but I knew inside that she hurt intensely and that in some way she blamed herself for the whole sad business. I would try to placate her, and she would positively quiver with pent-up emotion. I could sense the pain but could do little to alleviate it. Long before the holiday was up, I was praying for the summer to end.

The continued refurbishing of our home, apart from the great pleasure it brought into our lives, meant a lot more work for my wife. Dust and dirt seemed to accrue as if by magic and I had always tried to help out with the chores. One little job I enjoyed, which certainly was not a chore but great fun, was bathing Patrick and his brother Ian.

One particular night when Anthea was up to her eyes in curtain material, I was trying to keep things under control in the bathroom. It was whilst soaping down Patrick that my heart missed a beat as I made what I thought was a frightening discovery. Surely, I must be mistaken, but closer inspection proved my initial diagnosis was correct and I let out a yell that brought Anthea running. The two boys stopped their tomfoolery in dismay, startled at my shout, and frightened too at my expression. Their mother peered in and cried, 'What is the matter with you lot, why did you shout out?'

I pointed at Patrick and gabbled incoherently, my heart pounding. 'Slow down, what is it,' Anthea snapped, she too becoming agitated at my behaviour.

'Sorry,' I said, getting a hold on myself.

'It's Patrick,' I whispered. 'He has no testicles in his scrotum.' I don't know why I was whispering — the children could not understand.

My wife looked bemused. 'What?' she asked.

'Are you deaf? He's got no balls,' I shouted, my panic returning.

My wife looked as though she had been hit in the face by a wet kipper. She looked at me in utter bewilderment.

'How could this be?' I demanded. 'How come you did not notice this all these years? You are his mother, for God's sake,' pointing my finger accusingly and putting the blame squarely on her shoulders as I glared at her.

Anthea re-acted angrily. 'Well, you're his father, it is up to you to notice these things. You bath him as much as I do.'

I sat on the lavatory seat, appalled at my discovery.

My wife stormed off, shouting, 'You must take responsibility for this, I have other things to see to,' leaving me with the result of my findings.

Ian was standing up in the bath; he, too, had made a discovery. Fingering his navel, he looked at me in wonder and cried, 'Hole in there, Da Da, hole in there,' sticking his finger in his belly button.

A sudden thought made me carry out a hasty inspection of my other son, only to discover a pair of pings tucked nicely away. That was a relief — a proper chip off the old block. A sudden suspicious thought made me glance quickly at Patrick, only for it to be immediately dispelled. No, no way. That chiselled profile, that noble brow, could only have been inherited from one man. I castigated myself for even thinking such a thing and I assured myself that it was only the stress attacking my nervous system which was fast crumbling under the strain.

No sleep that night!

Holy Mother of God, can it be true? Had I fathered a eunuch? My eyes welled with unshed tears. I could handle the other business — it wasn't easy, but I could handle it — but this? You really did it to me this time, God. In every sense, this was below the belt. I cowered under the clothes in my misery. What would people say? My very manhood was being brought into question.

These things get out however much you tried to hush them up.

Somebody would talk. We would have to move away, that was for certain. I tried to be stoic in the face of this calamity. I needed to plan. It would have to be somewhere far away where nobody knew us. India might be good. I had heard there were many weird sects there. Who knows, there might be one that honoured a eunuch as one of noble birth. I could be a hero in India. I groaned in self-pity — why me, why bloody me!

The next morning, I tore into town to see our family doctor. On the way, I cast glances at Patrick who sat contentedly in the passenger seat — he loved the car and was never happier than when being driven somewhere. I found myself looking for signs of effeminate behaviour but could see none. In fact, with his crew haircut and slightly crooked nose he looked a right little tearaway, tough as leather.

Ushered into the consulting room after an anxious half hour in the waiting room, I blurted out the discovery of the night before.

Doctor Blythe did not seem greatly perturbed but then it wasn't his bloody kid, was it? He was not facing total disgrace.

'Let's have a look, shall we,' he said, smiling at Patrick who knew him from many previous visits and looked upon him as a friend, which indeed he was. Examining him and probing gently, he straightened up and said, 'Well, you can pull his pants up now, there is nothing to worry about,' and went on to explain. 'This is not unusual — in fact, quite common in small children,' he assured me.

'The testicles have remained in the abdominal cavity and not dropped down into the scrotum as they would normally have done by now. But no harm done, I assure you. We will give them another couple of months and if they do not appear of their own accord, he will have to have a small operation.'

I looked at him in a daze. 'You mean he has got them, there is no doubt?' I gazed at him beseechingly, hoping that I had heard him correctly.

The doctor looked at me sternly as if I was questioning his professional competence, and snapped back at me, 'Of course they are there — I said so, didn't I?'

I gabbled my thanks and, grinning inanely, hurried Patrick out of the room. In high good humour, I sang all the way home.

I broke the good news to my wife when I got home, and she looked at me sourly. It took a good few days of suitable boot-licking before I was allowed back into her good books. From many years of experience, Anthea knew how to deal with a craven husband.

Two months later and no sign of the 'will to live' appearing, so an appointment was made to see a specialist in Winchester. He suggested a suitable date for Patrick to go into hospital for the small but very necessary operation.

He warned me, 'There is just a small chance that your son might lose one of his testicles,' and seeing the look of horror on my face, quickly added, 'Of course, he will be able to perform quite well with one,' and he winked at me knowingly.

I found this of little comfort, thinking of the cold steel touching such an emotional and tender spot, and winced inwardly.

Our son went into hospital the following week, whilst we waited on tenterhooks for the result of the operation. I was in the waiting room alone, my wife having popped down to the cafeteria for a much-needed cup of coffee, when the surgeon entered the room, all smiles. 'Good news, Mr Mullen. Everything went as planned and Patrick is one hundred per cent.'

'You didn't—' I began, and he stopped me short with a raised hand.

'No, he is fully equipped and if I may say so, very well endowed,' and guffawed loudly at his own base humour. 'He, for one, has certainly nothing to worry about.' Was it just my imagination but did the surgeon sound rather wistful, if not indeed envious, as he hurried off on his rounds?

When my wife came back, I was able to give her the good news. Patrick was asleep but we were told that we could visit him that evening when he would have fully recovered from the anaesthetic. We drove back to Andover to report the latest development, which was all good news (I said we could not keep it quiet), to Anthea's parents, and to collect Ian who had been deposited with them for the day. We were able to quell their disquiet about Patrick's condition and there was general relief all round.

Later that evening, we returned to the hospital to find that the carpark appeared full, and as it was raining heavily, I decided to drop Anthea and Ian at the entrance porch to avoid them getting wet whilst I toured around to find a place. After nearly ten minutes, frustrated at every turn, I eventually managed to squeeze my car into a slot. I had just locked the car door and was turning round to make a dash for the front door of the hospital, when I heard a shout. Looking up through the pouring rain, I saw Anthea hurrying towards me carrying Ian, who by this time was a big lad, and I thought, 'What a silly woman, she will strain herself carrying that great child.'

When she got nearer, I could see that she was in some difficulty and she called out in a panic, 'Well, help me, he has fainted.'

It seemed that Ian, upon seeing the red antiseptic painted on his brother's thighs, had taken it for blood and passed out, hence the carrying operation. Ian came round almost immediately and showed no after effects from the experience. I laughed about it later, but my wife was not amused at my hilarity and again I was in the doghouse.

Patrick was back home in a couple of days, none the worse for his short stay in hospital. The rest of his holiday passed uneventfully, and he returned to Croome Court. Of course, his mother looked after him like a saint following his short stay in hospital and nothing was too much trouble for her. She baked his favourite flapjacks and made a real fuss of him. It was wonderful to see how much she mellowed during the last few days of the holiday, and I know she was genuinely sorry, in many ways, when she said goodbye to our son. I thought it sad that they clashed so frequently as they loved each other very much, and sometimes I really despaired for the future.

That was the pattern for the next nine years, with Patrick coming home for summer and Christmas holidays. The first week or so everything would be wonderful, before cracks started to appear in the relationship between Patrick and his mother. Maybe I should have done more but I was out at work all day and while I was around, I could see little to complain about in Patrick's behaviour.

He was a very placid boy, unemotional unless he was frightened, and it seemed at times that it was this lack of vitality which upset his mother, who herself was a demon of energy. I tried to do all the things a father does with his kids — playing ball in the garden, hide and seek when we ventured out into the country for a walk — but Patrick could not be energized, for want of another word, into playing a part in this fun. On the other hand, his brother, who was much younger, was full of life and up to all sorts of mischief, and again the contrast was stark between the two boys. They got on amazingly well together, though, and it was great to watch how Patrick doted on his brother.

Patrick was nine and Ian six years of age when we had our third child, which was again a little boy. We had hoped this latest baby might be a little girl but that was not to be the case. I think it would have been good for Anthea to have had another female in the family — a little girl for her to dress up and for me to spoil — but we were not obsessed with the idea and, in fact, were over the moon with our new addition.

For a time, we wondered if the new arrival might share a birthday with Ian, but in the end he came on the scene five days before his brother's date of birth. It was a time when expectant mothers were still expected to have their new baby at home with the help of a midwife unless there were good medical reasons for going into hospital, and as Ian's birth had been quite normal, my wife was expected to have this latest child at home.

I was not at all happy, as the old cottage in which we were living was only half renovated and, as such, left a lot to be desired so far as a hygienic environment was concerned. No posh bathroom — just basic facilities were all we had. We were lucky to have hot water but there was a distinct smell of drying plaster and plastic emulsion in the air. I tried to get the central heating installed in time, but on the all-important day, there were quite a few floorboards up and pipes lying all over the place.

Anthea was distinctly nervous about the whole arrangement, but her confidence was boosted by the fact that a highly efficient district midwife, by the name of Nurse McDonald, was assigned to assist her. She was close in age to my wife and in the process of making a number of pre-natal calls, she and Anthea became good friends. She was a rosy-cheeked Scotswoman with a lovely smile and cheery manner which engendered a reassuring atmosphere to the whole procedure.

A week before the baby was due, Nurse McDonald dropped a bombshell. If the baby arrived on schedule it would arrive on the midwife's day off.

'You are not to worry about anything,' she was quick to assure us. 'Nurse Rutter will be standing in for me and she is very experienced.' Seeing the doubt still on our faces she added, 'When you ring for the nurse, if you do not get an answer immediately you are to telephone me. You have my number and I will come at once. I have not planned to go anywhere as I shall be busy decorating my front room.'

Thus reassured, Anthea seemed content.

Not so yours truly.

Nurse Rutter was well known to me as a customer of the garage where I worked. We supplied her with a new vehicle every two years and thereby hangs a tale. The good lady was probably an outstanding midwife, her personal cleanliness may have bordered on godliness, but by virtue of the fact that she had two dogs who practically lived on the back seat of her car, she possessed a vehicle that stank to high heaven. We had to bribe our cleaners with a bonus every time it came to preparing it for re-sale after we took it in part exchange for a new one.

I did not dare divulge this tasty bit of information to Anthea, and as the day of the birth drew near, I was on tenterhooks. Would it arrive on Nurse McDonalds day off, that was the question? It would and did. It was mid-morning and my wife was in no doubt when her contractions began.

I looked at her and she nodded at my unasked question. 'Better ring the nurse,' she advised.

I nodded back, trying to remain cool although shaking with fright.

Picking up the telephone, I dialled Nurse Rutter's number. Upon hearing it ring once, I hung up again.

Then I rang Nurse McDonald and waited for her to answer, which she did after several rings.

'Is that you, Nurse McDonald?' I asked blithely.

'Yes,' she responded. 'That sounds like Mr Mullen.'

'I'm afraid Nurse Rutter does not answer. I am very sorry to bother you, but I think the baby is on its way.' I tried to sound apologetic.

'I will come straight away,' she promised, and was as good as her word.

Neil was born in our home, without any problem, at ten o'clock in the morning, and that evening was fast asleep in his little cot whilst his mother and I sat watching television. It was as uneventful as that. It was a strange feeling, however, to know that there was an extra person in the house whose life we were now responsible for looking after.

That is how Neil came into our world, helped by a sweet-natured little lady from Scotland to whom we owe a great debt. He was a beautiful baby and grew up to enrich our lives immeasurably.

Chapter Twenty

Patrick, too, grew into a fine young lad, with a strong physique and well-muscled. For a boy who was mentally retarded, he proved to have excellent co-ordination. He was particularly good at the high jump and I encouraged this sport when he was home on holiday by building a high jump in the back garden when he would play with his brothers.

The neighbours must have thought we were a crazy family as we all, including my wife, who had been an excellent high jumper at school, were seen leaping about like lunatics on the lawn. But it was great fun, even if I did suffer dreadfully the next day from stiffened joints. A sandpit was the best I could manage in the way of a landing area — not the softest of cushions, but then this was the era before the 'Fosbury Flop' and the inflated landing zone.

I had always been keenly interested in athletics, but owing to the type of work I did, which involved working in the evenings and weekends, I had been unable to pursue this interest. I had now left the cinema business, which had suffered greatly from the onslaught of the new craze — television. From something like four thousand cinemas in the country at the height of its popularity, the number had shrunk to a fraction of that total, with new closures seemingly being announced every week. The mighty silver screen appeared to have been outshone by this tiny upstart, but it would fight back with renewed vigour in the years to come. Although I had not been made redundant, I could see the writing on the wall, and made the decision to try a career move. This involved becoming a salesman with a Ford dealer which not only allowed me more free time with my family, but to take up athletics, for which I had always had a great love.

By this time, I was too old to make any impact in the sport as a competitor but the coaching of youngsters provided an outlet for my enthusiasm.

I helped form the Andover and District Amateur Athletic Club and within a year we were making our mark in junior athletics. As a coach, my philosophy was simple — I believed a twelve-year-old boy in Andover could run just as fast as a boy of the same age in Moscow or New York or anywhere else for that matter. What mattered from then on was in the form of training adopted by the youngster.

Of course, I was fortunate to have one or two outstanding young athletes in the squad, but the dedication shown by all of those youngsters was a revelation. Night after night, they would show up and work to the schedules I had drawn up for them. Often, too, they would descend on my home at weekends and tear into the huge garden we now possessed and help my wife with the clearing of scrub and weeds. They spoiled my kids rotten, and I recall, with real pleasure, all of us sitting drinking lemonade in the small orchard after a particularly strenuous afternoon working in the summer sunshine. Plans would be discussed at great length on how we were going to demolish the opposition the following Saturday. We were never going to just win, we were going to bury them. It was on just such a sunny afternoon that I coined a phrase that became the motto for the club namely, 'Nobody Wants To Know Who Came Second' — a phrase that almost became a battle cry among my young charges.

Their many successes drew the attention of the national press and I was constantly being telephoned by reporters. It was after the stunning victory of Andrew Barnett in the All England Schools' Cross-Country Championship at Leicester, that the television stations took an interest.

Andrew Harvey of the BBC and Tony Gubba of ITV made the journey to Andover to interview me but what could I say other than that these kids had found someone to take an interest in them. It was very clear to me that there were many such boys like them all over the country who could emulate them if only they had the backup needed. What was lacking was leadership — there was nothing wrong with the youngsters in the country. Kids will always rise to a challenge, and provided that challenge is focussed on something honourable and worthwhile, nothing but good can come of it.

Within weeks of these successes, Andrew Barnett had broken several world age records, for the mile and fifteen hundred metres. The club was now succeeding on all fronts and Marjorie, Countess of Brecknock, was gracious enough to become our Honorary President.

When I organised a huge two-day young athletes meeting at Tidworth Oval, she was kind enough to come along and stand for many hours presenting prizes and encouraging the youngsters to greater effort.

My greatest coup, however, was in persuading Charles Nicholls, a retired brigadier whose son I coached, to act as chairman, and he proved a tower of strength. The lessons that I learned from this great gentleman have been of wonderful value to me all my life.

Many local firms in Andover presented trophies for competition and took pride in being associated with the club. All of this success came about despite a total lack of facilities in the town. But success brings its own reward and it is because of the record-breaking achievements of these youngsters that the present-day kids of Andover enjoy the benefits of a proper modern running track. Their performances demanded that something should be done to provide facilities and although they came too late to be of any direct assistance to those early performers, nevertheless they were able to take pleasure in knowing that they were directly responsible for the new track.

Perhaps the most rewarding aspect has been the continued interest of those early members in the club. Not only the competitors themselves, but the parents of these kids, gave of their time unstintingly. Over a period of years, they raised thousands of pounds for much needed equipment. They were always on hand, too, to act as marshals, whatever the weather, and to provide refreshments when we organised race meetings. People like Ray Yates and Rose Oldacre — I could never have managed without them — they were the mainstay of the club.

Now forty years later, some of those same youngsters are still involved in the continuing success of the club by coaching and other help, putting back, with interest, some of the benefits that they received when they were much younger.

My very tenuous association with the media drew me to the attention of the Andover Carnival committee who had decided to invite the young lady who had come third in the Miss World competition to open this annual event. She just happened to also be Miss Ireland and someone decided, for some obscure reason, perhaps because I was Irish, that I was just the man to greet her on arrival and keep her amused until zero hour.

I agreed with alacrity, although distinctly nervous about the assignment. I duly met her at Andover railway station where she arrived with her chaperone, and I swept them off to lunch at the Star and Garter hotel. She was a most charming young woman, and both of us being Irish, we got along famously. I remember she had a tiny cold sore at the corner of her mouth which bothered her as I suppose she felt that it marred her great beauty — and she was beautiful. But this temporary tiny flaw failed singularly to distract me from her other more prominent features. To quote the famous columnist Donald Zec, on the occasion of his interviewing Jayne Mansfield, 'She was wearing a sweater so tight I could hardly breathe.'

I thoroughly enjoyed my short time with Miss

Ireland, and it was with considerable regret that after the opening of the carnival I took her, with her minder, to catch the train back to London. I never saw her again.

But I was becoming restless once more. I had long harboured the desire to have my own business and suddenly an opportunity presented itself that I could not turn down. It had come to our notice that a small family restaurant was for sale in the village of Milford-on-Sea, close to Bournemouth and the New Forest. It was called the Bay Trees Restaurant and occupied a lovely Georgian building situated in the high street. We fell in love with it at first sight, an offer was made, and duly accepted. It meant leaving Andover where I had made a lot of friends and helped build up a successful athletic club. I would miss all of this and more, but I was now thirty-eight years old and I had found a few grey hairs in my head. The time was ripe if I was ever going to succeed in business on my own and, having discussed it at great length with Anthea, we decided to make the move.

It was a wrench to sell the thatched cottage that we had so lovingly restored over five years, but at least the accrued value provided us with the capital to enable us to strike out on our own.

It was a sad farewell for us, and I was touched when the club made me a life vice-president for my services to it. Happily, there were now many well-qualified people to run things and I had no doubts that the club would continue to thrive. Subsequent successes would prove me right.

Patrick took a particular delight in looking after the

new baby and it was astonishing how gentle he was with him. Neil was a lovely baby — he, too, having enjoyed a normal delivery — and was a joy to have around. More reason to speculate on what might have been. He would gurgle mightily at Patrick's efforts to amuse him. Every day I told myself how lucky we were and how much worse things could have been.

There was plenty of evidence before us that this was the case when we visited Patrick. Apart from the very sad cases of physical disability, we heard stories of anti-social behaviour, and even violence, by the children of other parents, so much so that they were turned down by every school in the land. Those parents I really felt sorry for as they were isolated outside the system without any assistance from anyone. Patrick, on the other hand, was an excellent physical specimen and very good-looking into the bargain.

The nuns did a marvellous job of training him to be neat and tidy and to keep himself clean. He had perfect table manners and you could take him anywhere. His great difficulty was in communication and when spoken to by, perhaps, a stranger, he would just hang his head and mutter something unintelligible. Even then, his frustration was obvious as he often repeated the sentence, clearly annoyed with himself that he was unable to communicate properly and make an intelligent reply. Sometimes, there would be a hint of boorishness in his manner as he tried to hide his embarrassment.

As the time grew near for Patrick to finish schooling with the nuns, my mind was fully occupied with the thought of where next he should go for some form of training. I felt convinced that he could hold down some form of job with the right kind of tuition. But where was he to get this assistance?

The biggest shock was to come when we travelled to Besford Court, the senior school where he had been for the past four years, to collect him for the last time. He was sitting in the hall with his suitcase, quite alone, waiting for us. He was overjoyed to see us and scampered about, gathering up his belongings, clearly ready to go.

I was bemused, having expected at least some form of report with perhaps some recommendations about Patrick's future. But there was no final interview with anyone in authority — in fact, we had to go looking for a nun to let someone know that we were taking him away. The young nun just waved goodbye to us and that was the end of Patrick's nine years at the special school.

After succeeding in accomplishing what I considered to be a great job with Patrick, it was a tremendous let-down by the school just to turn him loose without a word of advice. We did not even get the chance of thanking the order properly for their kindness and efficiency over so many years. It was a bitter blow and we felt so disappointed. It was a tremendous let-down and neither Anthea nor myself ever quite got over it. It was the end of an era for Patrick, but it was the future we had to concern ourselves with now, and we braced ourselves for the challenges that lay ahead.

Chapter Twenty-one

Thus began a marathon letter-writing saga with the Hampshire County Council in an effort to find a suitable training establishment for Patrick. The file I now had on my son was inches thick as it contained scores of letters I had written over the years. I was convinced that, with the proper training, Patrick was quite capable of holding down a job — a simple job perhaps — but a job, nevertheless. He was eager and, for the most part, willing to try his hand at anything providing it was not too difficult, for then he would soon lose heart.

It was strange having him home permanently with us again after such a long time away. He was a big lad, still growing and had the appetite of a horse. Thanks to boarding school training, he was not a fussy eater and would scoff just about anything that was put down in front of him.

To quote his uncle Tom's favourite saying when he would come to stay for a holiday, which was almost every year, 'If it moves, shoot it — if it doesn't, eat it.' Tom would give his braying laugh which would have my kids in stitches. They loved their uncle dearly and looked forward to his visits enormously. It was a saying that was made for our dinner table, what with three boys with astonishing appetites. Their father was not far behind them either when it came to packing the food away. It was a lucky thing for us that we were now in the restaurant business where there was never any shortage of good grub. I guess when it came to variety of food, we were much better off than most families as we had the pick of each day's offering in the restaurant.

Patrick was in excellent health, never had a day's illness in his life and had a very amenable nature. True, there were many things he could not handle competently, such as money, the intricacies of which was quite beyond him. But there were positive sides. He was very strong physically and completely obedient, being very willing to please, even taking a pride in doing something well. It would be a tragedy if we could not put these very real assets to good use and enrich his quality of life.

We quickly discovered, however, that Hampshire was still near the bottom of the league table with regard to special places of learning for people like our son. With the notable exception of the splendid Compton Diagnostic Unit, for which we would be eternally grateful, the cupboard was bare. In our many meetings with doctors and teachers over the years, we had come to learn of the scale of the problem. At first, we were so inward-looking that we felt that we were the only couple in the country with a backward child. In fact, there were tens of thousands of children born with some disability, either mental or physical, every year. Each set of parents had to come to terms with this disaster in their own way, and it came to our notice that many found the disappointment too much.

The most common fact to emerge was that the father

often left home, never to return, unable to face a lifetime of looking after the child. Usually, it was the mother who was left to cope on her own or with the minimum of assistance from the child's father. Why was it so, I wondered, and was left to ponder my own reaction to Patrick's disability, which left me feeling very uneasy in my mind as I had little to be proud of in that regard.

As the months went by, we started to lose hope that we would ever hear anything despite the constant letters I wrote to the Hampshire County Council at Winchester, the administrative centre for the county. I reasoned that if I made a big enough nuisance of myself, someone in those offices would eventually get so fed up with my habitual complaining that they would do something — if only to get rid of me.

This strategy seemed to work, for finally we were offered a place in a training centre in Christchurch that Patrick could attend as a day pupil. We were living at Milford-on-Sea by this time, which was only fifteen miles away. Even more welcoming was the news that he could be picked up from our front door in the mornings and brought back each evening in a mini-bus, along with other youngsters who lived within the catchment area.

My wife and I were now running a successful restaurant in Milford—on-Sea and working flat out most of the time. Our two younger sons were at school all day, and we tried to involve Patrick in the restaurant by giving him simple tasks to carry out. Jobs such as helping with washing up, filling the beer crates with the empty bottles and keeping the yard clean and tidy. Although very slow, he worked at his own pace and coped with the responsibility very well. Once the job was fully explained to him, he could be left to get on with it just so long as we were not in a hurry to see it finished!

He showed particular interest in cooking and his mother went to great lengths to show him how to make simple things like flapjacks, a biscuit of which Patrick was particularly fond. Very few of them ever left the kitchen as he would scoff a whole tray of them, given half a chance. For all his backwardness, it was amusing to see him surreptitiously slipping a piece into his mouth when he thought nobody was looking. His mother, however, was very quick to notice and, pretending to be cross, would admonish him. 'Patrick,' she would exclaim sharply, and he would jump with fright and, with an embarrassed grin, try to justify his behaviour.

'Eh, just a little bit, eh, broken,' he would manage to stutter, clearly delighted with his subterfuge. He looked upon it as a game and his grin would break into a chuckle. He had a great sense of humour and loved any visual form of comedy.

'Mmm, it's well broken now,' his mother would retort, trying hard not to smile.

Among his other chores where he showed a good aptitude was in the garden. We were blessed with a large garden at the rear of the restaurant where we served cream teas in the summer months. This was hugely popular, and it was very much worth our while to keep the garden looking reasonably attractive, since clearly it was a valuable asset to the business. Here again, Patrick pulled his weight and enjoyed cutting the lawn and keeping things tidy. I felt that it was useful job experience for him whilst he waited for a new placement in a training centre. Like his father, he was lazy by nature and needed the discipline of a proper boss to keep his nose to the grindstone. His parents were too soft-hearted to set a proper work schedule for him, and a task was soon abandoned if a favourite television programme was due to be shown.

Although very willing to learn any new task, it was clear that he lacked the dexterity for any job that required skilful use of his hands.

Cutting up meat on his plate was particularly troublesome for him and was the cause of much rancour between him and his mother. It was one of those little things that caused her to get really annoyed with him.

'Cut it, Patrick, cut it,' she would shout. 'Don't hack. Do it like this,' and she would demonstrate, all to no avail.

'Leave him, Mum, leave him,' his brothers would implore, seeing another row on the horizon. Patrick always got on well with his younger siblings whom he adored. Always fiercely protective of them while they were growing up, he would seize them by the hand when crossing the road to make sure they came to no harm. I never heard a cross word pass between them, and Ian and Neil grew up accepting the fact that Patrick was a backward child. Having grown up with brothers and sisters, there was often a row between two of them which would thankfully quickly blow over. All the more reason, therefore, for me to have a sense of wonder that, to the best of my knowledge, my own children never fell out about anything.

Filled with optimism, we went along to meet the principal at Christchurch and to have a look around the facility. The amenities were meagre but the staff very dedicated — we decided that beggars could not be choosers and agreed to enrol Patrick at once as we were afraid that all the excellent work by the nuns would be lost if he was allowed to mope at home for very long. His learning curve had been interrupted for long enough and he needed to get his head down and do something constructive with his time.

He was picked up every morning by the school mini-bus which was driven by a lady whose own son attended classes and, of course, he was always aboard when Patrick took his seat. Either my wife or I were always on hand to see our son embark each morning, and we often commented on the attitude of the driver towards her son. It would be true to say he was garrulous, but he hardly deserved to continually hear the same command from his mother, 'Shut up, shut up, shut up.'

It became a family joke for years afterwards. When one of us became too talkative, the others would cry, 'Shut up, shut up, shut up.'

Although Patrick was as always most amenable, his behaviour towards his new place of learning was most noticeable. First of all, I should explain that there was no age limit at Christchurch. The council's budget did not stretch to segregation of any kind, so everyone was lumped in together. Not only young girls, old men, people of all ages, but persons of a completely different level of ability. So whilst there were one or two slightly more capable than Patrick in attendance, so there were many who were severely handicapped, both mentally and physically.

Many were obviously suffering from Downe's Syndrome, and this seemed to affect our son. Not in a dramatic way but, even with his limited ability to converse, it was clear, without any declaration on his part, that he knew that he was being treated as retarded. He felt above this grouping; I could sense it and his pride was hurt. I agonised over the matter but there was absolutely no alternative. He had to stay and make the best of it. At least he was being kept occupied, I consoled Anthea. Maybe something better would turn up, but I felt that it was a forlorn hope.

I remember, on one occasion, making an appointment to see the principal to discuss Patrick's progress, and when we were sitting talking in his study, which was on the ground floor, a face appeared at the window.

It disappeared almost at once and the principal groaned and made a gesture of despair. 'Stay perfectly still,' he warned. 'Don't make any sudden movement.' He rose to his feet and seemed to brace himself.

The words were hardly out of his mouth when the door burst open, almost taken off its hinges. The warning had hardly been necessary as the head that had appeared at the window had made my eyes pop but now, at close range with the rest of the body to support it, it made my hair stand on end.

Ugly does not quite cover it. The man was

enormous and completely shapeless. His face was extraordinary in the fact that nothing seemed to match. The hair was red in colour and quite straggly on one side, yet the other side was very short and almost yellow. One eye was almost popping out of his head and the other almost closed in a slit. One huge paw was rubbing agitatedly at one cheek, making it red raw, leaving the opposite side quite pale. Somewhere on his travels he had lost part of one ear, leaving him appear lop sided. He oozed danger and made a threatening gesture.

As he made towards me, he made a howling sound that froze my blood, and I recoiled as his buck teeth were exposed. Mister Wyatt was out from behind his desk like a rocket, shouting, 'Friend, Trevor, friend,' getting between this apparition and myself. 'It is OK, Trevor, Mister Mullen is a friend, he is not going to harm me.'

Trevor took some convincing but was eventually shepherded out of the room. I honestly believe that he felt cheated of a meal.

Mr Wyatt was most apologetic, and tried to make light of it. 'Trevor has been with us a long time. He is quite harmless but is very protective of me. He has this fixation that someone is out to harm me. I am very sorry if he startled you.' He laughed lamely.

I was not at all sure about the 'harmless' bit and brought the meeting to an abrupt close, grateful that I was still all in one piece.

We got to know some of the other parents whose children were enrolled at the centre and learned of the hardship suffered by many of them. People whose children were far worse off than Patrick. Stories of violence and abuse were common, and we secretly thought ourselves very lucky that, in Patrick, we had a son who was such a joy in so many ways.

I remember one couple with whom we became rather friendly. They, too, had a son who was retarded, but unlike Patrick, he displayed anti-social behaviour. His father once said to me, 'It's the doors that concern me, John, it's becoming very costly.'

I had no idea what he was talking about until he explained that his son was wont to kick in any or all of the doors in the house when he had one of his rages. Apparently, at these times, he was completely uncontrollable.

A very handsome youth, it was difficult to believe that he could behave in this way as he always appeared quiet and subdued. But I had the opportunity to see the other side of his character for myself. My wife had invited him and his mother to tea at our home, and as it was a warm sunny day, we decided to have tea outdoors.

Whilst our guests were in the garden, I went indoors to help Anthea and carry out a tray. Looking out of the kitchen window, I was in time to see the youth punching his mother quite viciously on the arm. Even more disturbing was the way in which he was glancing all around to ensure that he was not being seen behaving in this appalling manner. In doing so, he displayed an extraordinary amount of cunning which I never believed he could have possessed. Needless to say, I did not encourage the friendship between him and Patrick thereafter.

We attended all the usual functions organised by the centre, most of which were run in order to try and raise some funds. I particularly remember a sports evening when part of the fun was a football match — in essence, the fathers versus the pupils and staff. I was press-ganged into playing, although I could hardly ever remember kicking a ball in my life. One of the pupils, a huge young man named Andy Ryecroft, who weighed about eighteen stone, was playing in goal for the centre, and finding myself with the ball, I cantered towards Andy, who came out to meet me, his eye never leaving the ball. I did not possess the skill to dribble the ball around him and braced myself for the inevitable collision. I went down as though pole-axed, the breath completely knocked out of me.

Dazed, I looked up through a pain-filled mist to see Andy tearfully complaining to the referee that Mister Mullen was too rough. The referee put his arm around the goalkeeper consolingly and promised he would have a word with me about my unfair play. Without a hint of a smile and thrusting a yellow card in my face, he warned me about my future behaviour. The crowd loved it; as for me, I just wished he had given me a red card so that I could crawl away and lick my very real wounds.

On another occasion when the centre organised what they described as a carnival evening, we were encouraged to go along in some form of fancy dress. Various stalls had been erected in the playing field, selling all manner of donated goods; streamers and flags were everywhere, and a band was playing as we arrived.

There were plenty of volunteers to man the Aunt Sally stall and arrange various games for the children. In a small effort to join in the spirit of the evening, I was wearing a battered straw boater and an old rowing blazer, my wife deciding to wear a peasant blouse and sweeping skirt that she hoped gave her a slightly gypsy appearance.

Patrick was in high good humour, enjoying the colourful spectacle and even having a donkey ride. It was a Mister Donner, one of the young instructors, who really set things alight when he appeared dressed up as a rather well-built young woman. He was easily recognised, in spite of the deception, which I suppose was the whole idea. Amid gales of laughter, he strode among the crowd with a garishly painted face. There was consternation on the faces of many of the pupils who found it hard to understand this amazing transformation, not least Patrick, who stood there, his eyes boggling at Mister Donner's enormous boobs. Almost speechless, he pointed at the massive outcrop and stuttered, 'Mister Donner, he has those things, those things, ho, bloody hell.'

Incredulous, he looked down at his own chest as though frightened he too might suddenly grow these enormous protuberances. Looking wildly around, he clutched at my arm and then realised suddenly that everyone was laughing at the teacher's appearance and that it was all make-up. We were convulsed with laughter at the whole silly episode and Patrick joined in, his head hanging in embarrassment as he seemed to think that the joke was on him.

Chapter Twenty-two

It was about this time that I joined the 'New Forest Players' — a local amateur dramatic society. They were a highly talented group who put on four or five plays a year and made considerable donations to charity. I had always had a great love of the theatre from my early days in Ireland and had long harboured a wish to try my hand on the stage. When we lived at Andover, we went as often as possible to the old Salisbury Playhouse; indeed, we hardly ever missed a change of programme. In the late fifties and early sixties, they had an extraordinary array of talent at the repertory theatre established there. Young actors, like Timothy West, cut their teeth on the stage of the old theatre with its traditional proscenium arch. Leonard Rossiter was another actor who showed early promise of his comic genius at this theatre.

Of all the members of the extremely talented group who reigned here at the same time as Timothy West, I would have thought he was the least likely to succeed. The others far outshone him, and if anyone struggled with their lines, it was him. It was as though he had two tongues in his mouth. Of all the professions, this has to be the one which depends more on luck than any other. Timothy West is right up there with the best, but of his contemporaries at Salisbury Playhouse — I have not heard a word of them since those early days.

This was during the period when the programme changed weekly and this week's star was next week's butler. Rehearsals were going on all the time for future plays while the actors were appearing in the current week's production. It had to be the greatest training in the world. Later, they built a new and rather grand theatre in Salisbury, but to my eyes at least, the standard of acting dropped alarmingly. For the sake of economy, we were told that it was only possible now to put on five or six productions each year and the normal weekly run was extended to six or seven weeks. But then, did they really need so many assistant stage managers to run things smoothly?

Certainly, the new building was more comfortable, and you did not have to crane your head to one side to see round the head of the fellow in front of you as you did in the old edifice. They also found room, within the walls of the new palace, for a good class restaurant but this, too, soon deteriorated in quality. Last time I was there, I had a very disappointing meal.

Seeing an advertisement in the local paper that the New Forest Players, were holding auditions for their forthcoming pantomime, *Mother Goose*, I went along to see if I could capture a small role.

The 'Players' used the New Milton Church Hall as a base, and it was here that I attended the auditions for the forthcoming pantomime. There was quite a gathering, and it was with a wildly beating heart that I recited the lines required of me. I would have been quite content just carrying a spear for my first treading of the boards, but I was not to get off so lightly.

Due to the fact that, like all amateur companies, they were desperately short of men, I was given the huge role of Squire Stoneybroke. It was only after a great deal of pressure that I agreed to take on the responsibility. When I saw the number of lines I had to learn, I told myself that I must be crazy. The Squire is the character the kids love to hiss at, so I knew I was in for a baptism of fire in my first role on stage. I persuaded Anthea not to tell our own kids that I was in the show, and on the opening night, I had reserved four seats in the front row for my family.

The show was in progress for about twenty minutes before I made my entrance, and although I was dreadfully nervous and shaking like a leaf, I did manage to get my lines out. I did not dare even glance in my family's direction, but Anthea told me later that the boys did not recognise me under my makeup, but my voice was unmistakable. The three of them were open-mouthed in amazement as I spoke. When they realised that it was their dad, they were loudest of all when it came to the hissing part, almost out of their seats it seemed. I was not sure what I should deduce from all that, but I preferred to think that they were just getting into the swing of things.

It was the first of many parts I was to play with the group over several years, and I made many good friends there. After a while, I began to wonder if indeed I had any talent at all for acting as there was always that awful feeling at the end of a first night, with the old joke when actors will say, 'You were wonderful, how was I?'

I determined, therefore, to see about getting some formal training and enrolled with a well-known London drama school, New Era Academy of Dramatic Art, for an extended course. I was fortunate in obtaining the services of a qualified coach named Sonya Collyer, who was herself a talented actress, to prepare me for the examinations. We appeared together on stage several times in various productions, most notably that famous comedy by Ray Cooney, entitled, *Move Over Mrs. Markham*. It was the most hilarious script I had ever read, and rehearsals proved a riot as we could not stop laughing. Our director had an unenviable task in trying to maintain discipline over a very rowdy cast.

I teamed up with Sonya's husband Mike when we were cast as a memorable pair of ugly sisters, Tooty and Fruity, in a production of *Cinderella*. He was Tooty, I was Fruity!

I always harboured a fantasy of playing a great dramatic lead, but despite auditioning for many such roles, I was never lucky enough to be favoured with such a part. I always seemed to be cast as the comic in every production. The producer would smile sweetly, having listened patiently with his fellow judges to my reading of the part of the murderer, and then say, 'That was excellent, Johnny. Now would you be kind enough to read the part of the clown.'

Inevitably, I knew that that was the kiss of death for I knew who would end up wearing the silly costume.

Over the next couple of years, I laboured away at the examinations without any distinction, but finally, in the end, managed to obtain a gold medal for stage technique. It gave me great pleasure as it was an acknowledgement that I possessed some aptitude for acting. It saddened me, too, just a little bit, as I could not help thinking at what might have been if I had had the opportunity as a youngster to train properly for the stage. But I guess most of us could say the same thing about our lives. At the end of the day, we can achieve more or less what we want if we are determined enough to go after it.

I remember going to see a play being tried out in Bournemouth, among other places, prior to its West End debut. It was called *Baggage,* and starred Gerald Harper and that gorgeous actress Hannah Gordon. I took my seat rather early and could not help but notice a very attractive young lady sitting a few seats away, on her own. Nobody came to join her by the time the curtain went up, and she was still alone by the end of the play.

I thoroughly enjoyed the performance and wondered idly about the lovely young woman who seemed quite happy when she clapped vigorously as the cast took their curtain call.

The next day, I was sweating away in the restaurant when one of the waitresses came rushing into the kitchen to tell me that a famous actor, whose name escaped her, was sitting on the terrace and had ordered a ploughman's lunch. Curious, I peeped out and there was Gerald Harper sitting admiring my garden, accompanied by the mysterious lady of the night before. I remembered then reading that the actor had very recently got married and this young woman turned out to be his new bride.

Needless to say, I served the couple personally and

bored them both silly with stories of my own stage triumphs. Mr Harper and his wife were very gracious and avoided actually yawning in my presence, but they never returned for a repeat performance despite assuring me that it was the best ploughman's lunch they had ever eaten. I guess they did not enjoy the floorshow.

That was the year I had to have an operation on my leg. I had been in considerable pain for some time with a varicose vein in my left, and the doctor had made an appointment for me to see a specialist in Lymington hospital.

The consultant's name was Mr Chant, and he took one look at my leg, pronounced that the only solution was an operation, and advised me to see his receptionist on my way out.

'Next,' he bawled, and that was my sixty-second appointment over, after a four-week wait.

The receptionist consulted her appointments book.

Smiling sweetly, she declared, 'I'm afraid the earliest I can manage is July. I'll put your name down and confirm the exact date later.'

'Next,' she bawled.

This being the fifth of January, I was not greatly impressed with the urgency being given to the treatment of my poor leg. Talking it over with my wife that evening, I decided that it was time to make some use of my private medical insurance policy into which I had been pouring money for some years.

Anthea said, 'This is exactly the kind of situation that you have been saving for. I should get on and have it done.'

Taking her advice, I lifted the telephone and dialled Mr Chant's number in Southampton, where he had his private practice. A lady answered and said she was sorry that the doctor was out but would give him the message on his return. Sure enough, at ten o'clock that evening, the telephone rang, and it was Mr Chant himself.

'I received your message — how can I be of help?' he offered.

I explained to him who I was and that he had seen me that morning in Lymington hospital. In view of the long wait, I said that I would like to take advantage of my BUPA medical insurance in the hope that I might not have to wait such a long time.

'Very sensible, Mr Mullen,' he assured me. 'That leg should be seen to right away. Let me see, you live in Milford-on-Sea. I carry out procedures there on Mondays at St. George's Nursing home so it could not be simpler. I will ring the matron right away to make arrangements, and if you will be good enough to get yourself there on Sunday evening to check in, I will take care of your leg on Monday morning.' Stammering my thanks, I put down the telephone in a daze and looked at my wife.

'The consultant says he will operate on Monday morning,' I gasped.

This was Thursday night, so I had only three days to make all my arrangements for the running of the restaurant in my absence. I had completely forgotten to ask him how long I was likely to be in hospital, but the important thing was I was going to have the leg seen to without delay.

It was a marked example of the power of money, and I have to confess that I felt a little ashamed when I thought of the numbers of people who would have to wait many months for some relief from their pain.

I was familiar with St. George's for one good reason. In recent months, I had noticed a remarkable number of French visitors to my teashop in the afternoons. Now it was not unusual to hear foreign voices in the restaurant during the summer months. We usually received a lot of visitors from abroad on holiday in the New Forest area at that time of year, but not during the winter months. I mentioned this small phenomenon to Pam, my waitress, and she grinned knowingly.

'Have you noticed that they are all young, female and French?' she asked, her grin growing into a loud laugh.

Puzzled, I shook my head in ignorance.

'They are here for the 'op', she explained, in *sotto voce*.

'Sorry,' I said, leaning towards her, completely baffled.

'They are all here for an abortion,' Pam declared, loudly abandoning her discretion.

I cringed as several customers looked round at me — we were speaking on the terrace at the time. Seeing my obvious embarrassment, Pam waved away my confusion.

'Oh, everybody knows about it,' she explained. 'Abortion is illegal in France, but it is now perfectly legal in this country, so they are coming over in droves to rid themselves of their pregnancies. A short holiday in England and they are back home, working away, and none of their friends are any the wiser. St George's must be making a fortune,' she declared, dashing off to serve another customer and leaving me to ponder on ill winds and the like.

St. George's, in fact, was everything a worried patient might have hoped to find on entering a hospital for the first time. Elegantly fitted out, the reception area gave out an aura of comfort and repose. I was welcomed like an honoured guest at a five-star hotel and escorted to my private room, which was on the ground floor with a view of the garden. I noted the large television set, the telephone by the bed and the bowl of fresh flowers nearby. Most of all, I noticed the two nurses who it seemed were told to take care of me. They could have just stepped straight out of a Miss World line up. By now, I had almost forgotten why I was here, but I was soon brought back to earth the next morning when I was given what I think they called my 'pre-op' — an injection in the back of my hand.

A few minutes later and I was nearly, but not quite, out for the count, being blissfully aware that the two earnest young nurses were shaving my leg and moving ever closer to a very private part of my body.

Seeing my eyes closing, one remarked,

'Look at him, he is nearly gone already,' and laughed.

'Not quite, Blondie, not quite,' I tried to murmur, enjoying the moment, but drifted off into unconsciousness before my lips could form the words.

When I awoke, I was still in my room alone and

thought, disappointingly, that the operation must have been postponed for some reason. That is until I happened to put my hand down and felt the gauze on my thigh. It was only then that I realised that the operation was over, and I was back safely in my room. The relief was wonderful, but later I could not help but think what if it had not been successful. What if I had succumbed on the operating table for some reason? I would now be dead, but I would have been totally unaware of my own demise. Not a bad way to go, although I was very glad to be alive even if it meant I had now to continue worrying about the mortgage and all the stress of running a small business.

Yes, I was very pleased to be alive, but supposing I had a terrible illness for which there was no cure. Suffering terrible pain for which there was very little relief. Would I still be glad to have come through the operation or would I not have been much better off to have died on the operating table? I am not advocating euthanasia, but I think I can understand how some people might favour it — people whose quality of life has gone for ever, who perhaps feel that they are a burden on their relations. It is easy to imagine how they must feel, especially if they are bedridden and unable to carry out the simplest task for themselves. That easy injection and the promise of never waking up to pain and the feeling of wretchedness ever again. Yes, I am sure that it must hold a great attraction for some people.

It was a sadness for me when I left the area, as it was virtually the end of my so-called acting career. Despite many trials, I was never able to find another such talented company in my travels.

Chapter Twenty-three

Patrick was at Christchurch Training Centre for two years and learned very little that we could perceive, the only advantage being that he had something to do with his time. It was difficult to find out just what they did with their time, and far from improving, we could see that Patrick was becoming more lethargic, and lazy. Every evening he would return from the centre looking tired and fed-up, and I was certain that this was due to boredom rather than any hard work that was being asked of him.

What he really needed was constant encouragement and being pushed to his limits as we felt sure was the case when he was in the care of the nuns. Never at any time a boisterous youth, nevertheless, he had a certain liveliness which he appeared now to have lost and was beginning to act like an old man. I fretted about his future and wondered how we could improve things for him.

One dedicated young woman started a class in basket-making at the centre for some of the youngsters, at which Patrick tried his hand, but he was hopeless at it. He lacked the dexterity with his fingers required for that kind of work and easily became frustrated after a short while. In the end, he had to give it up.

We noticed this drawback, when he was very young,

on the countless occasions we tried to teach him to tie his shoelaces. Every morning we would go through the same drill of tying a bow, and often there were tears of frustration on all sides at Patrick's failure to do so. He just seemed to find it impossible to perform this simple task, but after what seemed like years, he did finally accomplish it.

The free bus ride to school was terminated after a while and Patrick had to travel by public transport which caused us a few headaches. Either my wife or I went with him a few times to make sure he knew where to get off and on before allowing him to venture on the bus on his own. We were on tenterhooks the first time he made a solo trip, but all was well, and he got off the bus with a big grin on his face. There was no doubting the fact that he enjoyed the challenge and he went off waving every morning. The regular driver got to know Patrick too and we had no real worries any more.

That is until one winter's evening when Patrick did not get off the bus at his usual time. One of us would always meet the bus, although it was only a very short distance from our front door. I stood open-mouthed as the coach pulled away, and I frantically ran alongside thinking that perhaps he had fallen asleep and missed his stop. But there were only a few passengers on board, and I could see at a glance that Patrick was not among them. I skidded to a halt in bewilderment.

Panic stations! What to do? I rushed home and telephoned the centre but could only raise a cleaner who assured me that everyone had left, and she was the only person in the building. I leapt into my car, leaving

Anthea by the telephone in case a message came through — the poor woman was quite distraught as I tore off in search of our son.

By now he was a big well-built lad and, physically, his mere size would deter most people from molesting him but there was always that worry that some louts would set about him. I went straight to the bus stop where I knew he caught his bus, but there was nobody there. My next stop was at the police station in Christchurch, where I was met with great sympathy by the desk sergeant. He took all the details and immediately alerted the local force to be on the lookout for Patrick. I told him that I would set off to tour the town in the hope of finding him and departed on what I feared might be a hopeless mission.

To my enormous relief, however, when I drove through the high street desperately scanning the sidewalks for any sign of my son, who should I see standing at the main stopping place for most passengers? Only Patrick, waiting patiently for his transport. It was difficult to know which of us was the most relieved as I pulled up beside him.

'That bus, Dad, that bus didn't come, it didn't. I waited, I did, that bus didn't come, bloody hell,' he cried out to me.

He was half laughing but I could see that he had been scared, the relief obvious on his face. I tried to play down the worry that we had experienced about his being missing and instead pulled his leg.

'We thought that you had left us, Patrick — gone away on holiday without us.' I punched him playfully on the chin.

'Going on holiday,' he repeated, in an incredulous tone of voice. Then, realising I was only joking, he gave his crooked grin.

'That bus, I waited ages, bloody hell, I got lost, I did,' he managed to stutter.

The expression 'bloody hell' was one he had picked up since going to Christchurch and not one he would have been likely to hear from the nuns. He only used it when worried or upset and it was a measure of his distress that he used it so much now.

I informed the police that all was well and when I made enquiries the next day, I was told by the bus company that Patrick's bus had to be taken out of service owing to a mechanical fault and there had been an interruption of the service. Patrick had waited a long time, and in the end, used his initiative to go in search of an alternative bus and had merely walked to the bus stop in the high street which was the next stop after his usual one outside the centre.

I tried to reassure Anthea that this was a very good test for Patrick, and he had come through with flying colours. But there was no denying that all three of us had a nasty fright through the incident. It served to remind us how vulnerable our son was in the outside world, and I wondered, not for the first time, whether he would ever be able to cope on his own.

During those two years, my file on Patrick continued to swell as I tried to get him accepted into some form of training programme which would equip him to hold down a job. I wrote countless letters to the education authority at Winchester, but I could never even establish that such a programme existed. I was continually told that there were the inevitable cut-backs that precluded any new initiative in this direction. Such funds as existed were desperately needed elsewhere and the facility at Christchurch was all that was available.

Later that year, I was told that Patrick's centre was taking part in a sports festival which included most of the training centres in the Southwest of England. The organisers had leased the Oval Stadium, Tidworth, from the army — an arena I knew well from my own involvement with local athletics. There would be several hundred competitors, and Patrick, who was an extremely fit young man, had been chosen to represent his county and would be taking part in several events. I was working flat out at the time as it was the height of the season, and as the sports meeting was a mid-week fixture, I found it impossible to get away until lunches had finished. The sports meeting would be well underway by the time I got to the stadium, but I hoped I would be in time to see Patrick compete in at least one event. We could not both get away from the business — the tea trade in the afternoon also being very important — but Anthea insisted that I go as athletics was more my thing than hers. I knew Patrick would be looking forward to seeing at least one of us present, and I felt it important that I make the effort to be there to cheer him on.

As the day of the festival dawned, I was delighted to see that we were in for at least a rainless day which was so important for any outdoor event. I had arranged for an extra waitress to be on duty that afternoon to help make up for my absence, as my conscience worried me about leaving the business at such a busy period. I rushed out to my car, on completion of the lunch orders, pulling my apron off as I went. I drove as hard as I dared to Tidworth, hoping to be in time to attend at least part of the meeting. I had no difficulty parking the car next to the stadium and found a good seat obtaining a grandstand view of the entire proceedings.

I soon spotted Patrick, who seemed to be performing well in the high jump without managing a winning leap. It was a pleasant afternoon, with warm sunshine now, and everyone seemed to be having an enjoyable time. There was a goodly crowd, doubtless with many parents among the spectators and every performance, however feeble, was cheered enthusiastically. The competitive spirit was evident, with every competitor giving his all, each effort being greeted with howls of support from teammates. I got quite caught up with the excitement and grew hoarse with shouting. Finally, it was the last event on the programme, and it was clear from the scoreboard that either one of three teams could walk off with the trophy if they could manage to win this four-hundred-metres final.

Seeing Patrick stripping off to take his place for this event, I could contain myself no longer and, jumping up from my seat, I ran into the arena. There was nobody to stop me as I vaulted the trackside fence, everyone being intent on seeing the final event. From my years of experience as an athletic coach, I knew where I must position myself to have the greatest effect. The gun went and they were off. I could see that Patrick, in his excitement, had gone off too fast, leading by a huge margin for the first one hundred metres before weakening and being overhauled by a strapping twenty-five-year-old. Patrick kept going, however, and gradually got his wind back, but could make no headway on the leader.

Patrick was still ten metres adrift when they reached the final bend where I was lying in wait. I could see the leader was struggling, and it was at this point that I let out a roar that could easily be heard above the din.

'Come on, Patrick, go, go for it!'

My son, who had no idea that I was present, did not see me, but he heard the familiar voice and having being in my company in this situation at many track meetings, knew what was required. His head went back, and with gritted teeth, tore down the track towards the waiting tape. Somehow, he managed to find the extra strength needed and overhauled his rival to cross the line for a narrow victory, his pursuers unable to catch him.

He was greeted with great cheers and his team-mates carried him shoulder-high towards the winner's rostrum where his team was presented with the winning trophy. I made my way back to the grandstand, delighted with my strategy. It was several minutes before I could control my emotions. I did not see Patrick to speak to until later that afternoon, as he was so involved with his friends and I did not really know whether he realised I was there or whether he thought he had just imagined he heard my voice roaring him on. I could see him looking around whilst on the rostrum, looking triumphant — he was so pleased at all the attention he was receiving.

He was absolutely delighted to see me as I shook his hand, congratulating him on a great victory.

'I won, Dad, I won the race, bloody hell. I was puffed out I was, bloody hell,' and he pretended his legs were about to buckle as he laughed aloud in his excitement.

It was a day that I was not likely to forget in a hurry, and I was just sorry that my former club members were not there to see it — I know they would have been just as proud of Patrick as I was. He would often attend training sessions when home on holiday and was greatly spoiled by all the young athletes in the club.

It was about this time that we decided to sell our small business in Milford-on-Sea and move to Salisbury. We had been in the restaurant business for seven years, and although we had built up a good trade, we felt it was time for a change. Our early enthusiasm had palled in the face of what amounted to very hard graft. On more than one occasion I was to hear a customer saying to a friend, upon entering our establishment, 'This is the sort of place I would like to take on when I retire. Isn't it delightful — what a pleasant way to make a living.' Words that would make my wife and I choke with laughter. I guess they would like to rise every morning at dawn and work until nightfall, with hardly a break in between, six days a week. Day after day, in a stifling hot kitchen, preparing endless meals with hardly time to have a bite oneself. The charm would very soon wear off — it did for me.

We always seemed to have endless problems with securing reliable staff upon whom we could depend. Young people seemed to look upon the catering trade as a stop gap on the way to something else. As soon as we had trained them into becoming useful to us, they were off to try something new. Many of them were girls who had taken their A levels and were just earning a few pounds, pending their exam results. As soon as the good news came through that they had passed they embarked on their real career, which, of course, was not serving high teas in high summer.

One could not blame them, but it made life very difficult for those of us who had to remain and get on with the job.

Anyway, we had had enough, and having obtained a good price, we invested the money in some property which was in need of doing up and I felt sure I could make a success of it. Anthea was overjoyed when she heard that there was an acre and a half of semi-derelict land that went with it and could not wait to get her spade sharpened. We had successfully accomplished a similar operation, some years before, on a spare time basis, so felt confident of our ability to do it again as a full-time job. It would mean working out of doors to a large extent — which pleased us both as we were fed-up looking like ghosts from working in a kitchen and seldom getting out in the fresh air.

This new move, of course, took us into Wiltshire and a breath-taking change of fortune for Patrick.

Our eldest son was now nineteen years of age and had grown into a good-looking and well-built young man. I had never known him to suffer any form of illness, not even a cold, and he looked the picture of health. We settled into our new home on the outskirts of Salisbury and much of my time was taken up with hard manual labour. We had bought two semi-detached houses which were in much need of refurbishment, and Patrick joined in enthusiastically in the laying out of the garden.

He would toil all day alongside his mother, whilst I got busy on the interior of the cottages. One was quite habitable, and we lived in this one whilst we prepared the other for sale. It was a delightful change from working in a restaurant with constant calls upon my time dealing with the general public. Here we were completely on our own, surrounded by beautiful countryside, and found it absolute bliss. It was the month of June and often we were able to knock off work and have lunch alfresco, sprawled on the grass and listening to the birds chirping away in the hedgerows. This sound was sometimes interrupted by the herd of cows, in the field next door, who would come to the fence and gaze with considerable interest at this new activity on their doorstep.

I had the idea that Patrick might well find his niche in the world as a gardener, because he showed a love of nature and had an aptitude for the work. Once he was shown how to do something, Patrick never showed an inclination to do it any other way, which was a positive advantage in many occupations.

I wasted no time in introducing myself to the Wiltshire Education Authority, and from the first meeting I had with them in Salisbury, they showed a keen awareness of our needs and the necessity for Patrick to have some form of training.

At this time, our son Ian, who was now sixteen years of age, had left school and commenced an apprenticeship at the Ford main dealer in Salisbury. He had always had an interest in cars and showed an aptitude for understanding anything mechanical. He had settled down well at his first job, and I was very proud of him. He was a boy who had matured early in life, and was very independent.

On one particular summer evening, Patrick and I decided to do some work in the garden and dragged the lawnmower out of the shed. This was a job that Patrick loved doing and eagerly helped me every time the grass needed cutting. He would happily trundle up and down, proud that he could operate the machine.

Try as I may, however, on this occasion I could not get the engine to start and silently cursed in frustration. At that moment, Ian arrived home from work and I called out to him to come and try his luck.

Patrick interrupted me when he heard that his brother was going to be allowed to have a go. 'I can do it, Dad, I can do it,' he insisted.

'Just a minute, Patrick, Ian will be able to get it going,' I said impatiently.

Ian bent down to take stock and made various adjustments, but despite every effort, could not get it started. He pulled continuously at the starting cord, and although it stuttered a few times, he had to admit defeat. All this time, Patrick kept interrupting, 'Let me try, I can do it, I can do it,' he kept insisting. By this time, my temper was getting short, and I told him several times to keep quiet as Ian was doing his best.

Finally, giving up, I said, 'We will have to leave it for now, Patrick — I will take it in for a service tomorrow — you will just have to be patient.' This from the most impatient of men.

Resignedly, Ian and I walked away to have our tea. We had just about reached the back door when we heard a splutter, and the lawnmower engine burst into life with a roar. This was as nothing to the roar of triumph let out by Patrick as he danced up and down in delight. Ian and I looked on in astonishment as Patrick yelled, 'Told you, told you I could do it.' He laughed aloud at our bemused faces and punched the air.

Our garden had a definite slope to it and Patrick had dragged the mower off the lawn onto the flat surface of the pathway and merely tugged the cord to make it start. We could only imagine that the petrol had not been getting through because of the incline and there were two very red faces that went into tea. Had Patrick just been lucky, or had he instinctively guessed what the problem was. We were never to know for certain. Suffice to say, Patrick was left to start the lawnmower on every subsequent occasion when we decided to cut the grass.

It was a delightful garden — one which gave my garden-loving wife enormous pleasure. She had it a riot of colour, seemingly, at every season of the year, though how she managed it I never knew. I was very much the labourer on the job, having absolutely no knowledge of the many varieties of flower and shrub. She would talk endlessly of the begonias, the dahlias, jasmines and clematis and vowed that she would one day grow a Lady's Slipper. I promised her that I would buy her a pair for her birthday if it meant that much to her — a suggestion that only made her groan in despair.

One great nuisance made its presence felt on the scene and that was the pigeons. They would appear at dawn and late evening and took seemingly great pleasure in pecking off the heads of every flower as soon as it bloomed. They were especially attracted to the much-loved begonias and my wife was in despair. What infuriated me more than anything was the fact that they did not eat the petals they pecked off — they did it out of sheer vandalism.

With murder in my heart, I consulted an old friend called George Ward about the merits of an air gun. 'Is a Webley air rifle capable of killing a pigeon, George?' I asked him.

George, who had worked for BSA for nearly twenty years and knew as much about guns as any man in the country, having been selling them for a living all that time, looked at me with a pained expression. He was more used to being consulted about the relative merits of a brace of Purdeys than a child's plaything. He was only five foot six inches in height and well known to have a hair-trigger temper every bit as sensitive as any of his guns. He drew himself up to his highest elevation and his face, taking on a decided puce colour, answered caustically, 'Yes, I should think there is every chance, John, provided you strike it in the eye in flight,' and stalked off, muttering something about imbeciles.

I never did buy that gun. Anthea was appalled at the thought and threatened to leave me if I brought one into the house. The pigeons continued to enjoy their daily ravaging of our garden.

Chapter Twenty-four

It took a couple of months and I think I was beginning to despair that we would ever hear anything from the Social Services, but one day, a social worker by the name of Mister Carpenter called to see us. I was working in the garden with Patrick when this strange-looking man drove into the drive in a battered old Ford. He had a wild head of hair and was wearing the almost obligatory sandals and beard of his calling, but in Mister Carpenter we found the man who had the greatest impact on Patrick's life and indeed on all our lives. He was the most cheerful and positive-thinking person we had ever met in that line of work. He sat in the garden, drinking huge quantities of tea, and explained the difficulties he was facing in finding places for all the young people in his care.

But one could tell that nothing daunted this young social worker and he was greatly enthusiastic about Patrick's future in this new facility he had found in Trowbridge. Up until now, Patrick had been attending a day school called Sarum Centre, near the old RAF airfield, as a temporary measure, just something to keep him occupied until a better alternative could be found. It meant taking him the four miles every morning and collecting him in the evening, but I did not mind as long as it led to something more permanent.

It was Mr Carpenter who found a place for our son in a splendid training centre in Trowbridge managed by a Mister Mason. It was organised by the local authority and was a newly built residential facility and well equipped. It was the best, by far, of any such place that we had seen, and we were very impressed. Each person had their own room which included basic facilities for making a pot of tea and toast. Main meals for the forty-odd residents were served in the dining room and we could not be other than won over by the cleanliness of the entire surroundings.

From the kitchens to the well-kept gardens, everything was immaculate. What impressed me most was the fact that all the residents were young and, for the most part, were on a par with our son so far as intelligence was concerned. This was a great relief to me as this was very much the kind of facility for which I had been looking. There was well-trained staff on hand to teach the residents basic skills which was an ongoing programme in this type of centre, Mr Mason's own wife often helping out.

It was the usual sad parting as we deposited our son in new surroundings. By now, Patrick had got used to being away from home, after his years with the nuns, and was now a young man. Even so, he hung his head in that familiar fashion and the tears were not far away as he hugged his mother and kissed her goodbye. He would not look me in the eye as I embraced him, but he did manage to raise his crooked grin as I warned him not to drink too many beers on Saturday nights. Patrick drank very little, but he was very fond of a shandy and it was a standing joke between us that he must never get drunk.

He settled in very quickly at Rutland House, his new home, and Anthea and I breathed a sigh of relief that at last we had found a good facility for our son. Within a matter of weeks, Mister Mason telephoned me and asked us to go over for a chat. With certain misgivings, we drove the forty miles to Trowbridge the next day, concerned that something had happened to upset the apple-cart. We need not have worried, as Mister Mason had already made a favourable assessment of Patrick's capabilities. Our son had impressed everyone with his easy-going attitude and had made friends very quickly. The principal, in particular, was anxious to see that Patrick should make the most of his considerable assets.

'I am convinced, Mister Mullen, that Patrick is quite capable of holding down a job, given the right training and encouragement,' he assured us, which was music to my ears. 'How would you feel about your son working in a supermarket, perhaps, helping to stack shelves, general handyman, something like that?' He looked at me, questioningly.

It was not what I had in mind for Patrick, but fate had dealt him a rough hand. However, at least it was something constructive. I felt certain that this opportunity would increase his self-confidence and add to his self-esteem. Being treated as one of the workers would make him feel proud, and more sure of himself. He would be gainfully employed and earning his own keep, which would be a tremendous step forward. He would have money in his pocket, cash to spend as he chose. He loved music and was always keen to buy the latest record in the charts. It was an exciting prospect and I looked at my wife who nodded immediately, a smile of delight on her face. I agreed wholeheartedly and Mister Mason went on to explain that it was not a *fait accompli* as yet. He had yet to make his rounds, as he put it. He had good connections with all the local business houses and was always on their backs to give his young charges a chance to earn their keep. Patrick was very obedient and anxious to please, two attributes which stood him in good stead when asked to do anything, especially if he was going to be paid for it. As a former employer myself, I knew how much I valued an amiable and cheerful worker by my side.

After another week had passed, Mister Mason telephoned us with the good news that Patrick had had a successful interview for a job at a local supermarket and would commence straight away. He had every hope that it would work out to everyone's satisfaction.

We celebrated with our other two sons who were now seventeen and eleven respectively. They were very impressed by the news and delighted for Patrick as they were very well aware of his difficulties. Big brother had finally made it and deserved their respect, which was gladly given. It was a huge red-letter day for us, as this had always been our objective — that Patrick would be self-sufficient or, at least as far as he could ever be, independent, with his very limited ability to communicate.

This new responsibility stretched our son to the limit, but the reports that filtered back to us, through Mister Mason, suggested that Patrick had made a good impression. Always neat and tidy, thanks to his training by the nuns for nine years, he now found that this was an asset in his new job. A very amenable chap, he was also well liked by his fellow workers who appreciated his amiable personality. On one occasion, when I visited his workplace to meet his boss, I was assured that Patrick was pulling his weight without any favours from anyone — a bit of news that thrilled me.

'If I show Patrick a particular job I want done, I know for a fact that it will be carried out exactly as he is shown — something I wish I could say about all of my staff,' the manager assured me. 'While you are here, let me introduce you to the head of Patrick's gang who is responsible for his daily schedule.'

He called up someone on the telephone, and a few minutes later there was a knock on the door and a huge man, with shoulders like an ox, entered. This turned out to be a Mister O'Shawnessy, who looked like he had spent most of his life in the boxing ring. He cut a formidable figure with his crew cut, cauliflower ears and a nose that had seen some hard action. He shook my hand, which made it difficult for me to steer the car home, and let it be known that Patrick was one of his lads and woe betide anyone that tried to mess him about. He bunched an enormous fist. 'Be Jasus, they will answer to me,' he growled. I smiled nervously at him and thanked God he was on my side.

Chapter Twenty-five

I came away from that meeting greatly reassured that our son had made a safe landing on firm ground. I was astonished at the kindness shown to my son by his employer and workmates. It was a great relief to know that he had fallen in with such good friends and was being well looked after. I knew that it was due in no small way to Patrick's own personality and his willingness to please, yet even so, things could have been very different in what was all too often a very cruel world.

It seemed strange meeting those people at his workplace, as they had no previous knowledge of me. Patrick was the person with whom they were acquainted, and I was unimportant to them. He was the young man who helped keep the shelves full of much needed stock, the guy who kept the place clean and tidy and generally made himself useful wherever assistance was required. He was important to these people, and I was not. It was a rare feeling and one which made me feel very good about his future.

In short, Patrick had a life. Not one that would suit everybody, but certainly one that suited him very well. He was functioning extremely well within his limitations and appeared to be very happy. He was well set up with an established routine, which was all-important for someone with his shortcomings. There was no sign of stress, which I would have noticed at once from his demeanour, and I could not have been more pleased

Patrick continued to live at Rutland House where he now contributed to his upkeep from his income at the supermarket. In other words, he was paying his way, unlike most of the residents as only a handful were capable of holding down any sort of job. We felt very proud of him. There were about forty residents at the centre with a small and dedicated staff devoted to their sometimes very difficult work. Not every youngster was as docile and easy-going as Patrick and there were many occasions when I am sure the carers had to show the greatest tact in settling disputes of all kinds. Even among people without any learning difficulties, living in close proximity, there were bound to be flashes of temper and a falling out among friends.

Excursions to other towns and interesting places seemed to form a major part of the routine at the centre, for we would often get a postcard from Patrick. By now, he was quite capable of signing his signature and writing his address, and although the writing was no more than a scrawl, nevertheless, it was quite legible. Yet again we were grateful to the nuns for another breakthrough, for it was they who had achieved what, at one time, seemed the impossible and taught him how to write. Not only was he now fulfilling every hope we ever had for him, but even surpassing it. He was living a very full life and was missing out on very little.

There were other moments when we sought to see

Patrick without him seeing us — it gave us great pleasure to see how he was coping on his own. I remember once when we visited Trowbridge and arrived in time to wait outside his place of employment when he was due to knock off work for the day. We saw him emerge from the staff entrance, wheeling his bicycle — we were thrilled when he first managed to learn to cycle and he was very proficient.

He was also very careful, as we were to find out when we followed him in the car and noticed how he never took any chances, especially at roundabouts. He would always pause and look in every direction before proceeding. Whoever had taught him at the centre had done a good job in instilling in him the dangers involved with traffic.

He had excellent awareness and it was a great relief to us to see him display it as we were very worried when we heard that he was cycling to work — something that at one time I would have said was completely beyond him. I was beginning to realise that we had been selling our son short — that he was capable of far more than we had ever imagined. Other people were more aware of his potential and were pushing him to achieve more than we, his parents, had ever believed possible. We needed to revise our thinking where Patrick was concerned. He had already outstripped our greatest hopes for him and had left us behind. It was time for us to take fresh stock of the situation and look at our son in a fresh light.

We discovered that there was a direct train service between Trowbridge and Salisbury, and in consultation with the centre, we decided that Patrick would be quite safe to travel home on his own if someone could put him on the train and we would meet him at the Salisbury end. If he could cope with the journey on his own, it meant he could come home at weekends if he was free of any other commitment — for instance, if he did not have to work Saturdays, which he had to do occasionally.

We regarded it as another important step in improving the quality of his life and increasing his options of how to spend his free time. The centre also frequently organised coach trips to various places of interest, often the seaside being a favourite choice, so he was a seasoned traveller.

The first time he made the trip home on his own, we were on tenterhooks, as it was the first real journey he had ever made on his own. There was no real risk as there were no stops between stations and he could not get off anywhere else by mistake. We just hoped he would recognise when he was at Salisbury and get off, otherwise he might go all the way to London, which was the eventual destination of the train. We need not have worried, as when it pulled in to platform five, the first person we saw was Patrick, whose head was craning out of the window.

When the train had stopped, he jumped out carrying his holdall and ran to his mother laughing with delight.

'We were worried about you, Patrick,' his mother said, kissing him.

'It was easy, I can do it, I can do it,' he replied boastfully, aware that he had accomplished something important. He had no qualms whatsoever about the journey. He really enjoyed the experience, and train journeys remain a great favourite of Patrick's to this day.

By now, our son was gainfully employed, earning a decent wage and contributing to his keep at the centre. In what amounted to handing over total responsibility for his welfare to the Social Services, we felt that we did not have the right to inquire too closely into his earnings or indeed his savings, which we were given to understand were in a local building society. He was able to purchase a new bicycle — a sports model with countless gears of which he was very proud and took great delight in demonstrating to us when we saw it for the first time.

He cycled round and round in the road to demonstrate his skill, and I had to curb his enthusiasm when he wanted to show us how fast he could ride on his new machine.

He would usually arrive home on Saturday mornings and stay until Sunday evening when we would take him to the station, and it was always a source of great satisfaction to see how he would go off smiling and wave to us until the train had disappeared from our view. He was now quite accustomed to being on his own, and when I thought back to those early days when we had to leave him at school and the emotional trauma for all of us when he would cry, it was a great relief to see how confident he had become.

His mother, feeling that he was now sufficiently independent to stand on his own feet financially, decided that he should bring home enough money at weekends to at least indulge himself in whatever past-time took his fancy without expecting us to pay for it. I was fully in agreement with this decision, particularly as my two younger sons were now fast growing up and I was determined that all three of my children should be treated the same, notwithstanding the fact that Patrick had a severe learning problem.

For all his limitations, Patrick could never be fobbed off with second best. For example, when sweet was being served at lunchtime, he would often be heard to say, 'Ugh, no cream?' and making a face — a trait that did not endear him, at times, to his mother, when busy serving up.

He was very fond of pop music, and knew the names of the various groups, certainly better than his parents. The walls of his bedroom were plastered with huge posters of the Beatles and Queen etc. and he loved to buy a record when home at weekends. These were not cheap, and he built up quite a selection of the 'top twenty' records over the years.

His mother would take him into the market on Saturdays, when shopping, and often something would take his fancy and he would ask her to buy it. It would frequently cost several pounds, and although we could afford it, we felt that he should pay for it himself. He never seemed to bring home enough money for these treats, and it annoyed his mother that the centre would send him home with just a pound or two in his pocket — certainly never enough to satisfy his needs or, should I say, wants. Patrick was now a young man with a young man's yearning for all the good things in life, and as he had the money, hard earned, I could not see why he should not have them.

We took the view that if he was not working and had no money of his own, we were quite prepared to indulge him as much as we might our other two kids. However, he was in the position to pay his own way in the world and was quite entitled to spend his own money any way he chose.

Why, therefore, was the centre keeping him on such a tight leash so far as spending money was concerned? What was the point in building up, what we suspected, was a substantial balance in his bank account (we were not privy to this information) when he was entitled to enjoy the simple pleasures available to all of us? On quite a few occasions we raised the point with Mr Mason, but the response always seemed evasive. It made my wife, in particular, furious when Patrick would come home with a couple of pounds in his pocket when a single visit to the cinema could absorb all of that and more.

I began to suspect that the people in authority were suspicious of us, that they thought we were taking Patrick's money off him for our own use and leaving him penniless. The thought appalled me, and I wondered how best I could allay their suspicions and at the same time make sure that Patrick was allowed enough pocket money to enjoy his weekends at home to the full. It was not that he was a complete spendthrift or extravagant — all he really wanted were a few simple pleasures like everyone else.

An idea finally formed in my head, and I sat down and wrote a letter of thanks and congratulations to Mr

Mason for the excellent progress Patrick was making, a feeling I truly held. In addition, I enclosed a cheque for the sum of one hundred pounds to buy any piece of equipment that he felt might prove useful to the youngsters at the centre.

From that day on, we had no further problem with Patrick's money. He always brought home enough cash to ensure that he had a good time and a major problem was overcome. My wife never knew of my duplicity and would often say smugly, 'You see, you have to be firm with these people and make them see the light.'

'Yes, dear, you are absolutely right,' I would reply in agreement, while smiling to myself.

Chapter Twenty-six

The people at the centre seem to have ingrained in Patrick a need to be extremely careful with money which allowed the only unpleasant trait in Patrick's character to develop, and that was an appearance of miserliness. It took a great effort to get him to take out his wallet and pay for anything, and, indeed, he had a tendency to turn away from you when he opened it as though afraid that you might see what was in it. I tried to make light of it, teasing him about all those moths flying out, but my humour, not surprisingly, was lost on him. Indeed, it was also lost on his mother, who was far from being amused at my light-heartedness over what she considered to be a ghastly trait.

This habit really infuriated Anthea, who was the most generous of people, and there was many a row over this unfortunate habit of his. In fact, the whole business of money was the only real failure of Patrick's over the years. Despite great patience by various teachers, he could never master the intricacies of the coinage. He could never be made to understand the value of any coin — it was quite beyond him.

He came to understand that he was usually on safe ground if he presented a note for whatever small item he wished to purchase. He was always chuffed when he was given a quantity of change, presumably imagining that he had come off best in the transaction. He would chortle when he stuffed the change in his pocket and tended to look around to see if anyone had observed his good fortune.

On a Saturday when he accompanied his mother to Salisbury market, she would first pay a visit to the bank to draw out some money from the cash-point. Patrick was always thrilled when the notes appeared out of the wall and would laugh out loud in amazement at this apparent bit of magic. I think he thought that his mother was a magician.

'Can I do that, Mum, can I do it? he would frequently cry out.

He loved his visits to Salisbury market every Saturday, when he was home, as his mother loved to spoil him. His muscles came in very useful, too, for carrying the shopping bags — a chore that he made his own.

The whole business of change was tiresome in more ways than one. For example, it was hard on the linings of Patrick's trouser pockets. It was a common sight to see Patrick approaching like the leaning tower of Pisa, weighed down on one side as he was by the weight of the coins in his pocket. He was wont to carry around enough small change to settle the national debt while still insisting on paying for an apple by offering the busy stall holder a five-pound note.

If Patrick likes one thing it is clothes. The nuns had taught him to be tidy in appearance and this lesson he had absorbed totally. Not only was he tidy — he was fastidious. By virtue of the fact that he earned his money by hard manual labour, stacking shelves with heavy boxes and emptying waste bins that built up a lot of muscle, he had a near perfect physique. He found it easy to find clothes to fit him perfectly and when he was dressed to go out, he looked immaculate. When he once attended a family wedding, he put his father and two brothers in the shade, his beautiful blonde hair making him stand out even more.

We frequently visited Patrick's training centre where he continued to live whilst working for the supermarket. He was now an adult, and although he would always be backward, like everybody else he matured and lost many of his boyish ways. I noticed more than once that when Mr Mason or one of the staff appeared in the communal lounge when we were having a cup of tea, Patrick appeared ill at ease. He would sit up straight, wipe imaginary crumbs off his trousers — all the small signs of stress with which I was very familiar having seen the evidence many times in the past. He was not worried — he just seemed unable to relax in this atmosphere and it concerned me.

Here was a young man earning his keep, and after a hard day's work, he was entitled to relax and literally put his feet up like the rest of us. But there was this headmaster and pupil relationship that existed, through nobody's fault, that prevented Patrick from fully enjoying his leisure time, and there seemed very little that we could do about it. Anthea and I discussed it at great length but decided not to raise the matter with the principal as there was really nothing that could be achieved by doing so. For one thing, it was the presence of authority that was causing the problem and Mr Mason could hardly be expected to leave. He was a very kind man — it was just that his personality demanded respect, an attribute for which he could hardly be criticised. Patrick just felt that he had to be on his best behaviour when the principal was around.

Fortunately, it was shortly after this matter had come to our attention that the suggestion was made that, if an opportunity arose, Patrick might prove a suitable candidate to share a house with several other young people with roughly the same degree of learning difficulty. Mencap was very keen to try to integrate such people into the community so that they could be as self-sustaining as possible. It was a policy that had been tried out in other areas and had been seen to work extremely well over the years.

We were delighted to give our approval to the scheme, as this would mean that Patrick would be out from under the gaze of the staff at Rutland House, however kind and well-meaning they might be. He would be truly able to relax in what would virtually be his own home and would be all the happier for it. Patrick had to wait some weeks, but the great day came when he made this important move, and with two young women and another young man, they moved into a terrace house in Trowbridge.

It was a well-built house in a fairly quiet road — rented from the owner by Mencap and provided a good home for the new tenants. A very kind lady, living opposite, was employed to keep an eye on them, help them with their weekly shopping on Saturdays and make sure they kept the place neat and tidy. It was exciting and challenging stuff for these youngsters, who found themselves fending for themselves in society for the first time.

Many mistakes would be made, but with the proper supervision, much could be accomplished. The work of such people who provide this all-important supervision is never fully recognised, and here I would like to pay tribute to Maureen Western, who proved not only to be a selfless and tireless worker on their behalf but became a real friend to those handicapped young people. Long after she retired, she made it her business to call often and see that they were all right.

The back garden of the property was, however, far bigger than they could cope with and really represented a huge challenge. My wife, who was a demon gardener, was equal to the task and would drag me over to Trowbridge to attack the wilderness that existed at the rear of the house. Many afternoons were spent digging and weeding, and gradually my wife licked it into shape. It was backbreaking work, but my wife loved it and it gave her the opportunity to contribute something constructive to the scheme. We felt greatly indebted to everyone associated with Patrick's progress.

Our son was still near enough to his place of work to be able to cycle to it and he was content there for many years. I never heard of any trouble between the residents who all seemed to get along very well. The experiment was a huge success — what one of the residents could not accomplish, very often one of the others could. It was always very much a team effort and on my frequent visits, in those early days, I sensed it to be a very happy household. I found Mencap, which is a long-established charity, to be a very caring and well organised association who do an enormous amount of good work for young people with learning difficulties. Without their efforts, a lot of the population would be living very sad lives.

Chapter Twenty-seven

Of course, life is not always perfect and there are invariably people ready to take advantage of those weaker ones in our society. Every town has its share of lowlife who prey on their fellow citizens instead of working for a living. It only takes a few twisted personalities to make life very miserable for so many others who are just trying to hack out a life for themselves.

I have never been able to understand why it is that, in an age when there is no real poverty in the country, we should suffer such a soaring crime rate. Rightly or wrongly, I have always associated destitution with crime, but I have to be wrong. In my childhood there was the most appalling deprivation, but crime on the scale we know it today, was unheard of. There are those who will argue that there is awful poverty existing in Britain today, but I have to say not the kind of poverty I remember. We did not eat Thursdays or most of Friday either — that is the kind of poverty I remember as a child. Now, being considered very poor is established when you cannot pay your television licence or buy a set of new tyres for the car. A lot of the crime is blamed on the drug problem, but I doubt that very much. If it is to blame, then it is only in the sense that much needed resources are spent trying in vain to curtail the traffic in illegal substances when they should be concentrated on chasing the real villains. I blame the media, in all its forms, for most of our problems in the area of crime. They have fostered a culture that is totally alien to that which was followed when I was young.

We were taught about honour, your word was your bond, your good name was sacrosanct. If you were involved in a fight, you fought fairly. Now what do we have. To foul and, above all, to get away with it is the smart thing. The sly trickster who can cheat some innocent person out of their savings is to be admired. What a rip-off, absolutely brill, people are encouraged to believe. The guy who insists on playing fair is an asshole and is invariably jeered. We see it on television, in films, in books and magazines. It is made out to be funny and clever when the hoodlum puts one over on the good guy, I could go on and on.

Many of us must ask, where did it all go wrong, when we are made to understand that the law persistently protects the lawbreaker and not the victims of his crimes. All too often the perpetrator goes free with a caution or a derisory fine, much to the chagrin of the arresting officers in the case. What must it do to the morale of hard-working policemen when they see this happen? The villain leering at them as they leave the courtroom and sticking two fingers in the air. If he goes free on a technicality, thanks to some slick lawyer, then it must feel even worse for the arresting officer. I feel sure that it breeds corruption.

Next time there will be the temptation for that officer to fabricate evidence to make doubly certain that the wrongdoer gets his just deserts. There spells the danger of the whole system of justice falling into disrepute. At all levels of justice, especially those of the local magistrates, there appears to be a total lack of common sense. Common sense seems to be the least common of the senses.

When Patrick was at work one day, three men called at the house declaring that they had been sent by the Social Services to 'sort out the garden'.

There was only one young woman at home — for some reason she was not attending the centre that day and she was bewildered by their presence on her doorstep, as her social worker usually kept her fully informed of any change in the routine. Taking it in turns to chat her up and allay her suspicions, they had no difficulty in persuading her that they were genuine workmen.

They were so confident and self-assured that she allowed them access to the back garden through the side gate, they spent an hour or so supposedly tidying up and eventually came to the door and demanded three hundred pounds for their efforts. Stunned, she tried to explain that she did not have that sum, and that all bills were settled by the Social Services. They were not best pleased and asked to use the telephone to obtain instructions from their employer about payment.

Confused and now very worried, having never encountered this situation before and under considerable stress, Patrick's friend allowed them to come in, and whilst one was supposedly telephoning, the other asked if he might use the toilet. Finishing the call, they told her everything had been settled satisfactorily and left.

It was over an hour later that she discovered that the housekeeping money, which was kept in a tin in the kitchen, was missing, the box lying empty on the shelf. Whilst one had kept her busy, the other had rifled the contents. It happens often enough to intelligent people — it must have been doubly easy to take advantage of a young person with learning difficulties.

Of course, the Social Services knew nothing about these conmen and the police were alerted. It was a shameful crime, but I suppose that the girl could consider herself lucky considering the amount of violence associated with this kind of robbery. Perhaps she was fortunate that they found what they were looking for so easily. The young woman might have been seriously injured. It was a very unpleasant incident to happen to anyone, and once again we were forcibly made aware just how vulnerable these young people were, living on their own in the community.

Patrick was the only one in the house who was capable of holding down a full-time job, the others making their way to the training centre each day, where they were kept occupied learning basic skills. Our boy had come a long way since attending Compton Diagnostic Unit, and when I looked back, the progress he had made seemed phenomenal. Here he was, holding down a tough manual job successfully and paying his way in the world. He had to get himself up in the morning, wash and shave, make his own breakfast and get to his place of work on time. Whatever the weather, he was on his bicycle, making his way through the town traffic and safely negotiating the many roundabouts he encountered — in Trowbridge, particularly, there appeared to be an abundance of these.

He had his own building society account, and to this day I have no idea how much he has in there. I am certain Patrick could not tell me, as counting still remains his biggest problem. It is sufficient for me to know, however, that he has enough money for his daily needs and can have a holiday when he wishes. In short, he wants for nothing. His progress in other areas more than made up for his lack of understanding of the coinage.

Could this be the same Patrick, I wondered, who was so terrified when we had left him with the staff at Compton Diagnostic Centre? It had been a hard decision, but when I looked now at this brawny young man who, although still severely handicapped, had nevertheless been trained to cope on his own with most eventualities that one meets during the course of a normal day. On his own turf he was quite at home and relaxed, and his parents were delighted to see it. He continued to have a good relationship with his two brothers, and although their lives went by very different paths, still he was always pleased to hear from them and would always ask after them whenever we paid him a visit.

Having worked hard all of our lives, like most other people, we had managed to save some of our earnings and now felt like spending some of it. Holidays had been few and far between at the beginning — we were so busy working and, in any case, could not afford it, but in recent years we had taken the boys abroad to Austria and France and enjoyed the experience immensely. Several times we went by ferry and train, and Patrick, in particular, was thrilled and excited at sleeping on the train. He always demanded the top bunk and would laugh delightedly as he clambered up into it, feeling superior looking down at his brothers.

We particularly liked the mountain walking and would return to our hotel ravenous after three or four hours tramping the well-marked trails. The Inn valley in Austria is especially beautiful and we returned many times to that area. They make cakes in that country like nowhere else on earth and it is certainly not the place to go if one wants to lose weight.

For a change of scenery, however, one year, Anthea and her sister decided to rent a villa in Spain which the two families could share, and have a proper family holiday. It was a country which I had never visited and, indeed, had no interest in at all. Bullfights and the like did not appeal to me in the slightest. I had heard tales of Benidorm and its high-rise apartment blocks, fish and chip shops and lager louts and much preferred the quiet mountains of the Tyrol.

I took much persuading, but with the rest of the family united in their decision to have a real change, I capitulated. I could not be left out of the Spanish adventure and agreed to go along with it. Having a great dread of flying (I later managed to conquer this fear, sort of!) it was agreed that I would leave by car a few days in advance of the rest of the party, who all loved travelling by air. I decided to take the Brittany Ferry from

Plymouth to Roscoff, and powered my way down south through France and Spain to reach the Costa del Sol in a little over two days.

As I approached my destination, whether it was the glorious sunshine or the tasty tapas I was able to buy at wayside ventas at ridiculously low prices, or just the magnificent scenery, I fell totally in love with Spain — a love affair that has lasted to this day. I found the whole atmosphere enthralling, and the easy going pace of life was enticing in the extreme. Although my Spanish was limited (it still is), thanks to my attending evening classes in Salisbury College for a few months, I was able to order a meal and make a few comments about the weather and surroundings at the many wayside inns I encountered. This attempt at conversation usually brought a torrent of quick-fire Spanish in reply which had me lost immediately. Nevertheless, I think my efforts were appreciated as I found people generally very friendly and welcoming.

Often, I would stop and have my cup of coffee mid-morning at a wayside inn of which there appeared to be one every couple of miles. I stopped for a snack at noon one day and sat on a terrace, which was shaded by masses of differently coloured bougainvillaea, and enjoyed a view over deep gorges to steeply climbing mountains beyond. As was usually the case, I had the place to myself at that time of the morning, the Spanish always eating a very late lunch, and it was the nearest thing to paradise that I can think of. The scent of the myriad of wild flowers coming off the mountain slopes was overpowering. Shades of amber, green gold and purple merged to form a pattern of infinite beauty and variety.

At first, I thought it was a trick of the light, but then what I thought was a moving shadow, transformed itself into a closely packed herd of goats moving at a leisurely pace through the bracken half a mile below me. As they drew nearer, I saw that they were accompanied by a lone shepherd. The dog that clung to his heels seemed superfluous as the goats moved in a very orderly manner.

They grazed as they ambled along, pausing now and again to nibble at whatever appeared edible. I noticed almost at once that one particular goat had fallen back, but neither the dog nor its handler paid any attention to it. The animal appeared to have sat down and, puzzled, I reached for my binoculars which I normally kept handy when travelling through such spectacular scenery. Training them on the dawdler, I watched in rapt attention whilst the animal gave birth to a new kid. The shepherd and the dog completely ignored this event, although they could not be unaware of what was happening. The herd and its minder continued blissfully on its way and I wondered at the owner's indifference.

When I mentioned it to the waiter when it was time to pay the bill, he explained that, after a short while when the new-born and its mother had recovered, they would continue after the herd and eventually catch up with it. No special attention was ever paid to such an event — it really was the survival of the fittest in these mountains. For humans and animals alike, it had always been a battle against the odds over the centuries. Not for the last time would I be surprised at the casual approach to animal welfare in Spain. It was with the greatest reluctance that I climbed back into my car and continued on my way.

I dawdled the last one hundred miles as I was so taken with Andalucia. Its mountain ranges are not quite as high as the Alps, but they are far less forbidding, rising more gently and almost constantly bathed in sunshine. The lower slopes give way to fertile ground which have been covered with olive trees since Roman times. This was part of the wealth that attracted the invader. The melting snows from the Sierra Nevada provide abundant water, and where I expected to find a completely burnt up landscape, I found green and lovely valleys. I approached Granada as dawn was breaking, having slept in the car for a few hours during the night, and I was blessed with the sight of the early morning sun rising over the Alhambra. There can be few sights more arresting than that of the fabled Moorish stronghold appearing gradually out of the dark red of dawn as though it were a mirage or straight out of a dream about the Arabian Nights.

The walls of the old palace glowed bright red and it was easy to see why it was so named — Alhambra being the Arabic word for red walls. I was almost sorry to reach my final destination, so much had I enjoyed the trip.

I found the villa we had rented for two whole weeks, and the family duly arrived by taxi some hours later. They were all relieved to see me, not least for the fact that I had taken a lot of their essential holiday gear with me in the car — snorkel equipment, loads of towels etc. It was one of the most enjoyable holidays we had ever had, and Anthea felt the same way as I did about this beautiful country. In short, she loved it. All the kids had a great time, spending most of the day in the water, and vowed they would come again next year. It took some getting used to the fact that you knew you would rise to certain sunshine every morning, and we would leap eagerly out of bed, thinking we were the first up, only to find someone else already in the swimming pool, however early the hour.

Always a sun worshipper, when we got back home my wife soon brought the conversation around to the possibility of buying a holiday home in Spain. I had rarely seen Anthea so excited about anything, and I was just as enthusiastic about the idea. We got in touch with agents and attended a sales presentation at a hotel in Bournemouth, where we were given details of some very attractive properties on the Costa del Sol. We pored over these for a week, some of which were stunning, and then, unable to contain our desire to see them any longer, I braced myself for the inevitable and we flew out for a weekend of viewing.

We spent several days being taken round by a very enthusiastic salesman who refused to let us out of his sight. I lost count of the number of apartments we viewed, any one of which might well have suited us, but we were always told that there was just one more that deserved a look. His company had arranged very pleasant accommodation for us, and after a day's viewing, having deposited us at our hotel for a much-needed shower, he was back again an hour later to take us to dinner.

Although many nationalities were represented, we were amazed at the number of British people who had bought properties, and we found the English language spoken just about everywhere. There was very little encouragement to speak Spanish. There seemed to be an endless choice of delightful restaurants boasting tantalising menus to choose from and the wonderful quality of life was very apparent. Our minds were soon made up to purchase something that would provide a holiday home for all the family.

However, always the cautious ones, despite the disappointment to the salesman, we refused to sign up for anything without first going home to think the whole matter over. We had heard the usual stories of people being conned by unscrupulous builders on the Costa del Sol and were determined not to be bilked out of our hard-earned savings.

We mulled over the various options and within a matter of days of our return we contacted the salesman again and bought a charming ground floor apartment near Marbella where, upon our retirement from business, we intended to spend a good deal of our leisure time. It had extensive gardens, beautifully laid out, an enormous swimming pool, tennis court and safe car parking right outside our front door.

Within four hundred metres of the complex was a small shopping precinct which boasted a supermarket, a bank and, most important from my wife's point of view, a ladies' hairdresser. I think that was the clincher. We had taken our time and refused to be rushed, and now I felt that we had made a good purchase — one that would give us good security and a delightful home in the sun. I little realised at the time how important a decision that was to prove for me in the future.

Chapter Twenty-eight

Whenever the centre held any kind of social function, the young people would always attend, and my wife and I tried as often as possible to get there as we knew Patrick enjoyed our presence. He was a young man who loved company and greatly looked forward to any get-together for whatever reason.

'Are you coming, Dad, are you coming?' he would shout over the telephone, when a forthcoming party was in the offing.

He always repeated the sentence as though unsure I was listening or perhaps to let me know how important my presence meant to him. In any event, I always tried to reassure him on both counts and promise him that I would be there on the night.

He always took great care with his appearance and looked quite the gentleman for these occasions.

These parties usually took the form of a disco held at a local hall or pub, with lots to eat, and not only the kids, but the parents, too, were encouraged to get up and take to the floor and usually were surprised to find that they thoroughly enjoyed themselves.

These functions served several purposes. They helped to raise money for the centre, enabling the management to purchase much needed equipment and finance excursions for the residents which were usually of an educational nature. Budgetary restraints only allowed for essentials to be provided for the inmates and additional money was always welcome. Every time we spoke to the staff, there was talk of never-ending cutbacks and we wondered where it would all end. Would it eventually mean the closure of the centre? Nobody knew for certain, and we just lived in the hope that it would continue in existence, for it was a desperately needed facility.

These functions also enabled the parents to meet and exchange views on their offspring. Parents of backward children often felt cut off and it was a comfort to find that one was not alone in this predicament. I know that I often came away feeling a lot better from having discussed Patrick's shortcomings with someone else in more or less the same predicament. In the light of other people's problems, my own often diminished considerably.

It was at one of the first of these affairs that we attended that we noticed (how could we not) Patrick's ability to dance. He possessed amazing rhythm and could keep time with an extraordinary display of steps. He had never taken any lessons, so where he got this natural talent from is anybody's guess — certainly not from his parents, who could just about manage a slow waltz at best. He was not the only one either, and we loved to sit out and watch these kids perform with such extraordinary skill. One could easily see the sheer enjoyment on their faces as they swayed to and fro, with a movement as natural to them as breathing.

Having qualified as a chartered accountant Patrick's

younger brother Neil had moved to America to further his career, where he had met a young woman and fallen in love. An impending marriage was soon announced and a party, consisting of his family and several friends, made the flight from England to Minneapolis where the wedding was to take place. Patrick was in a high state of excitement at finding himself boarding this huge aircraft, with the rest of his family, for the long flight to America and loved every minute of the trip.

It was a lovely ceremony in the local Catholic church, and afterwards, we were all entertained most royally at a reception. After the meal, a noisy disco was soon underway for the youngsters, with a talented group of musicians belting out some very loud pop music to the delight of the crowd.

Most of the young people were on the floor, and I watched Patrick as he sat at my table, his foot tapping away to the beat. Looking resplendent in a new suit bought specially for the occasion, he cut an extremely handsome figure. He would never have enough courage, however, to ask a girl to dance so I was pleased when this kind, middle-aged lady, seemingly aware of his shyness, took pity on him, grabbed his arm and dragged him onto the floor. I smothered a grin and thought, 'Are you in for a surprise!'

The look on her face remains with me to this day. Startled does not describe it adequately. Expecting a few stumbling steps from her partner, she was mesmerised as Patrick went into action. Poor lady, she soon found herself the centre of attention as the other dancers made room for Patrick to show off his technique. Neil, who had never seen his brother in action on a dance floor before, came running over to me and gasped, 'Dad, come and see Patrick.'

I laughed aloud and replied that I had seen it all before many times. In fact, he made his two brothers and most of the others look like stumblebums. Patrick enjoyed his moment of glory and when the music stopped, his companion made her way back to her seat in a daze.

'All right son, enjoyed that, did you?' I asked, grinning at him as he sat down to catch his breath.

'That lady, she can't dance, that lady. She can't dance, she can't,' and he laughed aloud, pleased with himself.

Patrick was fully integrated into the local community by now, liked and respected by his fellow workers, a regular at his local pub Saturday nights, even enjoying the odd game of darts, He attended local football matches and needless to say was an avid television fan. He could read, especially the TV and Radio Times which he would peruse at length, and would never miss out if there was a James Bond film on the box, the Ian Fleming hero being a great favourite.

But for Patrick's all-time favourite, one has to look elsewhere. No further, however, than Michael Jackson's video, 'Thriller'. He was enthralled with the special effects and never seemed to tire of watching it. Even now, years later, it still remains in his possession and is frequently taken out for a viewing.

The television, not surprisingly, remains Patrick's favourite pastime. In that respect, he is not very different from most of us when, after a hard day's work, it has become the natural thing to slump in an armchair and become, as they say, a couch potato. In that respect, I have to admit to being a television addict myself.

Chapter Twenty-nine

Patrick was about thirty when his mother contracted leukaemia. She was diagnosed on the 7th May and died on the 21st October. From being one of the fittest persons I had ever known — she had never had a day's illness in her life — she wasted away in just six months and was gone from us. She died in hospital from a massive stroke while undergoing chemotherapy. She had never smoked a cigarette in her life — an aerobic enthusiast who trained three or four times a week — it came as a shattering blow to lose her. She had a man's racing bicycle and on any fine morning was to be seen careering around the countryside, her pony tail streaming out behind her. She would reel off twenty or thirty miles as if it were nothing and arrive back home as fresh as a daisy.

We had a spare room which we referred to as the fitness room, and it was there we often worked out together. Aerobics was her passion and she would often persuade me to join her in a session — not that I needed much persuasion as I felt it was a great aid to my running. She had a great selection of music tapes that lent themselves to this form of training, and she would soon have me struggling to keep up with her, so fit was she all this time. I would stagger off to the shower, feeling drained after a workout with her.

I had retired early several years before, and it was one of the best decisions I ever made, for it meant that we were able to enjoy what turned out to be the best years of our married life. We had the time to really be together and share the fruits of what we had earned as a team. No more rushing to make deadlines or keep appointments or attend meetings. Our time was our own and we basked in the sheer luxury of it.

On this particular Thursday morning, she came in from the garden, where she always spent most of her spare time. She adored gardening and it was one of the great pleasures of her life. No weed would ever dare show itself whilst she was around. She was wearing her rumpled old tracksuit, which she always wore when working outdoors. In her hand she carried her ancient transistor radio which might well have been chained to her wrist, it seemed so much a part of her. It never left her side when she was working in the garden. She loved listening to music on the light programme and much preferred the radio to television. I looked up at her and frowned, as she appeared worried and ill at ease.

'What's the matter? Birds been at your flowers again,' I asked, surprised to see her in this mood.

'I'm glad it is next week we are off to Spain and not today — I feel dreadful,' she volunteered, as she joined me in the lounge where I was enjoying a cup of coffee while reading my newspaper.

Putting the paper down, I studied her in silence. It was so remarkable for her to complain about anything that I was at a loss for words.

'What seems to be the problem?' I asked, my eyes

following her as she moved to the window.

She rubbed the side of her neck. 'My glands seem to be swollen,' she muttered, half to herself.

'I should make an appointment to see the doctor,' I advised. 'You don't want to be unwell with our trip to Spain coming up.'

'Yes, I think I will ring up the surgery for an appointment,' she agreed, and went out into the hall to use the telephone. She came back a few minutes later and said that they could fit her in if she came at the end of evening surgery.

When she returned that evening, she said she felt a fraud as her glands no longer gave her trouble, but the doctor had said that if she had a recurrence, to come back and see him. All seemed well and we relaxed back into our routine. The weather was beautiful for May, with all her favourite flowers coming into bloom. I mowed the lawn, which was about all I was good for in a garden, and snored in my hammock when it was done.

On Saturday, Patrick arrived home for the day, bringing a young friend with him for company. His mother decided to take them both for a drive into the New Forest, stopping at our old restaurant in Milford-on-Sea for tea. It was typical of Anthea to put herself out in this way to bring pleasure to others, and I waved to them as they drove off. This was a particular treat for Patrick, as he loved to show his friends where he used to live, not to mention his love of cream teas.

On their return, my wife complained of a painful ankle, and when she took off her shoe and showed me the black discoloration, my heart gave a lurch. It looked very ugly and for some reason I felt a stab of fear. She could not remember bruising it which made me worry all the more. I told her she must see the doctor as soon as possible, but it was now Saturday evening and there would be no surgery until Monday.

Her ankle was much improved the next day and by Monday had almost returned to normal, but there was still some bruising evident, and I insisted she telephone the doctor for an appointment, to which she grudgingly agreed. I pointed out that we were leaving on holiday in a few days and that it was important to get it sorted out before we left, which she agreed made sense.

Fortunately, they were able to fit in an appointment for that day and when she returned, she said that she had been attended by a new young doctor at the practice who had been extremely nice. She could give him no explanation for the bruising, as she had not been involved in an accident. Apart from examining her ankle there was very little said, but the doctor had taken a blood sample for analysis and said he would be in touch.

Later that afternoon the telephone rang, and I went to answer it.

'Could I speak to Mrs. Mullen, please. This is Wilton surgery.' A man's voice.

Through the open window of the lounge, I could see my wife dozing in a sun lounger in the garden. She had found the work on the borders too tiring and was taking a rest. Normally a demon of energy, this was most unusual for her. It was a beautiful May afternoon, and everything was blossoming, but I felt very cold all of a sudden and my stomach knotted in fear. I knew without a shadow of a doubt that something awful was about to happen in our lives.

I went to the window and called out, trying to make my voice sound casual.

'Anthea, there is a call for you — it's the doctor.'

She rose instantly and hurried indoors. As I passed the telephone to her, she said, 'I don't like the sound of this,' looking at me with a wry smile and I could see the fear in her eyes.

I drifted into the lounge, wanting to hear what was said and yet not wanting to hear my worst fears confirmed.

When she hung up, she joined me, and I looked at her nervously.

Biting her lip, she volunteered, 'They have had the result of the blood test and an appointment has been made for me to see a specialist on Thursday morning at Salisbury infirmary.'

'Did they say what was the matter?' I asked.

'No, they just said I should see the specialist. What do you think it means?' She stared at me, obviously hoping for a simple explanation.

'Oh, it could be anything,' I assured her. 'Considering the discoloration, it might be some form of blood poisoning. Don't forget, he is a new young doctor and may well be over cautious. They will soon sort it out,' I added consolingly, not really believing what I was saying.

'As long as they sort it out before the weekend, that's all I hope. I don't want our holiday ruined. We fly out on Sunday,' she reminded me.

Not that I needed any reminding as we had been preparing for weeks for our next trip to Spain. The very next day after our return from a trip to our holiday home, a pile of parcels would start to build up in a corner of our bedroom — a pile that would grow as the weeks went by. These were items that my wife had decided were needed for our apartment and were a constant reminder of our next holiday abroad, which could not come too soon as far as I was concerned.

I drove Anthea into town to see the specialist on Thursday, and the first thing that was required before the interview was a further blood test. As usual, parking was a nightmare, the hospital car park being completely full. Many times I was to visit the place in the ensuing months, and I never once managed to park my car in the hospital carpark.

There was a lot of waiting about, both before and after the test, and I could not help but notice the ghastly appearance of those sitting in the consultant's waiting room in direct contrast to my wife, who looked like she was a candidate for the Olympics. Her ruddy appearance must have belied how she felt, for she never let go my hand all of the time. All the people present looked terribly ill, and I felt sure were not destined to remain long in this life. In fact, if the consultant kept them waiting much longer, I wondered if some of them would last long enough to keep this appointment. Eventually, however, Anthea was called in, by a burly woman in nurse's uniform, to see the specialist.

As my wife passed through the door, the nurse looked over at me and asked, 'Are you waiting for your wife?'

As I acknowledged that I was, she nodded significantly as though she felt that it was a good idea. Whatever false hopes I might have had up to that point were quickly dispelled, and my heart sank in despair.

When Anthea emerged a half hour later, she had a strange glitter in her eyes as I rose to greet her. We walked in silence out to the carpark before she spoke. Her voice was level and unemotional and she might have been telling me what we needed to buy in the market.

'He said I am sorry to be the bearer of bad tidings, but I'm afraid that you have got leukaemia.' She looked at me in that serious manner of hers. 'Not a nice thing to be told on such a lovely morning, is it?'

My mouth was dry, and I licked my lips as I tried to find some words of comfort at this terrible news, but I could not think of anything to say and just looked at her wretchedly.

She gave me a little hug which, for a woman as undemonstrative as my wife, spoke volumes about her feelings at that moment.

'I know,' she said, 'I know, but it is not as bad as it sounds.'

In the name of God, who was supposed to be comforting who I asked myself, feeling ashamed, and I hugged her fiercely in return.

'Apparently it is not acute, and he wants to monitor my condition by taking a blood test every three weeks.' She laughed. 'He seemed astonished when I asked him if it was alright if I went to Spain this week and he said there was no reason why not if I felt up to it.'

'And do you,' I croaked, finally finding my voice.

She squeezed my arm. 'You bet I do — wild horses would not stop me.'

Chapter Thirty

That was typical of my wife's attitude throughout her illness. Nothing would throw her — not even one ghastly moment that occurred some weeks after our return from that same holiday.

I read in the local paper about a new television series that had been mostly filmed in the Salisbury area and was about to start that weekend. A local mansion, situated about three miles outside the city, had been leased and would form the main setting for the series. I knew exactly where the house was located, and I suggested to my wife that we take a drive out to see it, if only from a distance, as it would add greatly to our enjoyment of the show if we saw the actual mansion used. We could not get close but had a good view of it through the trees in its park-like setting and looked forward to the first episode that evening.

A few hours later, we sat enthralled in front of the television set with our feet up. The storyline had, as its central character, a man of noble birth who was currently living in Hong Kong and played by the actor Peter Jeffreys. In the first episode, he was informed of the death of his elder brother who was lord of the manor, and that he had now inherited the title. He was to return immediately to England for the funeral and to take up his family responsibilities. Upon his arrival in

London, he went straight to his club to be greeted by an old friend who offered his condolences. Asked how his brother had died, the new lord of the manor looked straight into the camera and said, 'He died of leukaemia in Salisbury infirmary.'

I sat frozen in the chair and did not dare look at my wife, who was sitting across from me. It says much for her strength of character that she somehow forced a laugh and remarked, 'Are they trying to tell me something?'

It is possible that I have had worse moments, but I would have to think very hard to recall one.

I accompanied my wife to her second appointment with the specialist to whose care she had been committed.

I found him to be odious in the extreme. Sad, but true. He was the only man I have ever met who exuded self-doubt. It was all there in the twitchy shoulders, in the nervous hands that never seemed at rest, in the slicked-back hair and starched white collar. He was thin and pale faced and the light blue eyes behind the rimless glasses never quite met yours, despite the almost discernible effort of will to do so. He was in his mid-thirties, and I formed the impression that he, more than anyone else, was astonished to find himself in this position of authority.

At first, I tried to be charitable. Any doctor who loses most of his patients — indeed, one wonders if he ever saved any — must be affected badly by his lack of success. Perhaps being confronted daily by nothing but death could sour your view of life. But at least he could have adopted a gentle and caring manner towards all these unfortunates who were forced to place their trust in him. But his answer to my first and, indeed, last question, damned him in my eyes.

Having been introduced to him by my wife, I asked him meekly if there was any chance of a remission of the leukaemia.

He leaned forward over the desk and snapped, 'Zilch!' A spot of spittle spurted forth from his mouth as he spoke.

'Sorry I asked, Doc!' I was tempted to retort, but I kept my silence. After all, this was the man whom my wife had to put her faith in during her illness.

Arriving home fuming, I decided that whilst I might not be able to help my wife in any other way, at least I could ask for a second opinion. Indeed, having met the appalling creature in whose charge she had been placed, I considered it imperative.

Anthea had, for some years, been one of the voluntary mainstays at the local Imperial Cancer Shop, and now I felt that it was payback time. Having discovered that the trust supported a unit at St. Bartholomew's hospital in London, I decided to give them a call.

Having dialled the number, I sat in the chair, trembling at my cheek. Perhaps I was going over the top, but the sight of my wife sitting in the lounge and resting, with her head on a pillow, made me resolute. I was put through to the appropriate department and a woman's voice answered.

I explained the purpose of my call, telling her that I

would be very grateful if my wife, who had been in charge of the Cancer shop in Salisbury, could have the benefit of the opinion of the doctor in charge of the unit, as she had been diagnosed as having leukaemia.

'Can you hold on a moment, Mr Mullen?'

I acknowledged and said that I would wait.

The next voice that I heard was a jovial, cheerful shout. 'Hello, Mr Mullen, this is Professor Lister — my assistant has explained the circumstances. Can you bring your wife up to see me on Monday?'

I was stunned. This was Friday, the man to whom I was speaking was the man in charge, and I had got through to him in one minute, flat. My head was in a spin. I don't know what I expected, but certainly not this kind of attention.

I stuttered, 'What time, Doctor?'

'Would ten o'clock be too early?'

I agreed instantly. I wasn't sure how, but I would have her there in time, whatever it took.

I tried to croak out my thanks, but the professor interrupted, 'If it wasn't for people like your wife, Mr Mullen, I wouldn't have a job. Look forward to meeting you on Monday,' and he hung up.

It proved to be a long weekend, but Monday finally came, and we presented ourselves at St. Bart's hospital dead on time.

We were only kept waiting a few minutes in the waiting room, when the professor, wearing a bow tie, breezed in, full of good humour, and introduced himself. He swept my wife away, laughing, to his consulting room, with two nurses chasing them both. I marvelled at the contrast in his manner to the weedy individual at Salisbury Infirmary. Here was a man one could be happy to place your trust in — at least he made you feel better by his very manner.

There were an abundance of children running up and down the corridors, playing and all without any hair — all obviously undergoing treatment for the deadly disease. I looked around at the shabbiness of the whole area. I was squeezed into a child's chair, there being none bigger on offer, and studied the battered door in front of me. I counted the marks of five replacement locks — evidence of how long it had seen service and rough service at that. It seemed appalling that these dedicated professionals had to work in this run-down environment when so much money was wasted elsewhere.

We had to wait a week for the professor's report to find its way to Salisbury Infirmary and sadly the news was not any better. But at least we had met a great man, in every sense, who had not forgotten how to be human and to treat his patients with kindness and humour.

Our specialist at Salisbury made it very plain that he had been offended by the fact that we tried for an opinion elsewhere. Until the day my wife died, he had not a kind word to say to her.

Despite having been paying into BUPA for nearly twenty years, I discovered that that was of no help at all in the case of my wife's illness. I had imagined that if either one of us ever became hospitalised, at the very least we would be admitted to a modern hospital with every facility and enjoy the comfort and seclusion of a private room. Instead, my wife had to put up with the red brick Victorian edifice with its collection of tacky temporary sheds, which sprouted like warts from the central shambles that passed for Salisbury Infirmary.

During the six months of her gradual deterioration, my wife had to have quite a number of blood transfusions which normally took six or seven hours. Each time she was admitted, it was impossible to find her a space in a ward for this necessary treatment. She was put, instead, into a storeroom smelling of Jeyes fluid, and there she sat in a straight-backed chair surrounded by a collection of mops, buckets, toilet rolls and every kind of cleaning fluid on the market. Her good friend Joan Marchment, who was a justice of the peace, would sometimes sit with her and keep her company.

Having caught a glimpse of the horrors of the ward where the blood transfusions were normally carried out, with men and women jammed in together like sardines, I came to the conclusion that my dear wife, who was a very private person, was in all probability better off in the solitude of the stockroom.

During the months that followed, her condition gradually deteriorated and was causing concern not only to me but to her many friends. One of them suggested that she consult a man whom she had heard about who specialised in alternative medicine. He was a consultant from Blandford who visited Salisbury every Tuesday, and met with patients at a house in Castle Road where he rented a room that he used for consultations.

Having been given no treatment of any kind up to

this point, we both thought there was nothing to lose by giving it a try. Making an appointment by telephone, I found that his charges were extremely reasonable, which allayed a vague suspicion I harboured about the man being a charlatan. He was certainly not going to get rich on twenty pounds for a first consultation. I discovered that he was also an M.A. with a Ph.D. to boot.

I drove my wife to the consulting room but did not accompany her to meet the man, Anthea deciding she would just as soon meet him on her own. She told me afterwards that he was a charming gentleman who was accompanied by his equally cheerful wife. She was very sceptical, however, of his medical opinion which was that she might not be suffering from leukaemia at all but a different blood disorder. Having questioned her about any tooth fillings she might have had in recent months, he went on to explain that mercury was very often used for this purpose and could bring about similar symptoms as leukaemia.

Having had a filling not long before, of course, it raised hopes with us that this might be the case, but Anthea's doubts were well founded. Despite taking the health foods he recommended, which she bought from the local health food shop, no improvement was forthcoming in her condition and she remained very ill. It was a strange encounter, as the man was certainly not using his position for profit and made no attempt to seek any further involvement in the case.

When she was finally admitted to hospital for the chemotherapy, she found herself the only woman in a corner of a male ward albeit cordoned off to prying eyes.

During the twelve days that she survived in Salisbury Infirmary, I don't think she ever saw the same nurse twice. There appeared to be a permanent crisis so far as nursing staff were concerned, and the local health authority had to rely on 'rent-a-nurse' from some outside agency. Almost invariably, in Anthea's case, this turned out to be a male nurse and she never had the comfort of any form of relationship with another female during her final few days on earth.

Some months after she died, I received a cheque for one hundred and fifty-four pounds from BUPA for eleven days confinement — they could not make it for twelve they said, because my wife had died 90 minutes before midnight.

Ian had married some years before and was now the proud father of two fine boys himself, whilst his brother Neil was at college in London, studying to be an accountant. I had the unhappy task of informing them of their mother's death, and they both hurried to be with me and were a great comfort to me, although feeling an enormous loss themselves.

I did not have the courage to face Patrick alone with the dreadful news — how would he take it, would he understand what death meant? I was in a quandary. Ian and Neil agreed to come with me to Trowbridge to break the news to their brother, and I braced myself for what I thought was to come. He had no warning of our arrival — we just turned up at his house on the Sunday morning.

The door was opened by one of his friends who recognised us and ushered us inside, whilst calling out to Patrick that his dad was here. He was in the dining room, and when we walked in, he was sitting at the table having just finished his breakfast. He looked up to meet my eyes and immediately looked away to concentrate his gaze on the few breadcrumbs on the table. I knew at once that I hardly needed to say anything; Patrick was aware that something drastic had happened and was already prepared.

It was a very rare event for both his brothers to turn up with me and without his mother and he spent the next ten minutes sweeping imaginary crumbs off the table whilst as gently as possible I tried to explain the absence of his mother who was now in Heaven. Patrick knew all about Heaven from his nine years with the nuns and in the abstract I suppose he knew as much as any of us did what Heaven meant.

For certain he understood that he would not be seeing his mum again, and I know he felt the loss as much as the rest of us. His three friends fully understood as well, and they crowded round Patrick and hugged him as autistic youngsters are wont to do. I could see that he would have all the love and comfort anyone could wish for, and having discussed it with his brothers, we decided to leave him with his friends until the next day when we would all have had a chance to recover a little from the shock. The fact was we were all feeling shell-shocked and trying hard to come to terms with the enormity of our loss.

It was most noticeable that when we drove away from the house, Patrick did not come to the door to see us off — an unheard of thing to happen. Normally, he would walk out into the street, waving until the car was completely out of sight. Not today. Patrick knew that a great light had gone out of all our lives and especially out of his.

Chapter Thirty-one

I collected Patrick the following day and brought him home with me. On the way over to Trowbridge, I fretted about how he had coped since hearing the terrible news, but I need not have worried. He had recovered from what must have been a great shock, and was waved off by his friends to whom he waved back with a lot of his old humour. Nevertheless, I could see that he was agitated and wondered how best I could alleviate his worries. There was no easy solution — losing one's mother was a harrowing experience for anyone and had to be faced, however difficult it might be. For Patrick, it was going to be more difficult than for most people.

He was ready to talk about his mother, a fact that greatly pleased me. I had been very uncertain whether he fully understood that he would never see his mother again, but his stuttered questions proved me wrong. Not for the first time, Patrick had surprised me with his grasp of important matters.

As soon as we had driven off and were alone in the car, it was he who broached the subject of his mother's death first.

'Is Mum dead, Dad, is she with Jesus? Is she in heaven now?' He looked at me fearfully.

As I drove, I could see from the corner of my eye that he was staring at me as though hoping I might somehow bring her back to life.

'Yes, Patrick, Mum is dead, and she is happy in heaven.'

He stared through the windscreen, allowing this statement to sink in.

'Is Mum happy, is she, she is not hurting, is she?' he asked, a note of pleading in his voice.

'No, Patrick, Mum is not hurting. She has just gone to sleep and feels no pain.'

I felt completely at a loss for words. I just did not know what else I could say to comfort my son. Like all mothers since time began, Anthea had been the greatest force in her son's life and Patrick was going to have to come to terms with never seeing her again, and it was not going to be easy.

Patrick sat there trying to digest this information. He did not cry at any time, and I wondered how much he was holding back. He was quiet for the remainder of the journey, and later that day, I decided that he ought to see his mother for the last time. I wanted to be sure that he fully understood that his mother had gone for good and would not be returning. I was afraid that he might ask, in days and weeks to come, when his mother was coming back, and believed that if he saw her laid out at the mortuary chapel, he would be convinced of her death and learn to live with it.

So it was that we entered the chapel that afternoon, and my heart was in my mouth, for I did not know how Patrick would react. Would he scream and become hysterical and unmanageable? I had no idea, and I nearly had second thoughts about the matter and returned home with him. I admonished myself for such cowardly thoughts and put my arm around his shoulders protectively.

However, I need not have worried, for as we went through the door into the very cold building, Patrick clutched at my arm and was clearly frightened but otherwise quite calm. My wife lay peacefully and looked as though she was just sleeping. I had already visited the chapel alone the day before and had experienced that eerie feeling that I was not alone in the room — the very real sense of another presence. I had often heard it said by others in the same situation — now I had first-hand knowledge of it.

Patrick held onto me tightly as he gazed at his mother. He was scared finding himself in this strange place but otherwise very quiet. Clearly, he was very afraid, and I tried to console him as best I could that there was nothing to be afraid of, nobody was going to hurt us or his mother, and that God was watching over all of us. He remained calm, and as we left, after I said a short prayer, he put his arm around me as I cried, and I had the truly amazing experience of my son Patrick comforting me.

'Not cry, Dad, not cry,' and I could see that he was fighting back the tears himself.

My other two sons handled the sad event each in his own way. Ian expressed a wish not to view the body but to remember his mother as he recalled her best — full of life and vigour. Neil, on the other hand, made it clear that he could never accept that his mother was dead unless he saw with his own eyes, her body laid out in the chapel. I went with him for this moving visit and he came away reconciled, in part, to his tremendous loss. Being the youngest, I suppose he had been closer to his mother than his siblings in recent years. I had had to give him the terrible news over the telephone, and despite my warning to drive carefully, he had driven at breakneck speed to Salisbury. This attracted the attention of the motorway police, and he had been stopped for speeding. It says much for our police force that when told of the circumstances he was allowed to go on his way with a caution.

The funeral was held a few days later and there was a great turnout, as Anthea had been a very popular woman. Many could not get into the crematorium for the short service and crowded round the entrance porch, anxious to take part.

I looked at my three sons standing by my side and thought how proud Anthea would have been of them. They stood shoulder to shoulder with me and were a great support, as I was beginning to feel the strain of the occasion. I had never imagined in my wildest dreams that I would ever have to face this situation. Like most husbands, I suppose I had always believed that I would die first — women generally living longer than the male of the species. But we do not allow for fate to take a hand and dictate our future.

I let it be known that those who wanted a cup of tea afterwards would be very welcome in my home. Quite a few took up the offer, as many had come a long way and just wanted to take the opportunity to have a few words with me, as I did not often see them. It was wonderful seeing all these old friends all at once, but so sad that it had to be on such an occasion.

I was pretty well shell-shocked later on as I tried to concentrate on what people were saying and found it almost impossible to keep up a conversation. People were anxious to know what my plans for the future were now, and hoped that I would keep in touch with them. Although I did not, at that moment, tell anyone my mind was already made up to go and live in Spain, I desperately wanted to get away from the claustrophobic atmosphere of this house where, over the last six months, I had seen Anthea waste away and die. If I was ever going to recover from her loss, it was going to have to be somewhere else and not here where so much sadness had been borne.

I became vaguely aware of a small group of distinguished-looking gentlemen standing in a corner and idly wondered who they might be. Eventually, when I was free, they approached me, and Patrick, who had not left my side all afternoon, tugged at my sleeve and I could see he was grinning.

He obviously knew who they were, but before I could ask him their identity, they were before me. They had looked so sure of themselves but now, close up, they appeared shy, and they shuffled their feet with embarrassment. Two of them had beards, but the three others were clean-shaven and it suddenly dawned on me who they were. Instead of five confident men on the threshold of middle age, I saw before me a group of young teenagers desperately hoping that I was not going to give them a telling off for coming in second in an important relay.

Patrick, with his phenomenal memory, had recognised them immediately whereas I could not. They were five of my former young athletes whom I had coached a quarter of a century before. They had turned up to show that they had not forgotten how important my wife had been to the club and to them, particularly in those early years when she had worked so hard as honorary secretary.

Sheepishly, they conveyed their condolences and Patrick was all smiles as they shook him by the hand. I remembered how they had used to spoil him when he was home during the long summer vacations. He always accompanied us to the track meetings and attended training sessions. It was a thrill seeing them again — not only for Patrick but for me as well.

They were all very successful in their careers, the same competitive spirit serving them well off the sports field as well as on it. I felt very proud of all of them and felt humble at having played some small part in their development, because competitive sport plays a large role in the formation of a person's character. It is not all about winning — one has to learn how to deal with failure too, and that can be even more important at the end of the day. There are a lot more losers than winners in this world, but the important thing is to come away from defeat having learned something from it. We all have to go on with our lives and make the best of it. You are only a failure when you stop trying.

After the death of my wife, I decided to settle in Spain — a country Anthea and I had grown to love, having spent many wonderful holidays there. I had no qualms about the move as I already had a home there, which made the transition an easy one. Without my partner of thirty-five years, I knew it was going to be lonely at first, but I felt that I needed to make a fresh start. I felt that I was still young enough to accomplish it. What I wanted to avoid was to become a burden to my sons, all of whom had their own lives to lead.

Patrick was well established with a comfortable home and a sound job which allowed him a great deal of independence. He also benefited from the continued support and friendship of Maureen Western and others. This was what my wife and I had striven for all those years and it was now more than ever that I could appreciate that we had done the right thing by him. It had been very difficult at times — we might have appeared to be cruel, but Patrick had come through with flying colours. We had come to know many parents of backward children who had adopted a different point of view and had kept their offspring at home, never letting them out of their sight.

They even dressed them and cut up their food for them, so that the child grew up totally incapable of doing the slightest thing for themselves. They sat watching television day and night, grossly overweight from lack of exercise.

Surely this was cruelty, denying the child the opportunity of becoming at least partially self-sufficient and leading a more fulfilling life. What would become of that young man or woman when the parents grew old and eventually died. It would be a devastating experience being uprooted, perhaps in early middle age, and put into care, an experience for which they were not prepared.

This was the thought that had always been in our minds when thinking of Patrick's future. If we had adopted the same attitude as those others, what would I have been facing with my wife now dead. I knew for certain that I would not have been able to look after him on my own, and I would not now have the freedom of action that allowed me to make the decision to settle in Spain. Selfish it might seem to some, but for my son it was absolutely the right decision.

Left on my own at last, with my sons returning to their everyday lives, I came to realise fully the extent of my loss. I threw myself into the task of preparing to sell off all my furniture and effects — the collection of half a lifetime. I arose every morning at six o'clock, having slept very little, and laboured all day until midnight. I would fall into bed exhausted, but still, sleep was slow in coming, despite feeling drained.

I found it best to keep busy, but even so, at various times, the loneliness overwhelmed me, and I would find myself in tears without any warning.

The weeks passed, however, and I made one journey by car to Spain, taking with me those personal effects from which I felt I could not be parted. Three months after Anthea's death, I made my fond farewells to my sons and grandchildren and started out by car on the final trip to Spain, the car loaded down on the springs with the last of the bits and pieces that I wished to keep as cherished mementoes of my married life.

Chapter Thirty-two

The journey down through France and Spain was uneventful and I passed through the glorious Basque country on our wedding anniversary which made the trip especially poignant. Without doubt, this part of Spain has the most spectacular scenery. I was always amazed by the amount of timber standing and it reminded me of the fact that I read somewhere that Spain was formerly mostly comprised of a vast forest. Legend has it that at one time a squirrel could travel from Gibraltar to the Basque country without ever touching the ground. Apart from the Basque region, not much evidence of it now, I mused, thinking of the parched plains of La Mancha. Once I saw a wolf on the prowl down in a gully, but it slunk away as soon as it became aware of my presence. Even leafless, the trees were starkly beautiful, and I paused more than once to admire a particularly enchanting view. I endeavoured in vain, by talking to Anthea, to conjure up her presence by my side, wishing to share the magic with her. But I felt that she was with me in spirit and I took great comfort from that feeling. It was the 5th of January and we would have been thirty-three years married that day.

I had made this trip before in Anthea's company, and I remembered how much she enjoyed it. We had promised ourselves that we would return to more fully explore this part of the country, but sadly we had never got around to doing it. Like Northern Ireland, despite the terrible reputation for violence, we found the Basque region a very hospitable place. The people were warm and friendly, and we enjoyed some great meals in their restaurants. I put great store by the quality of their food!

That had been in warmer weather when the sun was hot on the mountainside. Anthea adored the sun. Now it was winter, and the air was much cooler, but still it was warm enough to get out of the car and wander about. Most of the restaurants were closed for the winter, but I found one that was open which had spectacular views and I enjoyed some tapas.

It seemed to take me ages to follow the tortuous road through the mountains, but eventually I was heading for Pamplona with the great plains of Spain ahead. I was driving a very powerful car, but being loaded to the gills, I had to drive more carefully than usual. Inside the car I had packed everything imaginable right to the roof. I had left a narrow tunnel of light through the baggage, just enough so that I could see what was happening behind through the rear-view mirror.

When the French customs officer, a tall man, with a twirly moustache and a military manner, swaggered up to the car and asked me if I had anything to declare, I replied, 'No, nothing.'

He opened the boot which sprang up under the pressure of the contents revealing not one inch of free space available for anything else. To my amazement, I had my first taste of a Gallic sense of humour (I didn't know they had one) as he pointed to the mass of suitcases and baggage and asked, 'Vas ees dees, tea bags? Ha, ha, ha,' and he laughed uproariously at his own joke and waved me on my way.

Being so laden down changed the handling characteristics of the car on the road, especially when the enormous forty-ton trucks which hammered along at a hundred and forty kilometres an hour overtook me. At that speed, when caught in the slipstream, I had great difficulty in keeping control of my vehicle. Although the highways were superb, nevertheless, it seemed like accidents waiting to happen to allow these monsters to drive so fast. Heaven knows how long it would take for those trucks to stop in an emergency. It hardly bore thinking about. They were virtually warehouses on wheels, and I gave them a wide berth, taking it steady all the way to the south.

My heart lifted as I entered what I liked to call home territory, and Andalucia appeared to be bathed in sunshine even at this time of the year. Unconsciously, I slowed down — I was in no hurry now and remained in the slow lane admiring the familiar landscape as I approached the coast and what was to become my permanent home for the foreseeable future.

I knew it would take me quite a while to settle down to my new life in Spain and I was right. Although I knew the area well, having spent quite a few holidays in our apartment, everything seemed strange without the company of my wife who had been my constant companion on every trip. I was only just beginning to realise how much fun and pleasure her presence had contributed to my enjoyment of life.

Everything reminded me of what I had lost. When I unlocked the front door of the apartment, I recalled my wife's words when we vacated it some eight months earlier. Was it only in May? It seemed a lifetime away.

She said, as I turned the key in the lock on departure, 'I wonder if I will ever see this little apartment again.' Words which drew from me at the time, a swift censure for even thinking such a thing. But I guess some instinct told her that she would never return to Spain. Could she have known, I wondered? Had the doctor told her something that she had not passed on to me? I was never to know for certain and I thought about it often on sleepless nights.

I remembered our last night in Spain before we returned to England. We had dinner in a lovely beach restaurant with the sound of the waves breaking on the sand beneath us. It boasted a small dance floor which beckoned a number of people to dance when a pianist began to play something romantic.

Rising from her seat, Anthea reached over and grasped my hand pulling me to my feet with what amounted to a command, 'Come and dance with me, husband.'

Being quite familiar with my two left feet, it was not an experience she would normally look forward to so she must have been feeling extremely wistful to say the least.

She was everywhere I looked, but I could not touch her. When I walked out on to our little terrace on my arrival, the Busy Lizzie, which had been a riot of white bloom when we had left eight months before, not surprisingly now lay dead and withered in its pot. It seemed to epitomise everything that had happened in the interim period.

Many kind people in the complex where my new home was situated tried to cheer me up, and I was very grateful but I knew that I needed a certain amount of time on my own to get over my loss. I found it so difficult to let go. I would talk to Anthea quite a lot in the solitude of my apartment and would without any warning suddenly burst into tears. She would never answer, of course, except once.

I had tried without success to get the washing machine to work — the washing being a task which had been the prerogative of my wife since our wedding day. To cap it all, the instruction book was in Spanish which did not help, but with my inability to understand even the mechanics of a catapult, it would have made little difference had it been in English and definitely not if it had been in Gaelic! Looking despairingly at the pile of grubby sheets, shirts, and other articles of apparel, I slammed the washing machine door shut and retired to the lounge.

I sat in the armchair disconsolate, bemoaning the luck that had left me in this state, when I noticed a blue-covered folder on the shelf beneath the coffee table. Anthea usually left helpful notes in there for the people who sometimes rented our apartment. We had found the summer months in Spain just too hot to cope with and as we could indulge our love for this country at any time of the year we chose, we found letting the apartment an easy matter at the peak holiday months. It brought in a useful sum of money, at least enough to pay the community charges. An added bonus was the number of new friends we made from this activity as people tended to return year after year.

Without any conscious thought, I now reached out for the folder and opened it. There was a loose-leafed note inside which contained some instructions in her familiar hand-writing, but my gaze was riveted on the heading. It said, 'John, this is how you operate the washing machine.'

I gulped, my throat constricting — I could hear her laughter and I cried a bucket of tears.

They say that time is a great healer and they are right. It worked for me.

The summer brought the crowds and the Bahia Playa complex where I lived filled up with holiday makers. It was good to hear the sound of children's laughter, and I found myself becoming interested again in matters happening around me. As always there were too many cars for the number of parking spaces available. This was an ongoing problem at the height of the season ever year, as we only had the narrow driveway which we all had to share. It was quite a common occurrence to find one's car blocked in and this could cause dissent among owners. Not only among owners, because many of the apartments were rented during the summer and people who rent never seemed to care where they abandoned their car.

There was one owner in the next block who had suffered particularly badly one week from these careless drivers. He had nearly been driven to despair as time and again he would emerge from his apartment to find his car hopelessly blocked in and would have to go around knocking on doors to find out to whom the offending car belonged.

He was possessed of a highly volatile temper, and when one morning he came out and found a little note on his windscreen, his response was not entirely unexpected.

The note, which had been written by a meek little man on holiday with his wife said, 'Sir, I am sorry to trouble you but if you could possibly manage to park your car just a tiny fraction nearer the wall, I could then park my car without difficulty. Thank you'.

'Apartment No. 34.'

When the holidaymaker emerged the following morning, he had his answer. The note on his windscreen said, 'BOLLOX'. 'Apartment 38'

Such were the little foibles displayed by the British on holiday. But apart from these minor breaches of etiquette, everyone seemed to have a good time and the summer passed quickly

After about a year I started feeling the need of company again, and I joined a local social and sports club. It was situated beach-side less than a mile from my home and I could easily walk there in the mornings without the need of a car. I started running every morning on the beach again, three or four miles, and with such a glorious climate I soon regained my zest for life. There was seldom anyone around when I ran, and it felt like my own private beach. I took up aerobics seriously, which got me fit again, and I made a lot of friends while doing so. Soon my mind turned to a sport that I had always wanted to take up. Skiing.

Not a sport that would spring immediately to mind when talking about Spain. In fact, the ski resort of Pradillaño in the Sierra Nevada mountains of Southern Spain is one of the best equipped in the world. Ally to that the fact that they are blessed with wondrous sunshine nearly all the year round and you are as close to heaven as you are ever likely to get in this world.

With the excellent motorway system now in operation, I can drive from my apartment near Marbella to the resort and be on the slopes in a little over two hours. But first I had to learn to ski which meant taking lessons, and so, fourteen months after the death of my wife, I headed for the Sierra Nevada. I had never been to a ski resort before but had seen films taken of this exotic background many times. Nothing, however, prepared me for the real thing. I was captivated immediately by the sight of the Veleta and the Monachil, the highest mountain in Spain, covered in snow and bathed in sunshine. The air was sharp and clear, and I felt breathless as I got out of the car. Considering that I was at a height of nearly ten thousand feet, this was not too surprising. Sucking in the clean invigorating air, I looked forward with great anticipation to my first week of skiing. Barnum was right — there is one born every minute!

Chapter Thirty-three

Having booked in at my hotel — I had decided to stay for two weeks — my next stop was at one of the many ski schools which run courses for all levels of skill. I thought the man looked doubtfully at me as I paid my fee for a five-day course starting the next day. Nothing like getting straight down to it, I thought, why hang about. Trudging through the snow, I could not help but marvel at the change of climate that existed between the coast where I had just come from in a matter of three hours and my present environment. It had been twenty-two degrees Celsius at home and here it was barely two or three degrees. The contrast could not have been greater as I sank my chin down into my anorak. Only then did I head for one of the countless ski equipment shops which hire out all the gear you need to go up on the slopes. I thought I looked terrific as I admired myself in the mirror at the store.

Years before, in a fit of madness, I had bought a pair of peds (thickly lined trousers) in the vain hope that it would provoke me into attempting a ski holiday, but they had lain in a drawer all this time. Now they were to be given an airing at last, and I was so pleased that they had not been wasted after all. Together with a well-lined anorak that I also possessed, I was reasonably well-equipped, clothes-wise, although I would not win any prizes for style, that was for sure.

It was only the next morning that I felt my first twinge of concern as I headed for the ski lift station to purchase my lift pass for the week. Now I know what Frankenstein's monster wears on his feet in all those horror films. Ski boots! They seemed to weigh a ton as I struggled to walk through the snow with the skis balanced precariously on one shoulder. More than once I nearly clouted someone on the head with the long skis as I slithered and stumbled along.

There was only a short queue waiting to go aloft, and with my ski pass now firmly fastened to my jacket, I staggered as best I could to the nearest lift, becoming increasingly worried as to the viability of this whole crazy enterprise. Thankfully, I was able to sit down and quite literally take the considerable weight off my feet in the small cable car, which seated four, on our way to the Bourguilles ski station. This is where we alighted and where I was due to introduce myself to my instructor and the class. Before I had even joined the group of learners for my first lesson, I was admonishing myself for my foolhardiness.

'You old fool, you've left it too late. Fifty-eight years of age, no wonder the man who took your tuition fee thought you were insane. He was too polite to say so but that is what he was thinking although he was happy to take your money — who can blame him. Look around you, do you see anyone over the age of forty?'

No, I could not. In fact, they all looked like they were no more than twenty. This observation was all too clearly confirmed when I joined the class and had my first look at my fellow students.

They were a mixture of boys and girls and not one of them was over twenty-one. They all looked very nervous, so you can guess how I felt especially when I had my first look, too, at my instructor for the week, and my heart sank to my large boots.

He was short, no more than five eight — ideal for a skier I guess — low centre of gravity. But the power of his presence seemed to make him taller, and he dominated his ten miserable pupils, me among them. I am sure he would agree with me that he was very good-looking, and a pair of piercing blue eyes looked out from a deeply tanned face, the colour of mahogany.

He was hatless, the purpose surely being to let everyone admire his beautiful golden locks which cascaded down on to his shoulders. He was wearing a one piece red and yellow ski suit, without doubt the latest fashion creation from Sergio Tacchini. Atop his golden crown, a pair of Bolle goggles perched flamboyantly.

He had met us as arranged by the ski club secretary, arriving at our rendezvous point in a shower of snow thrown up by his skis, seeming to decelerate from one hundred kilometres an hour to a dead stop within ten metres. It was certainly a very dramatic introduction and I felt well-rehearsed.

To the impressionable girls in our party, and I am sure to himself as well, he looked like a Greek god. I hated him. He was our ski instructor for the week-long course, and after taking one look at me, I knew with a sinking heart that the feeling was mutual, in spades.

In direct contrast to his majesty, I cut a very forlorn figure indeed, dressed as I was in an oddly-matched and ill-fitting suit together with cheap boots (even more ill-fitting as I was to find out to my cost) and a battered pair of skis which had seen many years of arduous service. But it was not just our apparel that clashed so conspicuously.

The mighty Zeus, as I was to come to think of him, his real name was Ricardo, was no more than thirty years old and unbelievably fit, whereas I had reached the ripe old age of fifty-eight. He spoke not a word of English and I hardly knew a word of Spanish — plenty of scope here for misunderstanding you might think, and you would be right.

To my jaundiced eye, our instructor appeared to be a show-off, a poser, a bighead — in fact, just about everything that I loathed in a man. I could hear him muttering what sounded suspiciously like curses to himself, as he took stock of me. The bobble hat pulled carefully down over my ears to conceal my conspicuous white hair and the big sunglasses to hide the myriad of wrinkles, did not fool him for a moment.

I could almost hear him gnashing his teeth and read his thoughts, 'What will they send me next. This is my mountain, I should be training champions. Instead, I have to put up with rich old buffers like this one, wasting my time, a refugee from a geriatric ward in Marbella.'

I shuddered visibly and not just from the cold as I tried in vain to out-stare him. I had the distinct feeling that this was going to be a lot tougher week than I had bargained for.

The only good thing I can say about the first day is that the weather was glorious. Once the sun had peeped over the top of the Veleta mountain, the early morning mist disappeared like magic. The air was crisp and stung the face with its freshness. That first day, however, was also notable for another reason as, with a potent mixture of pain and sweat, I slipped, tripped, stumbled and fell several hundred times. Every muscle in my body screamed to stop this nonsense. Common sense tried to prevail as I told myself I was too old, too fat and too unfit for this caper. I felt battered, bruised and beaten to a pulp, and it was revealed later that one big toe had lost its nail early on, thanks to an ill-fitting boot. No wonder I was limping!

They referred to this part of the mountain which they used for beginners as the nursery slope — aptly named, I thought, as I was made to feel like a small child again, trying in vain to remain in an upright position. The skis seemed to have a will of their own — I just could not control them however hard I tried. One would go one way and the other would determinedly make off in the opposite direction to dissuade it. I was in constant danger of seriously damaging a certain part of my anatomy of which I was particularly fond, and which had brought me untold pleasures in life. There was a limit to the risks I was prepared to take in the pursuit of skiing adroitness.

The method used to reach the top of what was regarded by the experts as a gentle slope, was by means of what they called a 'T' bar. This was a short bar connected to an elasticised rope which one grasped as it went by on a continuously moving line and deftly placed behind the thighs thereby drawing you up the incline. Did I say deftly? I found it almost impossible and having held up a rapidly lengthening queue for ten minutes as I struggled to accomplish this seemingly simple task, to the accompanying screams of the attendant, 'Cheat, cheat,' I finally got away.

I made a mental note to belt him one when I got back down again for calling me a cheat, only to realise later that the man only knew one word of English and he was merely trying to tell me that I was going about it the wrong way. Getting off was just as difficult and to avoid the final ignominy of being drawn back down the slope again when I reached the top, I adopted the simple principle of throwing myself on the ground to my utter chagrin. This elicited a stream of what I am sure was invective from Zeus, and howls of laughter from my fellow pupils.

The punishment ended at last after three of the longest hours of my life, and as I staggered to the chairlift to be borne away to my hotel and a hot bath — oh, yes, please, a hot bath — the last thing I saw was the leer on Zeus's face.

Having collapsed on the bed upon reaching my room, I managed, after an hour, to raise enough strength to remove my clothes. I gasped at the number of bruises I had collected and reluctantly decided enough was enough. My big toe, minus its nail, hurt like fury and I wasted no time in putting some salve on it. Where did I get the salve from, you ask? Listen, when I travel, I take my own personal chemist shop with me. I leave nothing to chance. I keep a mobile field hospital in the boot of my car. Well, you never know when you might require a quick appendectomy.

But today I had done my best and I was just too old. I had left it too late to take up such an arduous sport. During the night I turned and tossed, unable to sleep, and filled with chagrin for allowing that little poser to get the better of me. I could bet he would be laughing his head off in the morning when I failed to show up for the second day of the course. I was filled with self-disgust at my cowardice and bemoaned the fact that I had ever set out on this crazy scheme of mine. Who ever heard of anyone taking up skiing at my advanced age, I admonished myself?

By daybreak, after castigating myself for my weakness, I decided to give it one more day — after all, I had not actually broken anything, I pointed out. My first stop was the shop where I had rented the equipment, as I could not continue, under any circumstances, wearing those appalling ill-fitting boots. I was relieved and grateful to be able to swap the offending footwear for a better fitting pair.

Determinedly I set off for the rendezvous point with the other students, closing my mind to the thought of the pain to follow. Day two was much of the same, with Zeus now making fun of me as he impersonated my antics at trying to control the wayward skies for the amusement of the class. 'No like Juan,' he would say to the others in his couple of words of broken English, looking at me and waving his arms wildly in a very good imitation of my vain attempts to stand upright.

I retired to my room at the hotel at the end of the lesson, not only with a bruised body but with badly bruised pride as well.

Day three, and as I clambered into my ski suit, I gritted my teeth in anticipation of what was sure to be another painful day. By now I had almost mastered the dreaded 'T' bar, and as we assembled on the slope, Zeus proceeded to give us our first lesson of the day. Without the aid of ski poles, we were to glide down the slope, one at a time, and come to a halt by his side where he awaited our arrival.

I was last away as usual, and having seen everyone else achieve what appeared to be a very simple manoeuvre, I set off with severe misgivings. My nervousness was due to the fact that I had not yet mastered the all-important technique of stopping my downward progress when it was often very necessary to do so.

I was now moving at an ever-increasing speed without any clear idea of how to slow down, and panic quickly set in. Fifty miles an hour was soon reached, and fear clutched my entrails like a vice as I seemed certain to die on this mountain at the ridiculously early age of fifty-eight. The wind tore at my clothing and my hat was wrenched off, allowing my unusually long white hair to stream out behind me. With my lips forced back from my teeth in a gruesome grin, I must have looked like death on skis to anyone in my path.

Suddenly everything seemed to go strangely silent and in my bemused state I imagined that I had passed through the sound barrier. Everything took on a dreamlike quality as I approached a speed of Mach 1 and certain death. Time seemed to stand still, and with it, every being on the mountain.

Reality returned when my terror-stricken gaze fell on Zeus who was immediately in front of me, screaming like a dervish and waving like mad for me to do something — I did not know quite what.

However, I did see in the person of my instructor whom I was approaching at an awesome speed, the seeds of my salvation. He was directly in my flight path, and I now relaxed a little as I knew exactly how I was going to reduce drastically the speed of my downward rush.

My nemesis soon got the message as his look of anger swiftly changed to one of concern and then to one of consternation, moving on without pause to pant-soiling terror as I bore down on him like an avenging spirit of the mountain. Desperately he tried, with all of his considerable skill, to get himself out of my path, but to no avail. There just was not enough time to get away, and he knew to his horror that he was not going to make it to safety.

Then it was collision time, and after a bone-crushing encounter, I was grasping him lovingly but firmly to my bosom, and gasping aloud, *'Gracias, muchas* gracias,*'* in his ear as I bore him backwards down the slope. My outpourings of gratitude seemed not to be appreciated as he tried in vain to extricate himself from my clutches.

I was vaguely aware of all the other instructors

lining our route, none of whom I later gathered had much love for their comrade, making catcalls, blowing kisses and making lewd remarks at his predicament, caught as he was in my vice-like hug.

We finally careered into a large snowdrift, with my instructor, who was after all only a little guy, pinned underneath me, the breath completely knocked out of him. When he eventually recovered his composure, the air was blue with Spanish swear words, none of which I understood but was able to guess at from the raucous laughter of the other students and everyone else within hearing range.

He missed no opportunity to embarrass me in front of the others for the remainder of the lesson, and it was only pride that sent me back for more of the same the following day.

Yet strangely, a grudging admiration for each other was beginning to emerge as I slowly came to realise that Ricardo was a brilliant coach and the other learners quickly made progress. It was only me that seemed to be useless, partly, no doubt, due to my somewhat advanced age but also because I could not understand the instructions. For example, it was the last day before I came to realise that the word *cuña* meant to form a wedge with the skis, essential if you are a novice and wish to slow down, and was not a particularly obscene Spanish swear word.

The instructor, for his part, came to understand that I did not give up easily and began to look at me in a new light. After a particularly nasty fall, he came to my aid and was quite solicitous as to my welfare. It was on this, the fourth day of the course, that something seemed to click with me, and I finally solved the mystery of keeping my balance and retaining control of the skis.

This was the strange part. All the others were just normal youngsters who seemed quite content to have attained a reasonable standard of competency and were not ambitious enough to improve their skill still further. This drove Zeus frantic as he wanted every student to reach as near perfection as possible in the short time available.

With me it was different. I was always a competitor, having enjoyed cycle racing in my youth and later on athletics. Once having got the hang of this new skill and being basically pretty fit, I strove to improve my technique and soon left the others behind. It was such a thrill being able to master the technique at last and there is nothing more thrilling than haring down a slope at fifty miles an hour with the wind in your face. Just as long as you know how to stop!

By the end of the last day, I was by far the best of the bunch although still lacking many of the finer points of the sport. To my great amusement, Zeus was so proud of me and kept pointing out to the others how good I had become. Quite a turnaround from previous days. I guess he realised he had achieved the impossible — the equivalent of turning a sow's ear into a silk purse. The school had a final get-together in a local restaurant at the end of the course, and I was very proud and excited to receive my diploma of competency from the principal. It had been the toughest assignment of my life, but I had come through it and I felt a better person because of it.

I subsequently saw Ricardo, taking a class, a couple of times on the slopes over the next few seasons, and he always punched the air in a victory sign whenever he saw me. I think he looks back on my progress as a skier as his greatest achievement. I continue to enjoy my skiing immensely, but my advice to anyone is to take it up when you are young and do not wait until you are over fifty years of age!

Chapter Thirty-four

Sometime after emigrating, I decided to invite Patrick out for a holiday. I had spent much of my time moping around the apartment generally just feeling sorry for myself. There was very little else to do in such a tiny home except read, which I did voraciously. I was the only permanent resident on the complex during the winter months, and apart from the odd holidaymaker who came out from England for a break from the atrocious weather in that country, I had the entire place to myself for much of the time.

I was still missing my wife dreadfully and was sure that a visit from my son would help pull me out of my misery. Patrick, I knew, would also be missing his mother, and I reasoned that this could be a good move for both of us. We could be company for each other even if it was only for a short while. Once the decision was made, I found myself getting all excited at the thought of having Patrick with me again. We could have fun together because even though he was very slow with some things, yet he had a good sense of humour. I had seen him more than once with the tears running down his face, at something amusing he had seen on television. How he loved those martial arts films. The more outrageous the action, the more he seemed to enjoy it.

By now it was early summer, and the days were growing longer and warmer. I enjoyed the mild climate of Spain especially during the winter months, but now I was beginning to miss the season of spring which is my favourite time of year in England. I missed the sight of daffodils and crocuses pushing their way up above the ground giving advance warning of better days to come. The trees and hedgerows would be in bud and there always seemed to me a special smell in the air once Easter was past, as if telling us that another winter had been survived and now, we could get on with our enjoyment of life again.

Here on the Costa del Sol, the transition from winter to spring is much less noticeable, with the days getting just perceptibly longer but no great change in the temperature. When the clocks go forward as they do in April, it comes as a slight surprise to realise that winter has passed almost unnoticed, so mild has been the weather.

I was pretty certain that Patrick could manage the journey on his own as he had flown several times with us on holiday, and he showed every sign of loving it. He particularly liked it when the food and drink was brought round and was very partial to San Miguel! His friend Maureen took him to the airport by taxi and saw to it that he got on the right flight — I had this recurring nightmare that he might end up in Beijing, but I need not have worried. I waited anxiously at Malaga airport, and sure enough, I soon saw the blond head of Patrick coming into the arrival hall.

We had arranged that he would only take hand

luggage, thereby ensuring that he would have a smooth and quick exit upon arrival. He gave a huge grin when he saw me, and we hugged each other as of old. He looked in great shape and was obviously delighted with the whole idea of a holiday in Spain. I asked him how he knew where to go when he got off the aircraft and he pointed to a bearded gentleman carrying only a briefcase.

'I followed that man, I did. He sat in front of me.'

I laughed nervously and was grateful that the same man was not in transit to New York or some other far-flung city. Every year since, Patrick comes to Spain to visit me and it is a very precious time for both of us. For a week or so he is able to crash out and relax although he has to be careful not to get burned as his skin is sensitive. He takes a great interest in his surroundings and pleased to meet my friends, remembering many of them from his previous visits.

We have picnics on the beach and swim and in the evenings, head for Fuengirola where we find a different restaurant to eat in every night. In short, we do all the things that any family might do on holiday and the time goes all too quickly. The lovely thing about it is that although we are both sad when it is time for him to catch his flight, yet he waves goodbye with a big smile and is happy to return to his own home.

I usually see him on to the aircraft and the stewardesses are always kind to him when I explain that he might just need a little help in finding the right seat. Other than that, he has no problem with travelling and indeed enjoys every minute of it.

I often wonder how he gets on with the person sitting next to him. They must realise as soon as they try to converse with him that he has difficulty making conversation. I sometimes ask him what the person was like and he always answers, 'She was a nice lady, or he was a nice man.'

I can only assume, from this short statement, that most of his fellow travellers are extremely kind to him and I only wish there was some way I could thank them. He always gives the impression that he is enjoying life and his shy grin usually endears him to people.

When Patrick first went into sheltered accommodation sharing a house with other youngsters, the Social Services put his name down on the council waiting list for a flat which he was entitled to do as he is a wage earner and, to that extent, financially independent.

After the years rolled by, his name finally reached the top of the queue and he was allocated a very nice flat on a local housing estate. It enjoyed lovely views over farmland, and although I was concerned that he might get lonely living on his own, Patrick gave every sign that he was very contented without continuous company. His friends would visit him at weekends, and he was never really short of company if he desired it. He had continued great support from his friend Maureen Western who, although now retired, still kept in touch with Patrick on a weekly basis, concerned as always for his welfare.

But sadly, this very happy state of affairs was not to last very long. The ugly head of intolerance was to rear its head again as the local youngsters soon discovered that there was a weak one amongst them. Despite the fact that Patrick tried to keep to himself, being very shy, this was not to be tolerated by the vicious youth in the area around Francis Street in Trowbridge. Cat-calling, shouting insults and throwing things at his windows, they soon made Patrick's life a misery and caused him enormous distress. When he told me over the telephone I was devastated at the news as I had imagined everything was fine with him.

When I spoke to the Social Services about it they told me that they were already aware of the problem and sadly it was felt that it would be better if he returned to shared accommodation where at least he would not be so vulnerable to abuse. It was a painful decision to make as it affected not only Patrick, but some other young person who might have benefitted from living in shared accommodation.

So Patrick was driven out of his home — a flat for which he had been on the waiting list for many years — and forced to move back to shared accommodation. One can only hope that he will soon be enjoying the quality of life to which he is entitled like everyone else in the community. For my son has proven and continues to prove, every day of his life, that with a little consideration he can hack it with the best of us. Fate dealt him an unkind blow at the outset of his life, but he has largely overcome it thanks to a few very kind people who will never make the honours list but whose reward surely must be of far greater significance. Loud-mouthed yobs will never defeat him for he stands head and shoulders above them for courage and dignity. Shy and modest, he is the kindest human being I have ever known and will always be an inspiration to me. I am truly humbled by his example and very proud to be his dad.

Chapter Thirty-Five

My desire to keep fit brought me unexpected riches, namely through my membership of a local fitness club and in particular my frequent attendance at aerobic classes. Here I found myself among a mixed group of people, male and female, and of all ages and of different nationalities. Although I was one of the older members, age seemed to make little difference, and I was warmly welcomed to join the group for refreshments on the terrace after our exertions. This vantage point overlooked the enchanting La Calla beach where, much earlier in the day, I would join the squawking seagulls for my morning run. They were a fun group of people and in time they helped me, in no small way, to recover from my loss and to live a more or less normal life once more.

Over those first summer months, I felt drawn to the company of a young Spanish woman by the name of Marisol Barrera who was a regular member of the group and who, to my great good fortune, seemed equally happy to be in my company. She was very attractive, with an endearing personality, and had an excellent command of the English language, certainly better than my pathetic attempts to speak her native tongue. We always met as part of a group, but eventually I mustered enough courage to ask her out to dinner alone. I was a great deal older than her, old enough to be her father no less, so it was with bated breath and eventual delight I was to find that she readily accepted my offer. That was the beginning of a warm friendship that gradually developed into an enduring love that has lasted twenty-eight years. My wife, now of many years standing — I am truly blessed to have her by my side. Her family, too, have long since welcomed me into their midst and opened their hearts to me. I am pleased to confirm that my own family were delighted at my good fortune at finding happiness once more.

I have made it clear of my abiding interest in keeping fit, but after a year or two, in spite of my good fortune, I felt that something was missing in my life. Marisol held a position of considerable responsibility with a local internet company, and as a senior executive, worked long hours but was quite happy as it was a job she loved. It meant, of course, that I was alone all day, but I managed to keep myself busy as the villa we now shared had a huge garden, much of it on the side of a hill. I worried a little as whilst my body was in fair shape, I felt my brain, such as it, was lacked being tested to any degree. I had been an avid reader all my life and eventually the thought occurred to me that I might try my hand at writing a novel. The idea having taken root, I became obsessed with the thought and read somewhere that for a first attempt, a budding author should write about what they know. So, having decided to place the fitness club at the centre of my drama, I embarked on my first attempt at writing a book. No computer in those days so it was writing in long hand that it took me a year to complete the manuscript.

If I thought that the publishing world was waiting impatiently for me to finish my masterpiece, I was to be sorely disappointed. After many more months of canvassing every agent and publisher in the country, I possessed enough rejection slips to paper the lounge, aye, and maybe the dining room as well. Despite my disappointment, I had lost none of my love for the whole process of creating a novel and for my second book, embarked on the mighty task of writing about the invasion of the eighth century that brought the Moorish hordes to Spain. This took me nearly two years as it involved a lot of research, but possessing an enduring love of history, the task brought me much pleasure. Once again, I had the depressing experience of being turned away by publishers and agents alike, but eventually my persistence paid off and I saw my first book take its place on the bookshelves

'The *Pillars of Hercules* was not a best-seller but it was a modest success and brought to its author one of the proudest days of his life. Much encouraged, it was followed, in the course of the next fifteen years, by a further eight novels, and although I enjoyed writing every one, there is nothing to compare with the feeling of seeing one's first book sitting proudly on the coffee table awaiting to be admired.

Patrick retired when he reached the age of sixty years and although suffering the usual minor complaints associated with that age, continues to enjoy reasonably good health. It is frequently pointed out in the media of serious shortcomings in the Social Services especially affecting those in need of home support. I am happy to report that in the case of Trowbridge in Wiltshire, the public are very well cared for as experienced by my son Patrick over many years. He has been looked after with the greatest care by a dedicated group of professionals who have become his friends of long standing.

I continue to live out my life in Spain in the company of my loving wife, Marisol, who together with her family have greatly enhanced my existence in this wonderful country where I hope to end my days. Looking back over the years, I can honestly say that I have made many mistakes in my life but the decision to make my home in Spain was not one of them.

The End

Previously Published Works

High Impact
Vital Organs
Survival
Death Rate
The Snows of Sierra Nevada
Maranatha
The Ravensdale Conspiracy
The Wainwrights
The Pillars of Hercules (Publishers Book Guild)